POLICING
VICTORIAN
LONDON

Recent Titles in Criminology and Penology

POLICING VICTORIAN LONDON

Political Policing, Public Order, and the London Metropolitan Police

Phillip Thurmond Smith

Contributions in Criminology and
Penology, Number 7

Greenwood Press
Westport, Connecticut • London, England

Library of Congress Cataloging in Publication Data

Smith, Phillip Thurmond.
  Policing Victorian London.

  (Contributions in criminology and penology, ISSN 0732-
4464 ; no. 7)
  Bibliography: p.
  Includes index.
  1. London (England)—Police—History—19th century.
2. Great Britain. Metropolitan Police Office—History—
19th century. I. Title. II. Series.
HV8196.L6S65 1984   363.2'09421   84-6666
ISBN 0-313-24437-5 (lib. bdg.)

Library of Congress Catalog Card Number: 84-6666
ISBN 0-313-24437-5
ISSN 0732-4464

First published in 1985

Greenwood Press
A division of Congressional Information Service, Inc.
88 Post Road West
Westport, Connecticut 06881

Printed in the United States of America

10 9 8 7 6 5 4 3 2 1

To my family

Contents

Acknowledgments

The bulk of the research for this book was done in London over a period of several years. Most of the material can be found in the Public Record Office (P.R.O.) at Kew, Surrey, and is listed under the various "MEPOL" (Metropolitan Police) headings. The Home Office papers, also in the P.R.O., were very fruitful, but somewhat less so than the police papers, except for the more important events when reports and extensive correspondence were collected. The Parliamentary Papers, comprising Select Committees, Royal Commissions, and Annual Reports of the Commissioners, were also essential. But all of this must be supplemented by letters of public officials in private or public collections, by what few memoirs there are, and by newspapers and other scattered secondary material. Unfortunately, much of the correspondence generated at the level of police stations, such as daily reports, no longer exists, so that detailed studies of police work at a local level in London would be extremely difficult to conduct. Even the somewhat desiccated and sparse accounts from the police command levels provide little more than a skeleton which the historian is often hard-pressed to clothe.

My debts to British scholars are numerous. I thank Mrs. Jenifer Hart of St. Anne's College, Oxford, and Dr. J.J. Tobias, currently with the British Civil Service, for giving me guidance and encouragement in the early stages of my research. The Victorian and Edwardian Seminar at the Institute of Historical Research of the University of London was my intellectual home while I was in London and provided me with a good testing ground for some of my material. I thank Professor F.M.L. Thompson and his colleagues and my fellow seminar members for their helpful comments. I appreciate the help provided by Mr. D.T. Brett, F.L.A., Librarian of the Police Staff College (formerly Police College) at Bramshill House, Basingstoke. I was greatly aided by the staffs of the various other libraries and institutions listed in the bibliography. I thank Lord Blake (Robert Blake) for the use of the Derby papers at Queen's College, Oxford, and I am grateful to the trustees of the Broadlands Archives for the use of the Palmerston papers.

In the United States my greatest debt is to my graduate supervisor at Columbia University, the late Herman Ausubel, who welcomed me into British history and guided and encouraged me along the way. His passing has saddened a generation of his former students. I also thank Professors James Shenton, Carl Woodring, Otis Fellows, and Robert Nisbet, all of Columbia, for their helpful comments on style and content. Eugene Black of Brandeis University has made very perceptive comments as well. Joanne Hutchinson of Haverford College and Frank Gerrity, my colleague at Saint Joseph's, along with the others listed above, have helped me transmute a few of the more leaden passages, if not into gold, then at least into less opaque prose. For the stylistic and factual crimes that inevitably remain, I can only hope that they are of a magnitude to be regarded as "summary" and not "indictable" offenses, to use crime labels. I also thank my colleagues David Burton and Randall Miller for their constant encouragement.

Parts of this book have been given as papers before various historical conferences: The Northeast Victorian Studies Association meetings in 1977, 1978, and 1980; the New England Conference on British Studies in 1977, and the Duquesne History Forum in 1979 and 1983; and several other societies and conferences between 1976 and the present. A Saint Joseph's University Grant-in-Aid and a Cooper-Woods Travel Grant from the English-Speaking Union have been of great assistance.

I also thank my wife for typing the various manuscripts and for her infinite patience during the years her husband has been in the custody of the Victorian police.

POLICING
VICTORIAN
LONDON

Introduction

Police history in the so-called age of equipoise has only recently begun to attract much attention from professional historians. Most of those who have written on the London police have concentrated on the early years of the force and shifted their attention to the counties after the Chartist period, when the county forces were being established. Having been well entrenched and enjoying a comfortable amount of public acceptance by that time, the London police were put aside by historians until the fall of the Hyde Park railings in 1866 and the Trafalgar Square demonstrations of the 1880s brought the police out into the streets and into public attention again.

BOOKS ON POLICE

Within the last fifteen years or so police and crime histories have begun to appear with greater frequency as a newly-appreciated aspect of social history. The discipline was also perhaps nurtured by the establishment of criminal justice programs in many American colleges and universities, turning the subject into a minor industry. Those tilling the fields of police history do not work alone any more. The growing sophistication of the discipline shows the influence of the other social sciences, and particularly the use of social science concepts, definitions, and even methods, where they are appropriate. Also, no student of English police and crime developments could afford the myopia of ignoring American or European scholarship on the subject, and many of the recent works show a keen familiarity with broader scholarship.

The scholar of a generation ago would find the corpus of books on police history consisting almost entirely of what Roger Lane has called ''cop books,'' institutional works that show little awareness of broader social and political themes, and often devote much space to the solving of colorful crimes; questions of crowd disorders are mentioned briefly, if at all. The books on the London police were often written from a ''Whig'' viewpoint, seeing the advent of the Metropolitan Police in 1829 as an inevitable step in the march toward progress

and order. Such writers are also likely to exaggerate the corruption and inefficiency of the parish constables and watchmen before 1829, forgetting that very
real improvements were being made throughout the course of the eighteenth and
nineteenth centuries in London, which in reality made the break between the
old and the New Police much less sharp than older books would allow.

Of the general studies of the London Metropolitan Police, the most recent by
David Ascoli updates the still very sound work of Douglas Browne. To these
one can add the older studies by Sir John Moylan and George Dilnot, as helpful
introductions to the subject. The City of London Police, which has remained an
independent force within the larger metropolis, has its historian in Donald Rumbelow. For general accounts of the British police there are the books by Jenifer
Hart, T.A. Critchley, and W.L. Melville Lee. Charles Reith's tendentious and
somewhat eccentric books on the police are of value, and his *New Study of
Police History* is very full and useful for the early years of the Metropolitan
Police. J.J. Tobias' recent introductory survey, *Crime and Police in Britain
1700-1900*, conveniently combines crime, police, and punishment with legal
developments. His treatment of the law introduces readers to a subject often
buried in highly specialized works.[1]

For the mid-Victorian period, Wilbur Miller's *Cops and Bobbies* covers some
of the same ground I do, but his study is a comparison of the London and New
York police. Clive Emsley's *Policing and Its Context, 1750-1870* compares the
London police with the French police, and, to a lesser extent, with other European
and American forces. For the public order side of things and in the years I cover,
Donald Richter's recent book is the only general study of its kind to date.

F.C. Mather's *Public Order in the Age of the Chartists* most influenced my
original research, and Geoffrey Best's *Mid-Victorian Britain, 1851-75* gave me
the idea for a time frame, as well as interesting background material.[2]

OBJECTIVES AND ORGANIZATION OF THE BOOK

This present book attempts to steer a course between the existing accounts
and to discuss the Victorian Metropolitan Police from a somewhat unusual angle,
one not taken by the existing works, the police in regard to public order and
"political policing," which I roughly define as police control of, or surveillance
of, dissident or disaffected citizens to protect the interests or power of the
government.

We shall see how the police were a response to the demand for order created
by the needs of an urbanizing society in the transitional period between the pre-

industrial world of the eighteenth century and the Victorian bureaucratic state based on industrial capitalism.

What people in our own age think of when they hear the words "English Police" is an unarmed police force of constables who are ordinarily courteous to tourists, patient, and restrained in confronting crowds. This is an image based on the reality of what the public after 1829 demanded of the London Metropolitan Police, and in time, of other British police forces. The organization of the police, their powers and behavior, reflected very much the mentality of the police reformers and the articulate public and their reservations about establishing the London police in the first place.

The book falls roughly into three categories. First, there are the chapters that show the evolution of the police idea and its implementation from 1829 and discuss the leadership and inner workings of the force. A discussion of public order without a preliminary treatment of the personnel and operations of the police would be inadequate. The problems of keeping the peace were intimately bound up not only with the attitudes of the authorities and the state of the law, but also with the organization and functioning of the police and with the structural weaknesses and difficulties they faced. Also, the use of police in political spying or in the suppression of mass disorder was rarely a question of police decisions and tactics alone, but invariably involved other branches of government. Police actions, it will be seen, frequently reflected ambivalence in political decision making and also the need for compromise in balancing the competing demands of freedom of speech and action on the one hand with the preservation of peace on the other.

There are chapters that concern detection, surveillance, aliens, and threats to security—the other side of policing. This is what I mean by political policing, a label that would undoubtedly have offended the Victorian police commissioners. Where police surveillance was concerned, the authorities tried to reach a compromise between the Englishman's traditional aversion to internal spying and the need for adequate information, for example, with regard to the machinations of Irish Fenians or continental refugees in London.

Finally, there are chapters that deal with crowd control and public order, which of course cannot really be detached from political policing. Besides a discussion of the development of crowd control tactics, there are also episodes that one might consider case studies, such as the riots in Hyde Park in 1855 over sabbatarian legislation, or the Reform Bill demonstrations in 1866-1867. As in most of the other parts of this book we examine how the police functioned in practice, not in theory, in different circumstances.

In the chapters on crowd disorders I have been more interested in the police than the crowds, viewing the events as a problem of the use and abuse of authority, and the difficulties encountered. For this reason I have not attempted a sociological or psychological study of crowd identities, motives, and backgrounds, but rather have relied on existing studies for such information where it did not emerge from the documents I have used.

Because of the research of modern historians like George Rudé, E.P. Thompson, E.J. Hobsbawm and others, the "faceless" crowds in history not only have faces, that is to say, identities, but have been accorded a modest degree of respectability. We find that the "mobs" were not usually the criminal riffraff and scum of the earth ready to fill their pockets at the first opportunity, as portrayed by alarmed contemporaries. The participants often represented a cross section of the local working population, not people inevitably given to crime or violence. This observation would certainly hold true in the situations I discuss in this book. Nor, after recent research, are we likely to think of contentious crowds as seething, volatile, scarcely human masses, driven by primitive irrational urges, and ready to burst out in orgies of uncontrolled violence once the constraints of law and order are lifted for a moment.

A problem that surfaces in writing about public order is the nomenclature used for the events and participants. As Charles Tilly and Frank Munger have reminded us, words like "protest," "rebellion," "riot," "disturbance," "rabble," "mob," etc., prejudge the politics and intentions of the actors, and reflect the viewpoint of the authorities. The participants and their actions are then made to appear as anomalies or as a disease infecting an otherwise stable and healthy body politic. Some of the early writers on the subject of protest and revolution, working in the shadow of the events they described, or drawing from prejudiced accounts of contemporaries, did use pejorative terms, thus revealing their own biases which usually reflected a middle- or upper-class perspective. Tilly uses the term "collective action" to refer to situations in which sets of people pooled their resources to reach a common goal. It could cover events from total revolt to simple petition signing. Munger prefers the term "contentious gathering" for twenty or more people, instead of riot or disturbance.[3]

The historian should be aware of such considerations, but unless he wants to rework the English language he has little choice but to employ the words at hand while trying to rid them of the emotional baggage they often carry. Rather than annoy and distract the reader with the repetition of some arcane but "neutral" offerings from the social sciences (assuming I could find such suitable words) I have repeatedly fallen back on familiar words like "crowd" and even "mob." I beg the reader's indulgence that my use of such loaded words is not intended to express (at least consciously) indignation or social prejudice.

Critics of this book could accuse me of trying to write police history with the criminals left out, to paraphrase the historian G.M. Trevelyan. This is not far from the truth. In choosing to concern myself with public order and political policing, topics seemingly apart from the usual police duties of preventing and detecting crime (or more likely, performing services having nothing to do with crime), I have drawn a very thin line. I have done so merely as an organizational convenience, not because these concerns are in any way unrelated. No sharp distinction can be drawn between rioters and criminals; in any case both were criminals in the eyes of the law. Had I attempted to make this book a crime study as well, beyond the brief sketch in this chapter, its size would quickly have swollen to alarming dimensions.

STUDYING THE MID-VICTORIAN POLICE

As will be apparent, my concentration is on the years 1850 to 1868, during the time the police were under the control of Commissioner Sir Richard Mayne. He had been in that post since 1829, but had shared the command with Sir Charles Rowan till Rowan's retirement in 1850. I have chosen these years for the main reason that we are able to see a developed force in operation by the 1850s, one whose structure, components, and procedures were largely set, after the years of experimentation in the 1830s and 1840s. When one views the police from their starting point in 1829 what is striking is how little they changed over the decades. There were minor changes, to be sure, but no major reorganization. From a mid-century vantage point we may observe a mature organization at work.

Extending my coverage up through the 1880s, as a friendly critic suggested, would add little, I believe, to the observations made in this book. Also, research into the British archives is thwarted by the closure for a century of certain police and other official documents. Added to this is the extra vexation that some records that should be open are bound with later ones, and are thus closed. A study of public order later in the century will have to await a further volume.

In the 1830s there were organizational modifications that eliminated vestiges of the old parish police system and removed the last control the judicial magistrates exercised over the Metropolitan Police. The police thus achieved a certain organizational autonomy under commissioners answerable to the Home Secretary. In spite of command preferences to keep the police uniformed and open in its work, a small Detective Department was added in the 1840s. In the 1850s a single commissioner was appointed, a practice that has prevailed ever since.

In public order maintenance and crowd control the police had proved themselves capable of keeping order without weapons and without excessive violence. This was dramatically true in 1848 when the police stood off a large Chartist demonstration in London, and again in 1851 when the Great Exhibition in Hyde Park was kept orderly. On both occasions military units standing by were not used directly. Accordingly, middle-class property owners came to have even more confidence in the ability of the constables to keep the peace.

To social and economic historians the mid-Victorian years also have a certain integrity of their own. It was an age of relative economic and political stability, at least until the late 1860s, and seemingly free from the hardships of the thirties and the "hungry forties," hardships that had contributed to the complex working-class movement for political and social reform called Chartism. After 1848 a brighter economic outlook was in order, and working-class distress diminished somewhat, thus eroding support for Chartism. Concurrently, public fears about Chartism subsided and Victorians began to look forward confidently to what they believed would be a new era of prosperity, blessed with free trade, political liberalism, and a mutual accommodation of the social classes.

IMAGES OF THE CITY

The image one often has of the mid-Victorians is that of orderliness, of sobriety, of people circumspect and outwardly law-abiding—middle-class virtues that the Victorians themselves self-consciously touted, and to a degree followed. We should not let this somewhat pasteurized image mislead us as to the historical reality of the nineteenth century; neither can we afford to let our view of the eighteenth century be shaped by Gainsborough and Romney—Hogarth is a more realistic guide.

The truth is that rowdiness, drunkenness, and occasional rioting were also facts of life in the nineteenth century and were part of a long heritage of resistance to authority and even, to a degree, of lawlessness. Whether done openly or surreptitiously, dueling, cruel animal sports, bare-knuckle boxing, and public executions attended by hordes of idle, drink-sodden spectators, were part of the earlier Victorian scene. The same age that built churches in unprecedented numbers was also the age that shouted itself hoarse for revenge after the Indian Mutiny. In a country that in the Victorian age became the richest and most powerful in the world, about a third of its urban dwellers were living in poverty even at the end of that age.

We must also acknowledge that much of the London disorder was tame by Continental or American standards. The "June Days" in Paris in 1848 or the Paris Commune of 1871 had no counterparts in London; nor did London see the violent race and ethnic rioting that disfigured the growth of American cities in the nineteenth century. The agitation I discuss that took place in Hyde Park was anything but revolutionary—the ruling classes harbored few anxieties about this anyway. Participants at any demonstration were mainly curious spectators, often youthful, who found the events a source of excitement otherwise lacking in their lives. Far from being rioters and revolutionaries, the English crowds, often without real leadership, had a degree of spontaneity and were frequently protesting against what was perceived as an infringement of some customary "right" or an assault on traditional habits and pleasures. These crowd qualities are some of the characteristics that George Rudé has identified with what he has labeled the "preindustrial crowd."

The English mobs also showed a good-natured spirit, and even their battles with the police contained a fair share of rowdiness and horseplay. Challenges to authority often took the form of throwing rocks and breaking windows.

The relative passivity of the working classes and their reluctance to riot seriously for political and social changes was a source of continual disappointment for professional agitators and foreign observers like Karl Marx, who neither understood Britain nor could fathom the English refusal to get "a revolutionary education," as Marx put it.

Not a little credit must also go to the forces of order at the hands of the government. If the crowds were relatively restrained, so too was the government's response, in its preference for using unarmed police as the first line of defense. As Donald Richter has observed: "Victorian authority thus relied quite heavily on the ultimate good sense of the citizen body, a confidence frequently expressed by officials in times of crisis."[4]

Given the current preoccupation with urban crime, the non-scholar is apt to equate the growth of cities automatically with crime, and to see the manifestations of rapid urbanization as being inherently criminogenic. In this view crime and violence were to be expected. In quantity of crime this may well have been true, simply because urbanization meant that familiar controls were weakened, and more people meant more personal interactions that could lead to crime or violence; but that is as far as we can go. Scholars like Roger Lane have convincingly shown that far from breeding crime, urban conditions have put a premium on cooperation, personal discipline, and regular routine, which have, in Lane's words, "offered a powerful counter to the purely disintegrative forces of city living, resulting ultimately in the conquest even of unruly London."[5]

The negative view of the city owes much to late nineteenth- and early twentieth-century scholarship, particularly on American cities. The problem is suggested by a crude syllogism which assumed that the city is a product of the Industrial

Revolution, and that the cities automatically brought an increase in disorder. It followed therefore that the Industrial Revolution created these problems. In reality there were two great revolutions, urban and industrial, that occurred simultaneously: both were fed by the great increase in population which would have changed the face of society even if there had been no industrial revolution. As for London, it was never an "industrial" city and expanded largely because of surplus population. The second premise that cities meant crime is based on faulty data from prejudiced contemporary accounts or on questionable statistics.

CRIME TRENDS

The historical reality is that the cities throughout the nineteenth century, in America as well as Britain, seemed to have become more orderly, and late Victorians were certain that this was true of London. Recent scholarship on British crime has buttressed this view. The history of crime is not an easy subject to handle. Scholars who have worked in the area of crime history are aware of the statistical minefields through which they must tread, and the heavy qualifications with which they must surround their conclusions. Nevertheless, scholars writing in the past fifteen years or so have noted the appearance of a decline in crimes of violence and a leveling off of property crimes over the course of the last century, though even this cannot be accepted as conclusive.

Inevitably, the study of crime in any period presents problems of just what constitutes a crime, since what may be criminal at one time or place may not be (or might be ignored) in another. In no period can we know the incidence of "total crime," the number of crimes actually committed, because many crimes are never reported, and if they are reported, arrest, much less a conviction, may never occur. For most purposes the state will be concerned with selective enforcement of laws and the prosecution of people who are thought to pose a real danger. This "official crime" is, understandably, only a fraction of total crime, since it only includes offenses that have come to the attention of the authorities.[6]

The most accurate indication of the amount of crime in Victorian London would be those offenses known to the police or reported by the public, regardless of whether or not a successful prosecution ensued. If we jump to the other end of the criminal justice spectrum and try to determine nineteenth-century crime by studying the prison population, we would naturally have much reduced numbers, since few law violators ever got to prison. The historian studying Victorian crime would probably rely more on the figures for "crimes known to the police," but these statistics were only collected and published from 1857.

CRIME

The current debate on the subject in published works in English was opened by J.J. Tobias in his widely read *Crime and Industrial Society in the Nineteenth Century*, which appeared in 1967. Rejecting the criminal and judicial statistics as being unreliable, Tobias uses as his sources the evidence given before parliamentary committees, and books and articles written by contemporaries. Based on his wide reading, the picture he presents is a vivid one of Victorian London and its criminal underworld. According to him, while there seemed to be a general lessening in the level of violence in the first half of the century, there was no noticeable reduction in crimes against property from 1815 to 1850, although property crime seemed to taper off slightly after mid-century. From that time, it is quite probable that crimes of violence and property offenses did not rise in proportion to the increase in population. Juvenile crime was also significant, Tobias claimed, but it too dropped in the 1850s and 1860s.[7]

Another historian of crime, David Philips, has chosen to work mainly with police and judicial records in a limited part of England, the "Black Country" between Birmingham and Wolverhampton. In generalizing about crime, Philips feels that by the 1850s violence in public disorders was decreasing, but that the total level of crime was increasing, not decreasing. The surprising observation was that a crime rate which would have been regarded as alarmingly high in 1800, was accepted almost as normal in 1850: it was the cost of living in an industrial society. Crime was no longer linked to rebellion or social breakdown, but had simply become a social problem much like disease and poor drainage. Crime, in Philips' opinion, became "normalized" in English industrial society at some point in the period between 1830 and 1860.[8]

The best study to introduce a reader to the problems of understanding crime and of using crime statistics is the article by V.A.C. Gatrell and T.B. Hadden which considers crime from 1805 to 1900. This should be supplemented by a provocative study by Gatrell published in 1980. The authors show that in times of depression the nineteenth-century property offenses tended to go up, and in good economic times to go down. On the other hand, in times of depression crimes of personal violence such as assault and those triggered by drunkenness dropped, but with prosperity went up, suggesting that prosperity meant that more money was spent on drink. This was certainly true in the mid-1870s when drink consumption reached an all-time high, corresponding to a high level of drink-related assaults.[9]

These correlations worked till the 1880s when there appeared to be a reversal in the making which by the twentieth century meant that property crimes were highest in times of prosperity. But even this view has been revised by Gatrell. If property crimes did for a time coincide with prosperity, that began to break down between 1900 and 1908 when the old correlations returned and remained at least through the interwar years. In fact serious crimes like burglary and robbery swung up dramatically after 1900. The year 1908 was a peak year for larceny.[10]

The reasons for this have to do with the unfortunate conjunction of economic depression and high unemployment, combined with high food prices, a situation that existed most severely in the 1840s in the industrial cloth industries, and again in the Edwardian years with inflation, falling real wages and industrial stagnation. In both periods distress seemed to drive people to steal. The level of crime in the early twentieth century was up, but still below the high level in the 1840s.[11] Gatrell and Hadden dismiss the idea that juvenile crime accounts for either long- or short-term crime fluctuations. In his later article Gatrell suggested that the Education Act of 1870 and its compulsory clause (1880) probably did more than reformatories and the like to remove juveniles from the street and keep them from crime.[12]

If one can make any statement about crime in the nineteenth century that will find a reasonably wide consensus it is that crime was becoming less violent and was probably declining in proportion to the population from roughly the middle of the century. Why violence should lessen is not at all clear. Possibly the reason has to do with a general humanitarian outlook, and with the internal and external pressures exerted on its members by a more orderly and policed society, the same impulses that put brutal sports and punishments in bad odor with the public. Given the differences in police practices and reporting, one cannot be more specific about crime trends without looking at limited times and places. Since much local work must be carried out, comparative crime studies have been of limited value, but it is significant that studies in the United States and Western Europe have shown the same general pattern, even though the settings vary so widely. With this in mind one cannot see urban society and material progress leading to a permanently high crime rate. Nineteenth-century cities did indeed civilize their inhabitants. What part the police had in reducing the levels of crime and disorder will always be a moot question since the police were simply one of many elements used in the taming of London.[13]

NOTES

1. David Ascoli, *The Queen's Peace* (North Pomfret, Vt.: David & Charles, 1980). Douglas G. Browne, *The Rise of Scotland Yard: History of the Metropolitan Police*

(London: Harrap & Co., 1956). Sir John Moylan, *Scotland Yard and the Metropolitan Police* (London: Putnam & Co., 1934). George Dilnot, *The Story of Scotland Yard* (Boston: Houghton Mifflin Co., 1927). Donald Rumbelow, *I Spy Blue: The Police and Crime in the City of London From Elizabeth I to Victoria* (London: Macmillan, St. Martin's Press, 1971). Jenifer Hart, *The British Police* (London: Allen & Unwin, 1951). T.A. Critchley, *A History of Police in England and Wales, 900-1966* (London: Constable, 1967). W.L. Melville Lee, *A History of Police in England* (London: Methuen & Co., 1901). Charles Reith, *A New Study of Police History* (London: Oliver & Boyd, 1956). J.J. Tobias, *Crime and Police in England 1700-1900* (New York: St. Martin's Press, 1979).

2. Wilbur Miller, *Cops and Bobbies. Police Authority in New York and London 1830-1870* (Chicago: University of Chicago Press, 1977). Clive Emsley, *Policing and Its Context, 1750-1870* (New York: Schoken Books, 1984). F.C. Mather, *Public Order in the Age of the Chartists* (Manchester: Manchester University Press, 1959). Geoffrey Best, *Mid-Victorian Britain, 1851-1875* (St. Albans, Herts, U.K.: Panther Books, Ltd., 1973). Donald Richter, *Riotous Victorians* (Athens, Ohio: Ohio University Press, 1981).

3. Frank Munger, "Contentious Gatherings in Lancashire, England, 1750-1830," and Charles Tilly, "The Web of Contention in Eighteenth-Century Cities," in *Class Conflict and Collective Action*, ed. by Louise Tilly and Charles Tilly (Beverly Hills: Sage Publications, 1981).

4. Richter, *Riotous Victorians*, p. 167.

5. Roger Lane, "Crime and the Industrial Revolution: British and American Views," *Journal of Social History*, VII (Spring, 1974), 297.

6. David Philips, *Crime and Authority in Victorian England* (London: Croom Helm and Rowman and Littlefield, 1977), pp. 43-45.

7. J.J. Tobias, *Crime and Industrial Society in the Nineteenth Century* (Middlesex, U.K.: Penguin Books, Ltd., 1967), pp. 46-47, 134, 140, 142.

8. Philips, *Crime and Authority*, pp. 284, 287-89.

9. V.A.C. Gatrell and T.B. Hadden, "Criminal Statistics and their Interpretation," in *Nineteenth-Century Society: Essays in the Use of Quantitative Methods for the Study of Social Data*, ed. by E.A. Wrigley (Cambridge: Cambridge University Press, 1972), p. 371. Best, *Mid-Victorian Britain*, p. 240. See also V.A.C. Gatrell, "The Decline of Theft and Violence in Victorian and Edwardian England" in *Crime and Law: The Social History of Crime in Western Europe Since 1500*, ed. by V.A.C. Gatrell, B. Lenman, and G. Parker (London: Europa Publications, Ltd., 1980).

10. Gatrell, "The Decline of Theft and Violence," pp. 310-20.

11. Ibid., pp. 312-13.

12. Ibid., p. 307. Gatrell and Hadden, "Criminal Statistics," pp. 383-84. Two important collections which examine crime trends in both the United States and Europe are: T.R. Gurr, et al., eds., *The Politics of Crime and Conflict: A Comparative History of Four Cities* (Beverly Hills: Sage Publications, 1977). Hugh Davis Graham and T.R. Gurr, eds., *Violence in America: Historical and Comparative Perspectives* (rev. ed.;

Beverly Hills: Sage Publications, 1979). See also the useful bibliographical essays by Lane and Hay: Roger Lane, "Urban Police and Crime in Nineteenth Century America," and Douglas Hay, "Crime and Justice in Eighteenth and Nineteenth-Century England," both in *Crime and Justice, An Annual Review of Research*, Vol. II, ed. by Norval Morris and Michael Tonry (Chicago: University of Chicago Press, 1980).

13. T.R. Gurr, "Historical Trends in Violent Crime: A Critical Review of the Evidence," in *Crime and Justice, An Annual Review of Research*, Vol. III, ed. by Norval Morris and Michael Tonry (Chicago: University of Chicago Press, 1981).

1

From the Old to the New Police: The Search for Order and the Establishment of the Metropolitan Police

The Police of the Metropolis (its official name) that was established in London in 1829 was the first modern style professional police force, and came to serve as a model for other forces in Britain and elsewhere. Its organization, its practices and limitations, and its guiding philosophy of being a "preventive" police, designed primarily to forestall crime, reflected very much the milieu in which the force was conceived. The Metropolitan Police represented a comprehensive reform of London's antique system of decentralized parish policing. The 1829 act, however, should be seen as the culmination of a series of police reforms stretching back almost a century. The fact that London did not get a uniform, centralized police system till 1829 is testimony to the view that only minor changes to the parish police were needed, or that a centralized force would usurp local authority, cost too much, or pose a threat to liberties. The character of the London police, its freedom from partisan politics and patronage, and its limited role, represented some concessions to these and other concerns.

Although not established as an anti-riot force, the Metropolitan Police did have to serve in this function, and showed that it could supplant the military in confronting hostile crowds. In the realm of public order generally, the police within twenty years did much to inspire confidence among the propertied Londoners that law and order could be preserved and that massive urban disorder was probably a thing of the past.

THE URBAN WORLD

The relative social tranquility of the 1850s and 1860s was often contrasted with the turbulence of the 1830s and 1840s and again with the seemingly languid indolence of the eighteenth century. Charles Kingsley wrote of the time when "young lads believed (and not so wrongly) that the masses were their natural enemies and that they might have to fight, any year or any day, for the safety of their property and the honour of their sisters."[1] Certainly diaries, letters and newspapers of the day make it clear that such a view was widely held, contrasting the mid-Victorian years with the generation immediately preceding. Those same sources would show that this notion was not without some foundation, since Chartist disorder in the country had caused alarm, although not to the same extent in London as in industrial areas. In 1863 the Commissioner of the Metropolitan Police, Sir Richard Mayne, wrote to Lord Palmerston in a cautiously optimistic memo: "These times [the Chartist period] have been successfully passed, and are now almost forgotten, but we must not suppose that in some form or other dangers and difficulties will not again have to be encountered."[2]

The age of the Industrial Revolution had brought with it two discrete but simultaneous phenomena, urbanization and the rapid growth of population, both of which undermined the security of some of the larger towns and cities in England. By 1801 more than twenty towns in England and Wales had more than 10,000 people, while London, with a growth rate of between 18 percent and 21 percent a year from 1801 to 1870, was approaching 1 million. London's expansion was mainly in the out-parishes of Surrey and Middlesex, away from the administrative jurisdiction of Westminster and the City of London. London was dependent upon the structure of decentralized local government little changed for centuries, while other rapidly growing towns were constrained by local oligarchic governments better suited for agricultural villages or small market towns.

Confronted by a rapidly changing world, urban administrators were ill-equipped to deal with the overcrowding, the squalor and the chronic underemployment of the poor. Many of those who came into the cities looking for work lacked specific skills and were not readily absorbed into the labor market. London, never an industrial city but one of crafts and trades, had a largely non-industrial labor force up through the first half of the nineteenth century at least.[3]

To early Victorians there was little doubt that things were getting worse. As cities grew the old informal social controls of class, neighborhood, and shared values seemed to be breaking down, with the well-to-do middle and upper classes removing themselves from the poor. In London especially, the gulf between the classes seemed wider than ever as social segregation became more pronounced. Class divisions became geographical divisions, and districts of the metropolis began to acquire specialized functions and special identities. The poor were increasingly isolated and compressed in slums like St. Giles in central London, and were seemingly impervious to the common moral standards and influence of the upper classes.[4]

The eighteenth and early nineteenth centuries were still aristocratic and paternalistic at root. The whole polity was cast in the image of a predominantly rural society, emphasizing communal responsibility. It was a system that had weak central control, small units of local government, and other local bodies that functioned with a remarkable degree of autonomy. Bureaucratic ties were loose and paternalism and informal social controls were the matrix of society. It was this personal dimension that would slowly disappear over the course of the nineteenth century, to be replaced by a world regulated by administrative and bureaucratic institutions.[5]

The eighteenth century was hardly the age of Augustan repose that one might assume from observing the cultural artifacts of the time. The tenor of daily life was marked by crime, disorder, and popular disturbances that hardly sit well with the superficial literary and artistic images that a casual modern observer might mistake for the exclusive historical reality. There were disturbances over elections, agricultural enclosure, military recruiting, and excise taxes; there were food and price riots, these last two accounting for two-thirds of recorded riots. Much of this was "primitive" or "reactionary" violence, to use Charles Tilly's labels. This was violence more or less endemic to a rural, slowly evolving society, ranging from drunken brawls to food riots, where in the case of the latter, the goals were limited and the means were well understood (or even tacitly approved of) by both sides, and were no particular cause for alarm by the social elites. Damage was usually slight, as was personal injury. Violence in one form or another, whether in sports and other recreations, drunkenness, or public executions, was simply woven into the tapestry of English life.[6]

We shall have to wait until the 1840s to hear talk of the "dangerous classes," of an outcast subculture that was clearly defined as being a threat to the social order. The people of the eighteenth century harbored no such fears, nor did Englishmen think daily crime, however alarming personally, a direct threat to society until the second quarter of the nineteenth century.[7]

THE IMPULSE FOR POLICE REFORM

The legal system admirably served the purposes of the ruling classes in the pre-industrial age, and was far from being a hindrance to the cause of social order, given the ambiguities, obscurities, and absurdities in the law. "The criminal law, more than any other social institution, made it possible to govern eighteenth century England without a police force and without a large army," in the words of Douglas Hay.[8] It has been argued that with the decay of ecclesiastical authority and royal power the landed classes after the seventeenth century were able to secure their property rights through the law. Throughout the eighteenth century and well into the nineteenth, capital statutes multiplied so that capital offenses numbered well over 200 by the 1820s, making the criminal code the harshest in Europe. This is not to say that the law was imposed evenly or regularly: commutation of sentences, pardons, dismissals of cases, refusals to prosecute, and acquittals on the most minute technicalities marked the judicial process. The law served the cause of authority as well as the cause of order, and the use of technicalities to acquit men, pardons for the repentent, as well as exemplary executions, were a form of patronage in the hands of the propertied. The "irrational" legal system had a very definite purpose.

Toward the end of the century, however, police and legal reformers made themselves increasingly heard, taking up the arguments of the eighteenth-century Italian legal reformer Cesare Beccaria, that it was more effective as a crime deterrent to have a fixed code of less severe penalties that were more in keeping with the magnitude of the offense, which could then be imposed with greater certainty. In England Jeremy Bentham, that curious Enlightenment figure who straddled both ages and whose "rational" universal administrative schemes expressed an emerging liberalism, called for the complete overhaul of the criminal laws to redefine criminal responsibility and to crack down on the disobedient. Bentham and his followers were aware of an increase in crime, but they were more interested in law reform than in radical police reforms to solve the crime problem. It was this emphasis together with a modicum of confidence in the existing police arrangements that helped delay major police reforms until 1829.[9] By that time Robert Peel, as Home Secretary, had already inaugurated legal reforms which included the reduction of capital offenses. By 1841 there were only eight offenses for which death was prescribed, but in practice only murderers were then executed.[10]

If Britain was being transformed by an industrial age the social order was also being altered, as it could no longer maintain itself by hollow paternalism and on ritual displays of terror from the law. It would have to be founded on consent and on bureaucratic and economic efficiency. Middle-class liberalism, which would become a powerful force in the Victorian age, was slowly making itself felt, and already in the late eighteenth century it can be seen in the demands for the abolition of exclusively aristocratic government and corrupt and weak institutions. Bentham was part of this movement, and besides recommending legal changes, he pushed for the extension of political and religious rights and the removal from government of aristocratic vestiges. Efficiency and economy were regarded as being supremely important by Bentham and his followers.

Far from bringing with it a multitude of freedoms, applied liberalism would extend formal political rights but would sharply reduce the scope for "deviant" behavior. This stood in contrast to the earlier paternalist conception of order that allowed restricted political participation but tolerated a wider range of popular customs and behavior. In place of the traditional, almost fatalistic interpretation of crime as the symptom of timeless depravity, the reformers saw crime as a symptom of a society in crisis, a society whose household and artisanal economic bases were being eroded, and whose urban population was becoming more and more divided between the rich and the masterless underemployed poor.[11]

To this we must add another powerful impulse from the later eighteenth century: the growth of evangelical Protestantism, which was strongest among the middle classes and which in time would do much to alter the tone of nineteenth-century England. The manners and morals of the lower classes were increasingly being scrutinized, and rising standards of daily decorum brought an intolerance for drunkenness, fighting, brutal sports, and petty crime, as well as other disorders, that might have been viewed more indulgently in an earlier age.

FORCES OF ORDER

From the point of view of law enforcement, the eighteenth century was a formative period, although outwardly the institutions of order retained the functions and forms handed down from the Middle Ages, which were based on the ancient concept of community responsibility for keeping the King's Peace. The system in England and Wales was based on four officers including the annually-elected parish constable, the night watchman, and the parish beadle whose functions included minor administrative ones in each parish. Above these was the fourth figure, the unpaid justice of the peace (JP), whose responsibility was to maintain law and order and to mobilize the forces at his disposal against disorder. As a last resort the JP would be the one to read the Riot Act ordering the dispersal of a gathering, or even to call in the military. There were roughly 5,000 JPs, most of them landowners, so that their judicial status merely bolstered their social standing in the community. In London the Chief Magistrate at the Bow Street Police Office was the *primus inter pares* among the London JPs.[12]

The forces of order included, besides the army, the militia and the volunteers. The militia was organized on a county basis by compulsory election of the inhabitants, as with the parish constables, but substitutes were easily hired. The quality of the militiamen left something to be desired. In London in the late eighteenth century desertion and lack of recruitment left the militia at about half strength, thus rendering it less than reliable for handling riots.

Volunteer associations were formed and could meet specific emergencies after having been called by a magistrate. Composed of respectable citizens, these special constables were sworn in and "associated" as a body to keep the peace.

Such associations were formed during the Gordon Riots. Dressed in blue and scarlet, the London Association met for weekly drill. After 1794 they tended to be absorbed in the volunteer movement acting as a sort of "Home Guard" against insurrection while the army was engaged with the French. Although the volunteers were little used after 1813 the cavalry arm, the yeomanry, continued and was used to deal with disturbances in the industrial districts in the hard years after the war. Most of the yeomanry were small landowners who had the reputation of being particularly zealous in combating local disturbances. During the Napoleonic War years, they had made themselves conspicuous against the machine-breaking Luddites and again in 1819 at "Peterloo"—St. Peter's Fields—outside of Manchester, when they broke up a peaceful reform demonstration, leaving 11 dead and over 400 injured; and later in the agricultural and Chartist disturbances of the 1830s and 1840s. Repression, if not swift or efficient, was at least certain, if conciliation, philanthropy, or charity did not head off a civil crisis.[13]

Given the fact that before 1829 policing in London was a parish matter, the quality of law enforcement varied greatly with the zeal of the constables, and the sobriety and competence of the watchmen. The negative picture of the old parish system with drunken and aged watchmen, hired to keep them from being a drain on the parish poor chest, must not be assumed to be a uniform picture. Some parishes were competently policed; others did not bother hiring watchmen unless a crime scare panicked the residents into doing so until the scare blew over. In any case, there was no police "system" for London as a whole, since parish officials had no jurisdiction beyond their own parishes.[14]

THE POLICE IDEA AND ITS CRITICS

Modern historians have been puzzled as to why major police reform, instead of *ad hoc* tinkering, was not made before 1829. While we can acknowledge the numerous complaints by contemporaries, there was still considerable confidence—and inertia—that the system worked, and that the existing arrangements were capable of maintaining order. It was a conviction stronger than we usually admit. It was true, of course, that criminal law and police reformers were apt to stress the weaknesses in the old system to make a case for reform, a viewpoint picked up by later writers.

We should not, however, exaggerate the effect of the 1829 police bill, because very real improvements were made before that which smoothed the transition from the old to the "New Police," beginning with the 1735 act of Parliament that allowed two of the central London parishes to impose a compulsory police rate (local tax) on the householders, thus making the parochial watch a public service financed by statutory authority. The system still rested on the parish constable.

In 1749 Henry Fielding, the Bow Street magistrate, established a small group of detectives who would in time be called the Bow Street Runners. In 1792 under the Middlesex Justices Act, six more police offices—not yet called magistrates' courts—were set up under the Home Office, each with a small group of constables attached to it. Then followed the Thames River Police, attached to the Thames Police Office, the first regular professional police force in London, but whose activities were limited to patrolling the Thames.[15]

The calls for a more comprehensive police system were made by men like Bentham and Patrick Colquhoun, who wanted a professional, centrally controlled police for the metropolis, an institution likely to appeal most to the urban middle classes. Crime statistics were also being published after 1805 and helped make their point. The figures showed that committals to trial were steadily increasing (indeed, they went up by four and a half times between 1805 and 1842). Some contemporaries correctly pointed out that the rise in committals revealed a hardening of attitudes to crime and a greater willingness to prosecute, which inflated the statistics; this did not necessarily mean a large increase in crime. The years 1815-1817 probably did see some increase in crime, however, due to the demobilization of soldiers and to other postwar readjustments.[16]

Parliament responded to the anxieties caused by an apparent rise in crime with a series of select committees in 1812, 1816-1818, 1822, and finally 1828, to consider the issues of police arrangements, crime, the courts, and related matters. Except for the select committee of 1828, which gave the Home Secretary the power to establish a police, none of the other committees called for any drastic change in the parish system. They fell back on the usual prescriptions for more coordination among the police offices and the parishes to deal with crime. No consideration was given to mob violence.

The conservatism of influential Londoners and the reluctance to embrace drastic changes in the police system have led the writers of traditional police histories (most accounts, in fact) to stress the opposition to police reform as being largely due to the Englishman's traditional distaste for a ''continental'' police agency with heavy-handed practices and hordes of spies, all of which would subvert English liberties. Englishmen did, of course, have such fears, but these must not be exaggerated in retrospect. The few liberal Whigs and radicals in Parliament between 1790 and 1820 (who did not command a majority) were loud in their resistance, but the opposition, found in all social classes, was complex. ''Constitutional'' arguments—which were more muted than one might be led to believe—masked a variety of political and economic concerns.

The most persistent opposition to a professional police came from the working classes. In the 1790s the Home Office and the police offices, particularly Bow Street, used officers and paid informers to collect information about the London Corresponding Society, and later against radical sympathizers of Irish rebels, and to repress their activities.[17]

Critics today who stand with working-class police opponents of the eighteenth and nineteenth centuries, who see the police as a tool fashioned especially to keep the lower orders in their place, must realize that resistance to police reform from the ruling classes was also considerable. If the legal system and its abundance of property statutes accurately mirrored the indignation of the governors, so too did their preference for localized policing. If revolt and general lawlessness threatened from ''below,'' there was a corresponding menace from an overmighty executive from above.

The gentry, rural or urban, Whig or Tory, had inherited an antipathy to the encroachments of royal or governmental power, to a standing army and to a possibly despotic regime that might upset the balance struck in 1689 after the Glorious Revolution. It was an assertion of the virtues of local and voluntary peacekeeping over a centralized system that would usurp local authority. The gentry took very seriously their role of being unpaid JPs, since this status limited the office to gentlemen of traditional social standing and independence who were thus able to retain power and authority. To accept pay—and London magistrates were paid—meant to accept government control and discipline. Also, the JPs greatly valued their modest privilege of appointing the local constables, the loss of which patronage would be a blow to their pride as well as to their authority. Those village constables were obviously inadequate for maintaining public order, but they were sufficiently adequate for catching the few criminals one could reasonably expect to apprehend. The constables' shortcomings were simply the price to be paid for ''liberty.''

With these considerations in mind the rural gentry could speak through their Members of Parliament (MPs) about ''traditional liberties,'' ''continental spy systems,'' and the like, while at the same time resisting moves for a London preventive police which they knew would soon be copied in other parts of the country.[18]

In this light a select committee could publish its findings in 1818 with the warning that an efficient police ''would of necessity be odious and repulsive.... It would be a plan which would make every servant of every house a spy on the actions of his master, and all classes of society spies on each other.'' In 1822 another committee wrote in a similar vein: ''It is difficult to reconcile an effective system of police with that perfect freedom of action and exemption from interference which are the great privileges and blessings of society in this country.'' The forces of inertia, not repression, had spoken.[19]

This was hardly the last word on the subject, because for a variety of reasons reform sentiment was dissolving the opposition. With an apparent increase of crime and the weaknesses of the parish police system evident, together with radical agitation after 1790, a more receptive atmosphere was created for the establishment of a professional police force, better able to protect property.

By 1828 the various police agencies in existence included, besides the usual parish officials, a Bow Street Horse Patrol (1763) to police the major highways leading into London; a "Dismounted" Patrol (1821, officially part of the Horse Patrol) that operated closer in; a Foot Patrol (1805), London's first preventive police; and finally the Bow Street Day Patrol (1822) of 27 men, established by Robert Peel. By the 1820s, then, London was provided with a reasonably comprehensive and competent system of preventive policing, the collective result of the changes begun in 1735.[20]

THE NEW POLICE, 1829

Eventually the calls for a London police, loudest from business and commercial interests, resulted in the passage of the 1829 police bill, which established for the first time a comprehensive full-time professional police force, to comprise over 3,000 men under the command of two magistrates who were in turn answerable to the Home Secretary. The bill got through Parliament only because Peel prudently excluded the City of London from it. The City, which had its own police system, jealously guarded its autonomy, but it did set up a uniform force in 1839, very similar to that of the Metropolitan Police.

Peel and the two commissioners were of one voice in insisting that the police role was primarily to prevent crime, with detection being secondary. Just how much crime they could reasonably expect to prevent was never clear, if indeed such a thing could ever be clear, but there was the presumption that the police would be more aggressive in patrolling than the old parish watchmen whose jurisdictions were strictly limited.

The idea of prevention of crime was firmly embodied in the earliest police instructions and has remained so to the present day.

It should be understood, at the outset, that the principal object to be attained is the "Prevention of Crime." To this great end every effort of the Police is to be directed. The security of person and property, the preservation of the public tranquility, and all the other objects of a Police Establishment, will thus be better effected than by the detection and punishment of the offender, after he has succeeded in committing the crime.... The absence of crime will be considered the best proof of the complete efficiency of the Police.[21]

The preventive idea applied to the police was not exclusive to that body. Prevention was a principle dear to the hearts of men like Bentham and his followers, notably Edwin Chadwick. Chadwick, in particular, saw a centralized police—modeled somewhat after the French police—as one part of his concerted effort to fight the classic trio of social evils: poverty, disease and crime. The utilitarian principle that moved him and many other social reformers in the early nineteenth century was prevention. Just as the later public health and poor law reforms were designed to prevent unnatural rates of death, disease and pauperism, so were the New Police necessary to prevent an unnatural quantity of crime. It was the ease and profit of crime, and perhaps the thrill, that inspired criminals, not necessarily want; to thwart this impulse prevention seemed the cure, according to his analysis. Striking at the criminals was secondary to striking at the causes of crime. Neither Bentham nor Chadwick had any direct influence on the passage of Peel's act. The effect of "Benthamism" on the resulting police organization was tenuous at best, but the police idea did conform to the Benthamite notion of central control and of a paid professional service. The actual organization of the Metropolitan Police probably owes as much to Peel's experience in Ireland and to the Peace Preservation Forces established there in 1814, as to the schemes of men like Colquhoun, Chadwick, or Bentham.[22]

While contemporaries may have come to admire the police for their facility with crowds, it does not follow that the police that took to the streets in 1829 were conceived as or trained to be an anti-riot force. Public order concerns probably played but a small part in the establishment of the London Metropolitan Police, although some historians make crowd control the major determinant. Undoubtedly such concerns were present in the minds of men like Chadwick who realized the superiority of unarmed police over armed military in dispersing disorderly crowds before damage could be done and without the inevitable bloodshed that would accompany military intervention.[23]

One can examine in vain the select committees of 1816-1818, 1822, and 1828, or the parliamentary debates, looking for a discussion of the use of a police force to suppress mass violence or revolution. It may have been that contemporaries made no differentiation in the magnitude of disorder, assuming that a preventive police would keep minor disorders from ever getting out of hand; or it may be more likely that they expected to use the military anyway for serious rioting.[24]

Discussions of police reform revolved around the most prosaic of considerations, mainly how the parish police could be improved, and how coordination among the parishes could be furthered, how to effect changes which would not unduly alarm the parish officials or magistrates that their power and independence would be undermined. These were largely organizational questions, not philosophical ones about a radically different type of police. The lack of discussion on mass violence in the select committees would suggest that riot suppression would require other means.

The articulate public was sensitive enough about the centralized New Police, but had the proposed police been touted as an anti-riot force, and plans made to train and equip it accordingly, public outrage would have been insurmountable. As it was, Peel's bill was a logical evolution of the kind of thinking that had been going on for half a century, and was, in short, a triumph of conservative reform.

This is not to diminish the ingenuity of the experiment, for London now had a police force organized without regard to parish boundaries, and thus free from local political control and partisan politics. Central control might suggest that the police would be under political control, but the removal of the police from partisan politics prevented this and furthered public acceptance of the force. The new constables had to meet strict qualifications and were chosen by the commissioners who avoided patronage in selection. Seniority and merit were the bases for promotion.[25]

The commissioners, Charles Rowan and Richard Mayne, were appointed for life and did not change with the governments, so that they were able to exercise most of the real power over the police. They tried to create a police force wielding impersonal authority, while at the same time they maintained a tight bureaucratic control of their men. This reduced the scope of individual discretion that was characteristic of the New York and other American police forces.[26]

CRITICS OF THE NEW POLICE

Even after the passage of the police bill and as the two commissioners were assembling and training the police (Peel had little to do with this, leaving Rowan and Mayne with much latitude), there was less criticism than one might have expected. There were the inevitable hints that the English now had a continental spy system, or that the Tories, who created the police, could keep themselves in power vis-à-vis the police. In the House of Commons, one MP, a Mr. Lennard, said that the police were "a sort of military body" who could be dangerous under another Home Secretary than Peel. He recommended that the House "look with constitutional jealousy" and keep an eye on the police.[27]

There was also predictable opposition from the magistrates whose authority was undermined when they no longer had the watch forces to supervise. The Bow Street court lost its patrols except the Horse Patrol. Each office retained its complement of detectives (including the Runners at Bow Street), because the Metropolitan Police had none. The police court officers and Metropolitan officers frequently found themselves working at cross purposes, as magistrates often refused to issue warrants except to their own men. This confusion of jurisdiction was sensibly eliminated in 1839 when police authority was removed from the magistrates, leaving them with only judicial duty. The police offices were henceforth known as police courts. The Runners and other detectives were pensioned off and the Horse Patrol and Thames Police were absorbed into the Metropolitan Police.[28]

The loudest complaints from the propertied, respectable classes—the working classes were hostile to the police from the start—came from parish officials who no longer had any say about police arrangements, but who had to levy a police rate of eight pence in the pound (soon lowered to six). This was usually more (occasionally less) than many parishes were used to paying. Money complaints resounded for years.

By the mid-Victorian period the strident demands for lower rates had for the most part died down, as it became apparent that the reduction in crime was worth the expense. Nevertheless complaints were still made occasionally. The parish of Marylebone was perhaps most vocal on the issue, through its MP Lord Dudley Stuart.

There was little question that the Metropolitan and the City of London Police had a part in helping to reduce the general level of street crimes in London. In addition, Metropolitan officers often migrated elsewhere and helped establish town and county forces in other parts of the country or even abroad, thus carrying London police practices with them. But the London police served as more than an organizational paradigm for other departments. The temporary assignment of London constables to cover races, demonstrations, and other large gatherings outside of London was felt to have a "moral" effect far beyond the physical presence of the police. In 1837 Rowan testified that of the 2,000 to 3,000 men sent to the counties since 1829, "we have every reason to believe that their moral influence at such places has been as great, or perhaps greater than within their own district.'' During the Chartist demonstrations in 1842, Sir James Graham, Home Secretary, wrote to Peel: "We have had a quiet night in London, and the suppression of the tumults here [London] has had a magical effect in calming Merthyr Tydfil, and in allaying the excitement in distant quarters which waited for a signal from the metropolis.''[29]

The signal never came, and with the decline of Chartism the industrial North assumed a more benign appearance, for there working-class institutions that embodied the virtues of self-help, thrift, and sobriety seemed to have pacified the industrial proletariat. After the 1850s London supplanted "Coketown" as the focus for fears about urban existence within an industrial society.

THE "CRIMINAL CLASSES"

If propertied Londoners had lost their dread of revolutionary violence after 1848, they transferred their anxieties to what were variously called the "dangerous classes," the "criminal classes," or more commonly the "residuum," terms that vividly conveyed their fears. Even when the names—which were not used before the 1840s—were not specifically invoked there was the persistent image of a seething and volatile class on the lowest rung of society.[30]

Mid-Victorians came to forge a distinction between the respectable employed classes and the hordes of shiftless casual poor, apparently divorced from labor disciplines and established religion. The London labor market, with its masses of seasonal, unskilled, casual workers, barely distinguishable to many Victorians from criminals, also did much to define the residuum as a group apart from the respectable working classes. The locations of such people in urban districts as alien to the respectable as foreign countries, was particularly unsettling, given London's importance as the seat of the Court, the Parliament, the national government, and even more significantly, as the capital of a large new empire. Comparisons to Ancient Rome and its internal problems were invariably made.

After a quarter of a century of economic growth and rising standards of working-class prosperity, chronic poverty was no longer seen as the timeless and inevitable lot of mankind, but rather as a remnant of the past which progress would eradicate.

The existence of the dangerous classes was increasingly explained as due to moral or physical defects or to character weaknesses. Alfred Marshall was not alone in identifying the problem as a moral one. "The residuum," he said, "were those who have a poor physique and a weak character—those who are limp in body and mind.''[31] It followed that the battle was not against poverty, but against pauperism and its attendant vices of drunkenness, mendicancy, filth, bad language, gambling, and ignorance.

While it was unlikely that the residuum would join forces with the stable and respectable working classes above them, there was still the disturbing possibility that the forces of order and progress might be undermined by the idle and dissolute who were a volatile mass, ready to break out in a sudden mob disorder. It was in the East End of London where such a thing was most likely to happen, for this was a district whose malignant identity was firmly grounded by the mid-1860s. Only there, said the *Quarterly Review* in 1870, could a formidable riot take place, given the combination of 12,000 sailors "ready for a spree," and the 7,000-8,000 dock laborers and lightermen.[32]

Although such views were widely articulated they were overshadowed by the contradiction of complacency about the metropolitan condition. Respectable Londoners at the same time were convinced that the march of progress had provided an environment that was improving and would presumably continue to do so. Never before had they felt so secure or confident about the future as they did in the 1860s and 1870s.

By the 1860s noticeable improvements in London were making it a less noisome and a tidier city, even though appalling slums remained, seemingly impervious to law and order and the earnest labors of social engineers. The London police, of course, were but one factor among many in rendering the metropolis safer. The police, together with the improving machinery of justice, meant for London dwellers an increasing sense of security and protection from serious social disorder.

In London, however, the arrangements are so good, the security so general, and the complex machinery works so quietly, that the real danger . . . is too much forgotten; and people begin to think it quite a matter of course, or one of the ordinary operations of Providence, that they sleep and wake in safety in the midst of hordes of starving plunderers.[33]

If police vigilance were lifted for a moment, however, the "idle and desperate classes" and assorted criminals were ready to emerge. With an eye on the reform demonstrations of 1866-1867 the *Quarterly Review* wrote that such elements were always much more numerous than reform agitators. They were the "roughs and the dregs of the roughs—those dreadful creatures that are never seen in London assembled in mass, except at a fire, a Lord Mayor's show, or a reform meeting."[34] If, after the 1850s, "dangerous classes" were never endowed with revolutionary potential, they were still a disquieting presence in the midst of Victorian prosperity.

The London Metropolitan Police must be considered as one part of the development of the modern state of the nineteenth century, which itself grew out of an earlier society based on aristocratic control, paternalism, and on a weak central government. The force that was created in 1829 was the culmination of police reforms stretching back into the eighteenth century, which had slowly altered London's old police system based on the parish constable, the watchman, the beadle, and an antiquated legal system whose vagaries served the interests of the ruling classes.

If the eighteenth century presented a spectacle of a crude and at times barbarous criminal system, the stirrings of reform were also felt. Criminal law reformers like Bentham and Colquhoun began to call for a rational comprehensive police. Middle-class liberalism was also making headway in the late eighteenth century in demands for the abolition of exclusively aristocratic government and corrupt and weak institutions, in favor of government based on consent and operating with bureaucratic and economic efficiency.

In league with this liberalism were the powerful religious impulses from evangelical Protestantism that placed a premium on good behavior and on scrutinizing the manners and morals of the lower classes. There was decreasing tolerance for drunkenness, fighting, and other disorderly behavior.

If the atmosphere for police reform seemed propitious, those reforms were, as we have noted, delayed by the belief that parish self-government in London would be threatened by a centralized police system which might be used to subvert liberties or that *ad hoc* tinkering with the parish system was sufficient reform, in any case.

The system that Peel designed was comprehensive in its jurisdiction, but intended for a preventive role; it was not conceived or trained as an anti-riot force. The removal of the police from partisan politics, and the insistence that constables exercise restraint and impartiality and operate within strict limits, are adequate testimony to the serious reservations that the public had about such an institution in the first place.

NOTES

1. G.M. Young, *Victorian England: Portrait of an Age* (2d ed.; New York: Oxford University Press, 1969), p. 27.

2. Great Britain, Royal Commission on Historical Manuscripts and National Register of Archives, Broadlands (Palmerston) Archives, PM/C/14, 1863; by Permission of the Trustees of the Broadlands Archives.

3. John Stevenson, "Social Control and the Prevention of Riots in England, 1789-

1829,'' in *Social Control in Nineteenth Century Britain*, ed. by A.P. Donajgrodzki (Totowa, N.J.: Croom Helm and Rowman and Littlefield, 1977), p. 29. Francis Sheppard, *London 1808-1870*. *The Infernal Wen* (London: Secker & Warburg, 1971), p. 1.

4. David Philips, " 'A New Engine of Power and Authority': The Institutionalization of Law-Enforcement in England, 1780-1830,'' in *Crime and the Law*. *The Social History of Crime in Western Europe Since 1500*, ed. by V. Gatrell, B. Lenman, and G. Parker (London: Europa Publications, Ltd., 1980), p. 158. V.A.C. Gatrell, "The Decline of Theft and Violence,'' p. 269. G. Stedman Jones, *Outcast London: A Study in the Relationship Between Classes in Victorian Society* (Middlesex, U.K.: Penguin Books, Ltd., 1976), pp. 13-14.

5. Donajgrodzki, *Social Control in Nineteenth Century Britain*, pp. 21-23.

6. The terms are employed by Charles Tilly, "How Protest Modernized in France, 1845-55,'' in *The Dimensions of Quantitative Research in History*, ed. by W.O. Aydelotte, Allan Bogue, and Robert Fogel (London: Oxford University Press, 1972), pp. 192-255.

7. Stevenson, "Social Control,'' pp. 28-29. Allan Silver, "The Demand for Order in Civil Society,'' in *The Police: Six Sociological Essays*, ed. by David J. Bordua (New York: John Wiley & Sons, Inc., 1967), p. 20.

8. Douglas Hay, "Property, Authority and the Criminal Law,'' in *Albion's Fatal Tree: Crime and Society in Eighteenth-Century England*, ed. by Douglas Hay, et al. (New York: Pantheon Books, 1975).

9. Gatrell, "The Decline of Theft and Violence,'' p. 269. Eric C. Midwinter, *Social Administration in Lancashire, 1830-1860; Poor Law, Public Health and Police* (Manchester: Manchester University Press, 1969), p. 127.

10. Philips, " 'A New Engine,' '' pp. 156-57.

11. Michael Ignatieff, *A Just Measure of Pain: The Penitentiary in the Industrial Revolution, 1750-1850* (New York: Morningside Books, Columbia University Press, 1980), pp. 211-12. Oliver MacDonagh, *Early Victorian Government, 1830-1870* (London: Weidenfeld and Nicolson, 1977), pp. 12-17.

12. Tobias, *Crime and Police in England 1700-1900*, pp. 25-26.

13. Stevenson, "Social Control,'' pp. 30-38, 45-57.

14. Great Britain, Parliament, *Parliamentary Papers* (hereafter *P.P.*), 1828 (533), VI, *Report*.

15. Tobias, *Crime and Police*, Chapter 2. W.L. Melville Lee, *A History of Police in England*, pp. 155-95.

16. Philips, " 'A New Engine,' '' p. 180. Gatrell, "The Decline of Theft and Violence,'' p. 239.

17. Philips, " 'A New Engine,' '' pp. 171-72. A new study of London radicalism is J. Ann Hone, *For the Cause of Truth: Radicalism in London 1796-1821* (Oxford: Clarendon Press, 1982), see especially pp. 41-148.

18. Philips, " 'A New Engine,' '' pp. 159-60, 171-72. Victor Bailey, ed., *Policing*

and Punishment in Nineteenth Century Britain (Brunswick, N.J.: Rutgers University Press, 1981), p. 13. J.L. Lyman, "The Metropolitan Police Act of 1829," *Journal of Criminal Law, Criminology and Police Science*, LV, No. 1, (1964), pp. 144-50.

19. *P.P.* 1818 (423), VIII, *Third Report from the Select Committee on the Police of the Metropolis. P.P.* 1822 (440), IV, *Report from the Select Committee on the Police of the Metropolis.*

20. Melville Lee, *Police in England*, pp. 176-227. Tobias, *Crime and Police*, pp. 36-37, 50-56. *P.P.* 1822 (440), IV, *Report from the Select Committee on the Police of the Metropolis. P.P.* 1828 (533), VI, *Report from the Select Committee on the Police of the Metropolis*, pp. 20, 334.

21. *P.P.* 1830 (505), XXIII, *Accounts*, p. 406. Ibid., 1851 (66), XLVI, *Accounts*, p. 359. Ibid., 1871 (358), XXVIII, *Accounts*, p. 572. Public Record Office, Metropolitan Police Records (hereafter P.R.O. MEPOL) 8/2 *Police Instructions*, 1836. All the MEPOL documents consulted for this book were in the Public Record Office.

22. [Edwin Chadwick] "Preventive Police," *The London Review*, I (Feb. 1829), 272. Midwinter, *Social Administration*, pp. 128-29. MacDonagh, *Early Victorian Government*, pp. 169-70. J.J. Tobias, "Police and Public in the United Kingdom," in *Police Forces in History*, ed. by G.L. Mosse (Beverly Hills, Calif.: Sage Publications, Inc., 1975), p. 29.

23. Bailey says that the Metropolitan Police had been formed as a "para-military force" partly in response to the possibility of riot by the "dangerous classes." Victor Bailey, "The Metropolitan Police, the Home Office and the Threat of Outcast London," in *Policing and Punishment in Nineteenth Century Britain*, p. 101. Wilbur Miller wrote that while Peel's bill did not mention riot control, Peel devised his scheme in 1822 when the fear of insurrection was present. Miller, *Cops and Bobbies*, p. 8. Whatever was in Peel's mind in 1822 we cannot assume that he envisioned an anti-riot force. David Philips, citing Chadwick as a source, said people started to think of a force "specially trained for the purpose" of suppressing disorders. Philips, " 'A New Engine,' " p. 182.

24. *P.P.* 1828 (533), VI. The findings of the previous committees are discussed here.

25. Miller, *Cops and Bobbies*, p. 12.

26. Ibid., pp. 16-20. James F. Richardson, *The New York Police, Colonial Times to 1901* (New York: Oxford University Press, 1970).

27. *Hansard's Parliamentary Debates*, 3d ser., Vol. XXIV (28 May 1830), col. 1200 (henceforth *Hansard*).

28. Tobias, *Crime and Police*, pp. 90-91.

29. Moylan, *Scotland Yard and the Metropolitan Police*, p. 64. *P.P.* 1837-38 (578), XV, *Select Committee on Metropolis Police Offices*, qs. 2100-2101.

30. Tobias, *Crime and Industrial Society*, p. 61. G. Stedman Jones's admirable work deals with the casual labor problem in London's East End in the last half of the century. I have drawn much of my analysis in the paragraphs that follow from his book: G. Stedman Jones, *Outcast London*, pp. 11-16. See also V. Bailey, *Metropolitan Police*, pp. 94-96.

31. Quoted in Jones, *Outcast London*, p. 11.
32. "The Police of London," *Quarterly Review*, CXXIX (July-Oct. 1870), 123.
33. "The Police System of London," *Edinburgh Review*, XCVI (July 1852), 1.
34. "The Police of London," *Quarterly Review*, CXXIX (July-Oct. 1870), 122.

2

The Guardians: The Leadership, Structure, and Functioning of the Police of the Metropolis

Throughout the nineteenth century the London Metropolitan Police remained relatively unchanged in its organization and practices, although additional duties were added. If we ask how much the personal qualities of the commissioners had to do with the police, the answer would have to be that their influence was considerable. Although Robert Peel was largely responsible for creating the force, it was the two Commissioners, Charles Rowan and Richard Mayne, who, given considerable latitude, shaped the Metropolitan Police in its first forty years. Presiding over a quasi-military structure where the subordinate superintendents and inspectors made few independent decisions, the Commissioners exercised much personal authority. The public acceptance of the police was a continuing concern of the Commissioners who were content not to ask for broad police powers, and who made sure that the discretionary powers exercised by the constables on the beats were carefully circumscribed by rules and regulations.

What of the constables themselves? What effect did personal qualities, training, and discipline have on the character of the Metropolitan Police? The Metropolitan Police was composed primarily of young men, most of whom were from rural areas, and few of whom had served in the military. Few were from London, which was in accord with the police philosophy that the constables represented impersonal authority and were free from local patronage and influence. In spite of some military touches in police organization, the London police was very much a civilian force, which distinguished it from European police forces. All these qualities were significant, because they were adopted by other British police forces as well.

The successes and failures of the London police in the area of public order depended very much on the internal dynamics of the police. Also important was the legitimating of the police in the eyes of the public; the London police by the mid-Victorian period had gained the confidence of a considerable part of the upper and middle classes. From the working classes there was still some hostility and suspicion, something that would diminish noticeably only by the end of the century.

CONTROLLING THE POLICE: THE HOME OFFICE AND THE GOVERNMENT

The Metropolitan Police was only one force out of many in England and Wales, although it was far the most important one. The responsibility for the Metropolitan Police was vested in the Home Secretary, who combined the functions of a local police authority and of a central authority for provincial forces also under him. With regard to London he was personally and directly responsible for the administration and expenditures of the police, and for nominating the Commissioners. In these functions he was assisted by a small police section in the Home Office headed by an Under-Secretary of State who was in daily communication with the office of the Commissioner of the Metropolitan Police in Scotland Yard.[1] In actual practice the Home Office did little in the way of formulating long-range policies and was content to handle day to day matters on an *ad hoc* basis, and give advice only when specifically asked. A study of the Home Office papers shows that the Permanent Under-Secretary (a civil service post), particularly the capable Henry Horatio Waddington, played a large part in police administration and decision making. It was also obvious that his judgment prevailed on many issues. All the police orders and regulations of a general nature required the approval of the Home Secretary (who could overrule the Commissioner) as did any changes in police strength or any more serious matters of policy which were liable to raise public or parliamentary enquiry. The day to day administration of the force was left to the Commissioners of Police. Instructions from the Home Office to the Commissioners were almost always verbal, a practice which continued for many years, as the evidence so amply shows.[2]

In times of troubles the Home Secretary controlled and coordinated the activities of magistrates throughout the country and gave legal opinions, after consultation with the Law Officers of the Crown. In London, specifically in the 1830s and 1840s, he took a more active role in directing the police and the police court magistrates, for example, in having Chartist meetings banned. On his authority London policemen were loaned to the provinces in the 1830s and 1840s, and indeed overseas, to advise other countries in setting up their own police forces. Special constables could be called out as in 1848 and 1867, local yeomanry directed to other areas, and pensioners mustered to support the regular forces if need be.[3]

On another level the Home Secretary could invoke the royal prerogative of mercy to pardon accomplices in crime who were willing to betray their fellows, which, combined with the usual rewards for information, provided a useful means of securing indictments. The Home Office had its own staff of solicitors for routine advice, but on difficult matters other officials of the legal system were called upon. The Law Officers of the Crown, the Attorney General, and the Solicitor General assisted in drawing up royal proclamations, advised on prosecutions, and personally conducted the more important legal proceedings. They also advised on the expediency of certain courses of action, or of enforcing certain laws. The actual prosecution of cases was handled by the Treasury Solicitors.[4]

Although Parliament had the function of strengthening or regulating the powers of the central and local authorities, it usually preferred leaving the questions of public order and disturbances to the government, unless of course some scandal gave the opposition an opportunity to fire at the ministers in power. For example, the debates concerning the burning of shops in the Birmingham Bull Ring in 1839 did not reflect an attempt at combating disturbances, but rather, was an effort by the prominent Tories to investigate the conduct of the liberal magistrates of Birmingham, to discredit them and the Whig government that had originally nominated them.[5] We find relatively few parliamentary debates on Chartists in that period, and in 1859-1860 the anti-Ritualist riots in St. George's-in-the-East Church—an embarrassing and seemingly unsolvable conundrum for the Church of England—provoked more outraged speeches in both houses of Parliament than did the Hyde Park Riots of 1855 or 1866. This relative neglect of internal disturbance by Parliament was largely due to the assumption that enforcement was more a matter for the executive machinery, though, of course, London disturbances, as opposed to the usually more distant doings, always captured more attention.[6]

The days of Pitt and Sidmouth had passed forever, and any calls for parliamentary action against crime and disorder were more likely to be for an improvement of the existing laws rather than a demand for more crime categories, more hangings, or the suspension of civil liberties. Legislation for disturbances was controversial, hard to pass, and (it was usually argued) unnecessary. The parliamentarians were reluctant to create new laws where older ones could possibly serve. This would also avoid charges that constitutional liberties were being tampered with only for the sake of present contingencies.

THE POLICE COMMISSIONERS

Lower down the ladder of authority we have the Commissioners of the police. Even though the foundation of the force is rightly attributed to Peel, it was the two appointed Commissioners, Charles Rowan and Richard Mayne, who organized the police as best they could, having first received only Peel's general views on the subject. Peel had little to do with the police after 1829. The Commissioners were the ones who shaped the Metropolitan Police, doing so in response to the political and social setting in which they operated. No separation of duties between the two Commissioners was made. They were both responsible for choosing and training the men to staff the force, and to a great extent, for authorizing the expenditure of police funds.[7] Rowan and Mayne were actually non-judicial magistrates whose authority extended throughout the police district, that is from London into the seven counties into which the Metropolitan Police District reached.

Peel's choice for the first Commissioners could hardly have been wiser. Col. Charles Rowan was a forty-seven-year-old bachelor with a distinguished military record in the Napoleonic Wars. It was probably he who was responsible for the quasi-military structure of the force and who took particular interest in the training of the police. In the earlier years of the Metropolitan Police it was the diplomatic and affable Rowan who was heard of more than his colleague, though he shared his powers equally with the other Commissioner.

Richard Charles Mayne, aged thirty-three in 1829, had no experience for the job and had never held any administrative post. He was born in Dublin in 1796, the son of a judge of the Court of King's Bench in Ireland, was educated as a Pensioner at Trinity College, Dublin, receiving his B.A. in 1818. He then went up to Trinity College, Cambridge, as a Pensioner and took his M.A. in 1821. He was called to the Bar at Lincoln's Inn in 1822, and as a young barrister received his first assignment on the Northern Circuit.[8]

In spite of their differences in age and background the Commissioners worked together in harmony and there is no evidence to show that there was a serious disagreement between them in the twenty years of their joint commissionership. Both men signed each other's correspondence and inside and outside the force were known simply as "The Commissioners."[9] After the retirement of Rowan (then Sir Charles) in 1850, Mayne was in effect the sole Commissioner, even though a Captain William Hay was appointed to succeed Rowan. The two men did not get along, and the dual arrangement finally came to an end in 1855 with Hay's death. From 1856 Mayne continued alone as Commissioner, aided by two new Assistant Commissioners who had the status of justices of the peace. This arrangement would not only prevent the evils of a difference of opinion between two Commissioners, but would also help fill the gap in rank between the superintendents and the Commissioner, and allow for responsible superior officers to be on the spot and make decisions during disturbances—a failing for which the police were specifically criticized by the Royal Commission investigating the police conduct during the Sunday Trading Riots of 1855.[10] The pay of the

Commissioner was set at £1883 and that of the assistants at £800 each. As would become clear in the years between 1850 and 1868 Mayne was a man of decided opinion and great self-confidence, forceful and articulate in debate. He was also single-minded in his devotion to duty and punctilious to the extreme in administrative detail—qualities which would increasingly bring him a certain amount of public criticism in his later years.[11]

It was in 1855 that a nineteen-year-old clerk, Timothy Cavanagh, joined the police. Two years later he was transferred to Scotland Yard headquarters and had occasion to be introduced to Mayne, who was then in his early sixties. Cavanagh's memoirs leave us the following description of the Commissioner. He said that Mayne was about five feet eight inches, with a well-built, thin face, "a very hard compressed mouth, grey hair and whiskers, an eye like that of a hawk, and a slightly limping gait," which Cavanagh attributed to rheumatism. Cavanagh was understandably awed by the Commissioner who was for the most part feared, though respected, by his men and was stiff and formal in personal contacts with them. Cavanagh also said that Mayne frequently worked from ten in the morning till late at night, personally answering most of the letters he received.[12] Under his control the police functioned well as long as his faculties were undimmed; Mayne insisted on being involved with some of the most minute details of police administration. This dedication to duty, however admirable, placed a strain on him. In his later years he tended to ignore or defer pressing matters that needed a solution. "He felt, as many others have done, that he alone could carry on the duties of his office." Cavanagh also believed, as others did, that Mayne should have resigned years before his death in 1868 at age seventy-two. During Mayne's regime, on matters such as police organization, the detective force, and pay and pensions, the force virtually stood still in the face of growing pressure for changes.[13]

Mayne insisted that all correspondence from the two Assistant Commissioners had to pass through his hands. On the other hand, he never consulted his subordinates on matters of policy and rarely solicited their opinions. They were frequently kept in the dark, even in minor administrative matters that Mayne had handled personally. Where possible disturbances or other public occasions were concerned he would read the reports sent in from the field and would assign men as needed without consulting anyone, though informing the Home Office of his contingency plans for more serious events. In answer to a question asked him at the 1855 Royal Commission, Superintendent Nassau Smith O'Brien surprised the commissioners by replying that Mayne rarely asked his officers for their opinions. "It is not usual for Sir Richard Mayne to consult his superintendents?"—Answer, "Not at all."[14]

Mayne's Olympian bearing and the criticism of the police, particularly in the face of Fenian disturbances in the late 1860s, did little to endear him to the public at large. He increasingly came under attack in the newspapers, sometimes unfairly. This was partly the result of Mayne's increased visibility to the public as well as incidents in the 1850s and 1860s that brought criticism of the police. Most serious was the police mishandling of events connected with the Irish Fenians in the late 1860s, the subject of a later chapter in this book. Much of the criticism fell on Mayne's head, and there were demands that he resign. As the *Daily Telegraph* phrased it delicately: "Sir Richard has served for many years—so long, indeed, that a generous and enlightened public would gladly release him from any further exertions."[15]

They did not have long to wait: Mayne died in December 1868, touching off the expectation of numerous changes within the Metropolitan Police. There were calls for organizational alterations and a more military structure, or conversely to de-militarize the police completely. Others pointed out the need for more "educated control," that is, for better educated higher ranking policemen.

Mayne's successor, Sir Edmund Henderson, a former prison official, served until 1886; he made relatively few changes in police structure, although he did reorganize the detectives.

Richard Mayne was perfectly attuned to the mentality and prejudices of an earlier age. It could be argued that his faults were more with the limitations set for the force itself; but his own rigidity and insistence on running the force like a one-man show ossified the organization. By the time of his death Mayne presided over an establishment that had increased from fewer than 3,000 untrained men to almost 9,000 officers, enforcing a bewildering variety of laws, in an expanded police area. Mayne had simply outlived his time. He reacted against any proposal that would have raised fears of a police state. He was not the man to ask for broader powers or seek structural changes that would alarm liberals or embarrass his superiors at the Home Office. Mayne's own brand of conservatism kept the police in the 1829 mold. On the other hand, his scrupulous honesty, his sense of fairness, and his eagle-eyed control over the behavior of his men greatly enhanced the reputation of a police force which in any case was the first of its kind and had been considered a risky experiment from the beginning.

BECOMING A POLICEMAN

Leadership problems notwithstanding, to the public the police presented a professional and organized image that for the most part inspired confidence. The *Edinburgh Review* expressed itself in the following sanguine tones:

Nor can clearer proof be given of perfect discipline than the fact that 5,000 men, in the prime and vigour of life, with moderate wages . . . exposed in an unusual degree to the worst temptations of London, and discharging, for the most part during night, a very laborious duty, always irksome, and often dangerous, are kept in complete control without any extraordinary coercive power.[16]

The requirements for joining the Metropolitan Police included being under thirty, and if married, having not more than two children, being at least five feet seven inches tall, "intelligent," able to read and write "plainly," and providing at least two character recommendations, which were always checked. These minimal qualifications were sufficient to weed out large numbers of applicants, many of whom were grossly unqualified. Timothy Cavanagh was one of 37 successful applicants out of 140 in March 1855.[17]

Although literacy was a constant requirement after 1829, the Commissioners were prepared to overlook this on occasion. Rowan estimated that not as many as 1 in 100 was illiterate. There are numerous references to the fact that many policemen were barely fluent with the written word. This became more obvious and embarrassing after 1869 when the Civil Service Commission started administering promotion examinations. The superintendents soon began complaining that some of their best men were unable to pass the examinations, thus retarding—though not absolutely blocking—their promotions. Educational classes were set up in A Division and later in each division, though the constables had to pay the instructors out of their own pockets. It appears that instruction was given in such subjects as reading aloud, writing from copy, writing from dictation, arithmetic (to simple proportion), spelling, English grammar and geography. After this a certificate of proficiency could be granted.[18]

If the candidate's qualifications and references were otherwise satisfactory he moved on to a brief inspection by the police surgeon. If all went well there he was then informed when to report to the drill ground for training and where to lodge. Wages were ten shillings a week during training. Each preparatory class numbered about thirty men, who were required to parade at the Wellington Barracks drill ground for several hours each day six days a week for a fortnight. Close order drill and saber practice constituted the bulk of this training. After 1868 groups of police were also sent for riding instruction at the school of the Life Guards.[19]

During the two weeks' training the superintendent of A Division assembled the whole class for one afternoon a week to instruct them in the normal duties of a police officer. The men were also given a small instruction book which they were required to learn off-duty and about which they were quizzed regularly by their inspectors during the first six months of duty. After the two weeks the fledgling policemen were sworn in at the pay of fourth-class constables (nineteen shillings a week) and were assigned to patrol the busy streets of the West End in the company of an experienced constable for a week. After this brief exposure to street duty the men were finally assigned to their divisions and to section houses where they would lodge and take their meals. Married men were required to live in the sub-section of their divisions.[20]

A constable's first assignment was to night duty in a division police station. After that he patrolled with an experienced constable and was also exposed to courtroom procedure. When he knew his particular beat well, he was then sent out on his own, armed only with a truncheon, a rattle, and a notebook and pencil, walking his beat at an average speed of two and one-half miles an hour. "Perfect command of temper is indispensable"; therefore, the truncheon and rattle were to be used only when absolutely necessary, when the constable was in danger of being overpowered.[21]

An article in the *Quarterly Review* wrote admiringly of the police training and its obvious success in keeping the peace, and of the transformation by which "a wild young fellow, who perhaps only a few months before knew no restraint, should become a machine, moving, thinking, and speaking only as his instruction-book directs; and so wonderfull are the powers of organization that such an [efficient] officer he generally becomes." And on the beat: "stiff, calm, and inexorable, he seems to take no interest in any mortal thing; to have neither hopes nor fears, . . . an institution rather than a man." The author then hastened to assure his readers that off-duty policemen were very human.[22]

The policeman's dress was designed to be just conspicuous enough, but not "military" or in any way provocative. The occasional Victorian photograph might catch a view of a "bobby" (so called from Robert Peel's first name) on his rounds, an often youthful figure under a very tall hat and wearing a long frock coat. The original dress was a suit of blue cloth with a single breasted frock coat with white buttons. A standup collar was worn over a thick leather stock encircling the neck which would prevent someone from strangling him, but also made movement of the head difficult. An embroidered loop on the collar bore the policeman's division letter and number. He wore a tall chimney-pot hat, which weighed over a pound, and which had a shiny glazed leather top, and leather reinforcing strips down each side.[23] In 1865 the hat was changed to a Roman style helmet similar to the ones now worn.

Police drill was not limited to their "basic training" but was continued as a regular part of police activity, since the reliefs were always inspected in formation and marched to their posts by the sergeants. Until 1854 constables were drilled twice a week all year long. Some criticism of the drill appeared in newspapers in 1868 which prompted the Home Secretary, Gathorne Hardy, to point out that since 1854 the constables drilled an hour a week in good weather during the summer only. This also apparently included saber practice. In 1853 F.M. Mallalieu had testified on police training before a Select Committee and said that "the men in the Metropolitan force are now well drilled, and made efficient in the practice of the sword."[24] Since police duties primarily consisted of pounding the beat and acting as a riot squad in emergencies, drill was felt useful for giving precision to mass movements against mobs, or as the *Saturday Review* phrased it: "A body of men who bungled and floundered about when surrounded in close quarters, or confronted in the open streets, would be worse than useless as preservers of the Queen's peace."[25]

TRANSMITTING INFORMATION

At the beginning of a day's duty the men paraded for up to fifteen minutes before beginning their beats and again when coming off, which thus extended their work day. After they assembled the sergeant called the names and read out the daily police orders, ascertaining that the men "are all perfectly sober and correctly dressed and appointed." This was done with the relieved parties as well. In addition each constable had to write up reports during his free time, which for many less adept with the written word must have been a slow process.[26]

Each day police orders were sent out to the station at 6:30 A.M. giving special instructions, numbers of police to be employed, general regulations, resignations, dismissals, fines and punishments, and arrangements for public occasions. These orders were read to the assembled men.[27] Information about a day's activities filtered up as written reports to the superintendents who in turn transmitted this information to the Commissioner on a sheet of "occurrences." The superintendents were also required to appear in person at Scotland Yard regularly, though not daily as had been the case in the early years of the force. For some this commuting involved considerable distances.[28]

News of crimes or other events that must be made known throughout the force were reported to the central station of the division. From there the particulars of the crime were recorded on "route papers" which were disseminated throughout the police network by policemen-messengers. Each station had to record the details of the route papers and the time received and send them along to other stations. There was constant traffic in such papers throughout the day. By this means news could be spread to all but the most outlying rural stations in less than two hours. From 1857 on the process was simplified by issuing printed police orders from Scotland Yard.[29]

This task was immensely speeded up by the introduction of the telegraph to various stations in the 1850s. A telegraph had originally been installed between Scotland Yard and the Crystal Palace in 1851, and after that it was used by a few stations to notify fire brigades of fires. Telegraphs were also being slowly introduced to connect Scotland Yard to certain divisions, and used for more conventional police purposes. By 1867 the network was complete to the principal and sub-divisional stations in each division. By 1868 the Commissioner and the two assistants had telegraphs in their private residences and had men there to operate them.[30]

Summoning individual constables from their beats to meet some emergency was done simply by having a sergeant or inspector twirl his rattle continuously until all the men were assembled.[31]

Being thus prepared for duty the policeman, by his very presence and carefully defined duties, became more than simply an agent of legitimate coercion but a representative of the values of the "center," an "official representative of the moral order in daily life."[32] "The mob quails before the simple baton of the police officer . . . well knowing the moral as well as physical force of the Nation whose will, as embodied in law, it represents."[33]

POLICE DEPLOYMENT

The Metropolitan force was far and away the largest police force in Great Britain. In 1851 it had 5,551 men, compared to the 806 and 445 men of Liverpool and Manchester respectively. The whole police district of 688 square miles was mapped into divisions which were in turn broken down into sub-divisions, sections (run by sergeants), and individual beats which a single constable patrolled. The divisions had been drawn up with reference to the population and crime rates of a given area, which meant that the densely populated high-crime districts had the smallest divisions. They did not conform at all to the parish boundaries and often included several parishes, a fact that made it convenient for the police authorities to resist the occasional demands for parish control of the police, which would have been virtually impossible given the existing arrangements.[34]

As for the distribution of constables, there was no set police/population ratio. The heaviest concentrations of police seem to have been in those "border" neighborhoods that separated rich and poor areas—an attempt to keep thieves from invading the fashionable quarters. There was more than a little truth to the police axiom: "You guard St. James's by watching St. Giles."[35]

The beat system was a development of the old night watches. A policeman patrolled his given beat in a specified time (perhaps from seven to twenty-five minutes in inner London) inspecting the property and keeping his eyes out for suspicious characters. Because the beats overlapped, he would periodically meet constables from other beats. Approximately two-thirds of the police force were placed on night duty, with the heaviest concentration of them on duty between seven and ten o'clock. Each constable was on duty for eight hours straight.[36]

Besides the usual anti-crime activities the police had to keep order upon all occasions of state, such as the opening of Parliament, levees and drawing rooms, and for any disturbances in or near the houses of Parliament. The royal palaces were also guarded. Police were also regularly dispatched in large numbers to the races at Ascot and Epsom Downs or other events outside of London.

Any temporary vacancies among the men were made up from the body of 300 reserves who were attached in groups of 50 (later 56) to the six central London divisions. Each group, led by an inspector, could be assembled rapidly in case of public tumult and sent where needed. They were also useful in areas where a higher crime rate justified temporary fill-ins. In practice the reserves spent most of their time acting as general flunkies around the stations and conveying messages. They were also dispatched to investigate complaints and answer calls for police assistance. Vacancies in the reserves were filled from among the better policemen with at least a year's experience.[37]

THE SUPERINTENDENTS

The officer responsible for the policing of his division was a superintendent. His area of responsibility actually exceeded some English counties in population. Unlike a county chief constable who had a group of superintendents working under him, the Metropolitan superintendent had no staff and was expected to control some 200-400 men and perhaps visit twelve to fourteen station houses regularly. He personally had to handle important cases and submit reports to Scotland Yard, as well as report directly to the Commissioner two, perhaps three days a week. While the duties of the superintendents were considerable their actual power was circumscribed by the Commissioner, so that the latter made all decisions of any weight. Complaints, for example, were sent up the hierarchy to Mayne who then instructed the superintendents on what action to take, a lengthy process that made immediate redress impossible and raised the suspicion in the public mind that nothing would be done. Complainants also had the option of appearing at Scotland Yard, which was a quicker process, but the entire burden of proof of a policeman's misconduct would be on them.[38]

The organizational weaknesses of the police came increasingly under fire as their duties multiplied. One pamphlet by "Custos," written in 1868—"Custos" perhaps being a senior police officer—considered the gap in rank and social status between the Commissioner and the superintendents a serious weakness that hampered the subordinates in making quick decisions. Custos decried the fact that the superintendents were too close to the men in social status to "stimulate the moral guidance and admiration." What was needed was an "officer corps" of educated men more elevated socially.[39]

WHO BECAME POLICEMEN?

That the police never had an "officer corps" was no fortuitous development. From the earliest days of the police the Home Office and the Commissioners were set against employing gentlemen as inspectors and superintendents, preferring to let men rise from the ranks. Home Secretary Peel expressed the matter clearly in a letter in October 1829: "I have refused to employ gentlemen—commissioned officers, for instance—as superintendents and inspectors, because I am certain they would be above their work." They would probably have refused to associate with their colleagues of equal rank but lower social attainments and would have degraded the latter in the eyes of the men. Peel continued: "A sergeant of the Guards at £200 a year is a better man for my purpose than a captain of high military reputation."[40]

Three years' experience seemed to confirm Peel's preferences. Charles Rowan in 1834 told a Select Committee that the thirteen ex-sergeant-majors who were appointed police superintendents had worked out well, and that they "are not disinclined to do what men of superior requirements would think beneath them." "Reduced gentlemen," he said, might find it painful to mingle with their social inferiors who made up the bulk of the force. While Peel and the Commissioners were in agreement as to the qualities required, Rowan, as an experiment, had made superintendents of two former army commissioned officers: they were both subsequently considered failures, in contrast to the other superintendents.

In the 1880s the head of the Criminal Investigation Department experimented with bringing in from the outside "gentlemen of good education and social standing," to be detectives, as an effort to upgrade the quality of the department. It did not work: there was no substitute for experience.[41]

In an age when police were regarded as little better than unskilled or at best semi-skilled laborers, it was no surprise that Peel preferred not hiring "gentlemen" below the rank of commissioner. Moreover, the work was uncomfortable, often dangerous, and would hardly be expected to attract men of gentility any more than would the low pay, since it had never been felt worthwhile to pay the police any but the barest minimum; the numbers wanting to join the force, however, were usually plentiful. In addition, the police authorities did not want to create a class-ridden bureaucracy subject to the pressures of patronage, and not completely pliable from above. The public for its part had no enthusiasm for supporting a police apparatus bloated with sinecures.

Unfortunately, we do not know as much about the individual constables as we should like to know, but the scattered sources allow us to make some observations about the kinds of men attracted to police work.

In spite of Chadwick's recommendation that the majority of the constables be middle-class, most were in fact agricultural laborers; accordingly, few came from the London area. With a nod toward the later "urban degeneration" theory in which cities were supposed to cause human physical deterioration, the *Quarterly Review* in 1856 attempted to put this in perspective:

Intelligence of a certain kind, however, may be carried too far; your sharp Londoner makes a very bad policeman; he is too volatile and conceited to submit himself to discipline, and is oftener rejected than the persons from other parts, with whom eight-tenths of the force are recruited. The best constables come from the provincial cities and towns. They are both quicker and more "plucky" than the mere countryman from the village—a singular fact, which proves that manly vigour, both physical and mental, is to be found in populations neither too aggregated nor entirely isolated.

The article also said that London had sharpened the brain of the Londoner but "unstrung his sinews and cowed his courage." Residents of the other large cities were better fighters though less sharp-tongued than Londoners.[42]

Testifying before a Select Committee in 1853 Inspector F.M. Mallalieu chose not to make such a fine distinction on police origins. He said that the number of soldiers in the Metropolitan Police had declined, and when asked if soldiers made suitable policemen, answered: "I never considered them the most efficient men for the purpose; I have been rather disposed to think that the intelligent part of the agricultural labouring community after training make the best policemen." Given the stupefying boredom of military camp life, heavy drinking and alcoholism were notorious among soldiers. It was perhaps for the same reason, or because of the sedentary nature of their work, that tailors and shoemakers also made poor policemen, claimed Mayne in 1834. (He did not elaborate, but they constituted respectively 6 percent and 1.5 percent of the police in 1832.)[43]

The *Quarterly Review* seemed convinced that most of the police came from the Home Counties, but this is doubtful. It may have been a coincidence, but of the 41 policemen who testified before a Royal Commission in 1855, and whose origins were stated, 6 were Irish, 1 was Scottish, and 1 was Welsh; the remaining 33 came from a scattering of English counties, mainly in the southern half of the country. None of the men came from the built up areas of London; 2 were from outlying districts, and 2 came from Surrey, probably the agricultural portion. Since most of them were young their residency in London would not have been long enough to qualify them as Londoners for our purposes.[44]

This would seem to agree with later evidence. A survey of 300 entrants to the Metropolitan Police from November 1872 to February 1874 showed that 91 men or 31 percent came from the land, 12 percent from the military services and 5 percent from other police forces. The remainder came from a wide spectrum of primarily manual jobs.[45] At the end of the century Llewellyn Smith, a thoroughgoing exponent of the theory of "urban degeneration," writing in Booth's great study of London, estimated that, unlike the army, 70 percent of the London police in the 1880s came from the provinces, and that "the strength and steadiness of the countryman is here of the greatest service." In December 1888 out of 13,624 Metropolitan policemen just under 11,000 were born elsewhere and only 2,716 (20 percent) were born in London. Smith made no mention of the low wages which might appear more attractive to the country than the city lad, though his colleague G.E. Arkell suggested this in a later entry in Booth's study.[46]

Even as late as 1913 the preference for agricultural laborers remained strong. The American Raymond Fosdick, writing a comparative study of European police systems, reported a conversation with the Metropolitan Commissioner Sir Edward Henry, who said: "We like to take them right from the plow.... They are slow but steady; you can mold them into any shape you please." The head of the police training school told Fosdick that Londoners knew too much, "too much that is detrimental to good discipline. You have to knock so much out of their heads before you can begin their training." Fosdick estimated roughly that only 20 percent came from London, with 60 percent of the men being country born and bred.[47]

Since the police were supposed to be agents of impersonal authority and free from local politics or social ties, official prejudice against native Londoners was an important consideration. The Home Office and the Commissioners felt that taking men from outside London would avoid any excessive familiarity between the police and the people and would allow the Commissioners to mold the recruits as they saw fit. Some other English cities flatly refused to employ policemen who had been their residents for varying periods of time. By way of contrast the New York Metropolitan Police in this period were expected to reside in the wards in which they served and to be well known to the local inhabitants. This policy would insure that they would be regarded as pillars of the community and thoroughly subservient to local political control. The residence requirement would also lessen complaints that the constables were like an alien army of occupation.[48]

Men from other parts of the British Isles also joined the Metropolitan Police. In 1854 out of 5,700 police 145 (2.5 percent) were Scots and 370 (6.5 percent) were Irish. The numbers of Irish policemen were never large. Mayne told the 1855 Royal Commission that while there was no objection to employing Irishmen as such, he preferred not to assign them to Irish areas of London. He did not explain why, but it can be assumed that since policemen were not widely popular in largely working-class areas, Irish policemen certainly would not have been well received among their countrymen in, for example, Camden Town. Perhaps Mayne feared that lack of respect by the community would have prevented them from enforcing the laws.[49]

Family prejudice against policemen may also have discouraged young men from entering local police service, though the evidence for this suggestion is highly tentative. Scotland Yard detective Robert Fuller recalled in his memoirs that like so many of his colleagues he was a born countryman. "Town-bred fellows, as a rule, do not take kindly to this occupation, and if they do take it up they lose caste with their friends." Fuller's London relatives practically disowned him and forbade the mention of his name in their home after he joined the police. For him things improved in later years, he added.[50]

Although critics of the police in the early years were likely to think of them as disguised soldiers, few constables actually did come from the military, roughly 1 man out of every 6.3 in 1832. Among the higher ranks the percent of ex-military enlisted men was greater. In fact 13 of the 17 superintendents had been sergeant-majors in the army, chosen for their experience in enforcing discipline and for teaching drill to the new police force. As they retired, new men who had risen from the police ranks took their places. By 1859 none of the superintendents had been in either the army or the navy and only 25 of the 170 inspectors had done military service.[51]

Figures from the 1870s show that about 1 out of every 8 policemen had been in the military. In 1894 Arkell estimated that 14 percent of the recruits had been soldiers, which is about 1 out of every 7 policemen, probably a reliable average for the whole century. Thus the military presence in the Metropolitan Police was not very great. In this they differed from Continental police forces who drew their rank and file and many of their leaders exclusively from the military.[52]

If such figures would not support the charge that the police were disguised military, at least the public could rest even more assured in knowing that the police got more intelligent men than the army, according to the *Quarterly Review*. As proof of this: "The former [the police] learn all their movements in a fortnight, whilst the latter require at least two months."[53]

PROMOTION

Promotion, according to the standing instructions, was by tenure and "activity, intelligence, and good conduct." In a letter in 1829 Peel acknowledged that the principle of promotion from within the police could not be rigidly maintained, especially when the expansion of the force required many additional men, but that preference should be given to policemen already serving.[54] The Commissioners had attempted to avoid patronage and pressure in the selection and promotion of policemen, though it was some years before the public took this seriously, if ever. It is clear that Mayne was prepared to push up the promotion ladder capable men of obvious talent. Timothy Cavanagh, who had been a clerk, joined the force at age nineteen in 1855. His writing abilities did not go unnoticed and in less than two years he was transferred from a beat into A Division to the Clerk's Department and was promoted to sergeant in January 1857. In December 1860 he was advanced to inspector at the age of twenty-four, a little over five years after joining the force. Another individual Cavanagh knew was a former army sergeant and was made police sergeant after only a few months.[55]

Police turnover was a serious problem in that age, since the pay was low, starting out at nineteen shillings a week for a constable, which was about the level of a semi-skilled worker. Besides low pay, the hours were longer and the discipline more constraining than many young constables had bargained for, and many either went into other work or even into other police forces at a higher rank. Police service was a good recommendation for further employment.

The biggest turnover in police numbers came, as one might expect, within the first eighteen months of a constable's career. In fact, an investigation in 1874 found that over half of all recruits left after less than two years' service. About 13 percent of the Metropolitan Police left for one reason or another in the 1860s, a figure that declined to 4.8 per cent in 1895. Hanging on to police was the hard part: getting them in the first place was easy.[56]

DISCIPLINE

While the police could be assured of public scrutiny of their behavior, the public was often not aware of the quasi-military discipline within the force. Any citizen with a grievance could take it to a magistrate, and upon proof of the validity of the complaint, have the constable fined or even imprisoned for a month, after which expulsion from the force was usual, unless the Home Secretary ordered otherwise.[57] The Commissioner kept an eagle eye on the various newspapers each day for complaints or references to the police and frequently replied in writing to the complainants. Command supervision within the force was constant and often irksome, since sergeants kept a journal of the faults and misconduct of the men under them, and inspectors often checked the private quarters of policemen. This record influenced promotion. Unmarried constables living in section houses (barracks) were even more under the watchful eye of their superiors.[58] Since civilian clothing, even off-duty, was not permitted until 1869, a constable was conspicuous wherever he went, to say the least. Even retirement was no refuge from the long arm of discipline. Pensions could be cut down for men with mixed records. William Harris had his pension discontinued for having been convicted of an indecent offense in 1868. The next year another pensioner had his pension suspended for six months for obstructing a constable in his duty and was warned that another infraction would stop it completely.[59]

The Commissioners felt compelled to curb the zeal of some of their officers in abusing or spying on their own men. One verbal order of 1849 warned sergeants against hiding on the beats to entrap constables doing something wrong. Sergeants were also told not to speak in an irritating manner or use "improper language" to their men. Ever true to the principle that the London police were primarily a force for deterring misconduct by their obvious presence, whether with regard to the public or to the force itself, Mayne insisted that officers should deter their men from committing infractions.[60]

We can get a good idea of the kinds of misconduct that would result in dismissals or compulsory resignations from the London police by reading the daily police orders. A sampling from the years 1857 to 1860 runs the gamut from the familiar to the bizarre: "Dismissed . . . convicted of horse stealing previous to entering the Metropolitan Police." "Absent from duty and found in bed the worse for liquor." "Absent from his division, and found concealed under a bed." "Inside a cow shed, and milking a cow, when on duty" [dismissed]. "Being in a filthy state from vermin" [compulsory resignation]. "Marrying a common prostitute; called upon to resign." "Continuing to live with his wife after reporting he had found another man in bed with her" [compulsory resignation]. The last two remind us that the burden of Victorian morality often lay heaviest on those who were to enforce it.[61]

ALCOHOL AND THE POLICE

That drink was a problem among the police should surprise no one familiar with the role of alcohol in Victorian society. Drunkenness was an occupational hazard that must be reckoned with seriously at virtually all social levels. The police were no exception, and four out of five dismissals in the early years of the force were for drunkenness, according to Commissioner Rowan. Police orders required the dismissal of constables found drunk on duty, but Rowan admitted in 1834 that this depended on the constable's record. Often, nominal five shilling fines were levied. Conviviality at the Christmas season brought the obvious temptations of drink, and each December the Commissioners issued in the police orders a stern warning against drunkenness on duty, threatening dismissal for violations. Mayne usually kept his word, and on one occasion mentioned by Cavanagh dismissed all 60 men reported for drink one Christmas. Some had over 20 years' service. Another year he fired three inspectors, one having 28 years' service. The three fought their dismissals unsuccessfully in court.[62]

Drinking on duty, though not necessarily to excess, seemed to have been normal and was often ignored by the supervisory officers as long as it was reasonably discreet and did not interfere with duty. Beer and spirits were a good deal cheaper and more readily available than most other drinks, and were widely considered a good antifreeze against the cold weather. Certainly indulgence in alcohol was a panacea for the long hours on duty, the darkness, and the cold, and was facilitated by the convenience of a capacious top hat or helmet.

The problem was indeed a serious one, and an examination of the police orders shows that in December 1858, to take one month at random, 38 out of 51 dismissals (74.5 percent) or compulsory resignations involved drink. The figures for May 1858, presumably a drier, less festive month, showed that 22 out of 39 dismissals were alcohol related.[63]

According to J.P. Martin and Gail Wilson police drunkenness decreased steadily and was comparatively rare by the turn of the century. While the authors did not expand on this, it can be surmised that careful selection and supervision of the police played an important part. Also significant on a larger scale were the social developments that made the pub and drink less central to Victorian life: for example, societies, organized sports, and other leisure-time activities, and the growing availability of cheap non-alcoholic beverages. In addition, standards of public decorum concerning alcohol showed less tolerance of public and private drunkenness. Many trades and societies had considered drinking masculine and sociable and even necessary for good job performance. Workers often took a dim view of colleagues who either abstained from alcoholic beverages or were conspicuously more moderate in their use. Attitudes, however, were slowly changing, and the decline in police drunkenness no doubt reflected these.[64]

THE POLICE AND PUBLIC OPINION

The discipline and tight supervision of the police all had the purpose of providing a police force that performed as it was supposed to and also enjoyed widespread public support. By the 1850s the police could take some comfort in knowing that there was a widespread perception that they had been successful in making London safer from crime and the streets more orderly than before, a perception that was grounded in reality. The police did indeed enjoy considerable support from the middle and upper classes, those segments of society whose views exclusively constituted "public opinion" for the Victorians. Any attempt by a historian to gauge that opinion must necessarily force him to rely heavily on the more articulate levels of society, and risk the obvious distortions and biases of those sources—if indeed it were possible to chart such opinion accurately.

We have already seen in Chapter One something of the opposition to the foundation of the police. We should briefly examine some of the public attitudes toward the police from the 1830s. The Metropolitan Police took to the streets at the beginning of England's constitutional crisis over parliamentary representation when the new industrial, professional, and commercial middle classes sought enfranchisement. The Reform Bill of 1832 brought them the vote but separated them from the working classes who remained disfranchised. The middle and upper classes then were united in support of the existing social order and the defense of their property. Where previously many in the middle classes would have worried about a police that might curtail liberty and exercise arbitrary power, now by the mid-1830s they began to demand that the police do more to keep the peace. Also the propertied classes were finding new uses for the police. There were demands that the police remove peddlers and other annoying individuals, capture stray animals, regulate traffic, do something about street litter, unsafe buildings, gambling, loitering youths, and the like. In other words, by the 1850s the cries were loud that the police should be everywhere. The middle classes approved of the expansion of the service role of the police because they probably benefited most from a professional police. Middle-class acceptance of and dependence on the police reflected a growing trust in the government and their identification with the social order.[65]

In spite of police successes there was always some criticism, and in the 1860s there were demands for a more vigorous police to deal with the "crime wave" (such as it was) and the "dangerous classes." While there were those who assailed the police for their lack of military efficiency, most complaints were limited to specific abuses of power. Modern readers of a century-old edition of, say, *The Times*, will find a familiar refrain in the "Where were they when we needed them?'' letters, and the common complaints of policemen paying more attention to servant girls than to a brawl down the street.

''Constitutional'' arguments that the police were a repressive force were aired from time to time. Critics were ready to read a sinister interpretation into police drill, or the adoption in 1864 of the Roman style helmet to replace the old reinforced top hats.[66] The Reform League, which had its own grievance after skirmishing with the police over the use of Hyde Park in 1866, recommended that they be made a truly civilian force and be put under ''civilian'' leaders and returned to local—presumably parish—control, a call which echoed demands made by some parishes all along.[67]

Perhaps more persistent criticism of the police came from the working classes. Summing up widely held complaints by the lower classes Lord Dudley Stuart, MP for Marylebone, a persistent critic of the police in general and of the high police rates (local taxes) in particular, pointed out in 1849 that many of the police ''were prone to exceed their duty and oppress the people.'' While gentlemen might find them useful for getting home from a party, the ''people'' would tell you that ''wherever a policeman was found there was a petty tyrant.'' He attributed these failings to the low level of education among police.[68] Four years later in 1853 he suggested in Parliament that the police were not worth the money they cost, especially since the need for them had declined after the disturbances in 1848. He wanted to reduce their numbers and recruit a higher class of officers to control the constables better, and to prevent such incidents as the lethal mob crush at the lying-in-state of the Duke of Wellington the preceding year. Stuart's views on upgrading the police leadership closely followed those expressed by Edwin Chadwick in his testimony before the Select Committee on Police in 1853.[69]

In an age in which one's social status was fairly accurately represented in clothing, shabbily dressed workmen might well be ''moved along'' in areas like Mayfair and Belgravia unless they had obvious business to attend to—all of which contributed in no small way to the fund of ill will toward the police felt by many in the lower classes. One writer to *The Times* of 16 June 1851 signing himself ''A Lover of Justice'' said that he had witnessed ''acts of very arbitrary and insolent interference, generally with the lower classes of the community.'' He went on to say that the poor rarely made complaints. ''They bear many small injuries in silence rather than incur the displeasure of so powerful a body.'' In 1864 the *Spectator* wrote that

there are few residents in London who have not at some time or other observed instances of oppression and brutality perpetrated by a policeman against the poor and vicious.

Prompt obedience is in such cases often enforced by what the policeman would call a push and the bystander a blow, and resistance is "obstructing a constable in discharge of his duty."

The article concluded: "People in good clothes are generally safe."[70] George Holyoake, the journalist, writing much later, also had harsh words for the police. "Sir Richard Mayne, as all Metropolitan Commissioners do, treated the working class as a criminal class, and more frequently attacked them than assisted them." Holyoake said that by contrast the City of London police had maintained much better relations with the working classes.[71]

Hatred of the police by costermongers and other street venders had become almost traditional by the time of which Henry Mayhew wrote, the 1850s; his section on costermongers has numerous references to this. The venders were prohibited from selling in certain parts of London and in many others were forced to keep moving, a form of harassment particularly galling for their trade. They condemned the police roundly. "The poor costermongers," reported *Reynolds' Newspaper* in 1863, "have had their stalls ruthlessly swept away by the zealous and lynx-eyed police, who allow the foul ravishers of infant girls and the red-handed perpetrators of mid-day murders to roam at large, to repeat their revolting outrages." According to Mayhew the "costers" formed a tightly knit group who were "nearly all Chartists"—the term by then being almost a portmanteau epithet for any political dissident. "In case of a political riot every 'coster' would seize his policeman." To "serve out a crusher" (assault a policeman), even if prosecution would inevitably follow, was considered a mark of bravery. Mayhew wrote that some young men had been imprisoned up to a dozen times for this offense, and could always look forward to enhanced prestige upon their release—and a money subscription—from the costermonger community.[72]

Chimney-sweeps were also reported for their anti-authority (mainly anti-police) sentiments as well as for their Chartist leanings, and would supposedly welcome any mob tumult that might take place.[73] Other trades and callings, such as prostitution, also brought unwelcome attention from the police. One witness before a Select Committee in 1834 complained that in the Commercial Road in the East End he had seen crowds of young prostitutes, some no more than nine or ten years of age. The witness claimed that the police levied contributions from the older women shepherding them, in exchange for non-interference. Many years later Sergeant-at-Law William Ballantine said that prostitutes around Regent Street were allowed to solicit openly only after paying off the police. Ballantine said on "several occasions" he had seen policemen pick up money from a window sill or a post where a female had placed it. The Christian Socialist

J.M. Ludlow, in writing to the *Spectator* to complain of police violence during the 1866 Reform Bill demonstration, said that police blackmail of "omnibus-drivers, streetwalkers, publicans, &c.,—is so frequent as to be taken as a matter of course by the victims." Ludlow was scarcely an unbiased observer, but his observations were confirmed by others.[74] It is hard to judge the reliability of such charges, but in 1908 a Royal Commission on police took up the issue and concluded that it could not be substantiated that police sought or took bribes from prostitutes. Testifying before the same Commission the Secretary of the National Vigilance Association said that in hundreds of interviews with "unfortunate women" over the course of twenty-one years not one had ever made a charge against a policeman of levying blackmail or exacting bribes.[75]

Complaints about police in the Victorian years often reflected ethnic biases to "account" for some undesirable behavior. Ludlow said that on the outskirts of London "where the policemen were better known individually, and more under the control of local public opinion, they are stupider and more respectable; but they are far from immaculate even there." He was convinced that the policeman had degenerated from being a "self-reliant, trustworthy Englishman" and had become "too often unmistakably an overbearing Irish ruffian." Although a small percentage of the police were Irish, anti-Irish sentiment was such that people were likely to attribute police brutality to Irishmen on the force. In 1834 when hostility to the police was still relatively strong, Thomas Morris, a hatter from the East End, said that the majority of the police were the "lower order of Irish. . . . Those men are red-hot Irishmen, just imported, who run out and strike every person they meet."[76]

Much of the hostility shown by the working classes toward the police had to do with the police interference in a variety of customs and entertainments of the working classes. Not only did the police monitor drinking habits by enforcing pub and beerhouse hours, but they also intervened to block a number of leisure activities: brutal sports, fairs, foot-racing. "The police came as unwelcome spectators into the very nexis of urban neighborhood life," in the words of Robert Storch.[77]

However annoying the police presence could be to the working classes in London, their response was relatively tame compared to the massive shows of resistance to the introduction of police forces in some of the towns of the industrial North in the 1840s, where troops had to be called in from time to time to protect the constables. The overbearing behavior and brutality shown by some of those policemen toward workingmen only exacerbated the resentment.

Assaults on London policemen were prevalent enough—there were 2,858 arrests for such assaults in 1869 alone—but the tight control by the Commissioners and their insistence on correct behavior by constables helped facilitate working-class acceptance of the police over the course of the century.[78]

The turning of country lads into urban policemen was never an easy process, but even if their training was rudimentary, their job still required, more than anything, a controlled temper and a strong arm. By 1852 the police were a reliable enough fixture of urban administration that the *Edinburgh Review* could state confidently that "there is no longer any room for great improvement in our police system." When a respected periodical could write this way, things had indeed changed in the thirty-three years the Metropolitan Police had existed.[79]

By the 1850s and 1860s one was much more likely to hear favorable comments, especially from the middle and upper classes. "Their conduct has been so exemplary as completely to have removed the original dislike. . . . They are now looked upon as a constitutional force, simply because we have got accustomed to them."[80] Alexander Herzen, one of the numerous Continental *émigrés* of the mid-Victorian years who found London a more receptive home for their political activities, paid his own compliment: "Until I came to England the appearance of a police officer in a house where I was living always produced an indefinable disagreeable feeling, and I was at once morally on my guard against an enemy. In England a policeman at your door merely adds to your sense of security." Another foreign observer was quoted as saying: "I never speak of the London Police Force without raising my hat."[81]

By the 1870s, with the increase in literacy and the proliferation of cheaper newspapers and magazines for a wider public, various social groupings could express their own opinions in print more easily. This, it was claimed, added a further restraint to police practices and behavior. The *Quarterly Review* felt that the critical press had helped improve the police. "The whole population of the metropolis are reporters for the newspapers."[82]

CONCLUSION

To our modern age that takes police professionalism for granted nineteenth-century police training and practices seem rudimentary, but then the world the Victorian bobby moved in required little more of him than a keen eye, common sense, a strong arm, and a dose of courage. As we have seen, these bobbies operated within a more restricted definition of policing than did their Continental counterparts. Given the public skepticism about a uniform London police and about entrusting the constables with extensive powers, the Commissioners were concerned about public opinion and about the behavior of the constables whose discretionary powers were limited.

That the police were usually successful in their basic role of patrolling the streets and even in confronting crowds is certain, but also certain is that the conservatism of the Commissioners (and Mayne's rigidity in particular) created problems for the police in time. The Commissioners, however, were not solely to blame. Pay was low, pensions were inadequate, and discipline was often heavy-handed, leading to a high turnover in the police. Another area of weakness, was in the area of detection, and here the attitudes of the Commissioners and the public distaste for "spying" impeded the creation of a large detective force.

We have seen how important the Commissioners were in structuring the force, and how the initial decision by Peel to keep the police free from partisan politics and patronage went a long way toward establishing the Metropolitan Police as an organization that represented impersonal authority, and one that in time received considerable public approval. The Commissioners' tight control over the organization meant that their own perspectives from the top translated readily into police policy. The impact of Rowan and Mayne is still evident today with the British police as a whole.

NOTES

1. Moylan, *Scotland Yard*, p. 72.
2. *P.P.* 1856 (2016), XXIII, *Report on the Alleged Disturbances of the Public Peace in Hyde Park on Sunday, 1 July 1855* (Royal Commission), q. 6637. (Henceforth Royal Commission, 1855). *P.P.* 1833 (718), XIII, *Report from the Select Committee on Cold Bath Fields Meeting*, qs. 5, 6, 108-9, 4750, 4789. *P.P.* 1833 (627), XIII, *Report from the Select Committee on the Petition of Frederick Young and Others*, qs. 4075, 4082, 4085-87.
3. Many of the observations in this section and the sections to follow were drawn from F.C. Mather's useful book, *Public Order in the Age of the Chartists*, esp. p. 38. See also David Philips, " 'A New Engine.' "
4. Sir Edward Troup, *The Home Office* (2d ed., London: G.P. Putnam's Sons, Ltd., 1926), p. 251. P.R.O. Home Office Papers ("H.O.") 65, *Police Entry Books* (concerning the Treasury Solicitors).
5. Mather, *Public Order*, p. 30.
6. Ibid., p. 31.
7. MEPOL 2/5814 (4 May 1848), Memo from Mayne. Ibid., 2/34 (26 Nov. 1849), Memo from Mayne. *P.P.* 1834 (600), XVI, *Report from the Select Committee on the Police of the Metropolis*, q. 432.
8. *The Times* (London), 29 Dec. 1868. G.D. Burtchaell and T.U. Sadleir, eds., *Alumni Dublinenses* (Dublin: Alexander Thom & Co., Ltd., 1935).
9. Reith, *A New Study of Police History*, pp. 127-28. Charles Reith, *The Blind Eye of History* (London: Faber and Faber, Ltd., 1952), pp. 151-52.

10. *Hansard*, Vol. 140 (4 Feb. 1856), col. 180.

11. Browne, *Rise of Scotland Yard*, p. 138.

12. Timothy Cavanagh, *Scotland Yard Past and Present* (London: Chatto & Windus, 1893), pp. 75-76.

13. Ibid., p. 79.

14. MEPOL l/46 (28 Oct. 1859). Royal Commission, 1855, q. 12,271.

15. Christopher Pulling, *Mr. Punch and the Police* (London: Butterworths, 1964), p. 79.

16. "The Police System of London," *Edinburgh Review*, XCVI (July 1852), 10. For more about daily police activity see Miller, *Cops and Bobbies*; also Finlay McKichan, "Constabulary Duties: The Lives of Police Constables a Century Ago," *History Today*, XXX (Sept. 1980), 32-37. See also P.T. Smith, "The London Metropolitan Police and Public Order and Security, 1850-1868" (Ph.D. diss., Columbia University, 1976).

17. "The Police of London," *Quarterly Review*, CXXIX, 98. MEPOL 8/3 (1871), p. 97. Cavanagh, *Scotland Yard*, p. 2.

18. *P.P.* 1834 (600), XVI, q. 61. *P.P.* 1870 (150), XXXVI, pp. 35-36, 43. MEPOL 4/36, *Instruction Book*, 1871. MEPOL 8/3 (1871), p. 97.

19. MEPOL 4/36 *Instruction Book*, 1871. H.O. 65/8 (15 July 1868). All H.O. documents cited are in the Public Record Office.

20. *The Times* (London), 25 July 1855. *P.P.* 1871 (358) XXVIII. MEPOL 4/36 *Instruction Book*, 1871. MEPOL 8/3 (1 June 1870). By contrast the New York police received no formal training until 1853, and then only drill for riot control purposes. Richardson, *New York Police*, p. 68.

21. MEPOL 4/36 *Instruction Book*, 1871.

22. "The Police and the Thieves," *Quarterly Review*, XCIX (June 1856), 171.

23. C.T. Clarkson and J.H. Richardson, *Police! History of the Metropolitan Police* (London: Field and Tuer, Leadenhall Press, 1889), p. 66.

24. *P.P.* 1873 (839), XXXI, p. 297. *P.P.* 1870 (150), XXXVI, p. 5. *Hansard*, Vol. 193 (29 June 1868), col. 344. *P.P.* 1852-53 (71), XXXVI, *Select Committee on Police*, q. 2869.

25. *Saturday Review of Politics, Literature, Science and Art* XXVI (14 Nov. 1868), 654. "The Police of London," *Quarterly Review*, CXXIX, 128.

26. MEPOL 8/2 *Instructions, Orders*, 1836. J.P. Martin and Gail Wilson, *The Police: A Study in Manpower: The Evolution of the Service in England and Wales 1829-1965* (London: Heinemann Educational Books, Ltd., 1969), p. 22.

27. MEPOL 7/27 (5 Feb. 1866). MEPOL 8/3 (2 May 1866).

28. MEPOL 8/2 *Instructions, Orders*, 1836.

29. W.H. Wills, "The Metropolitan Protectives," in *Old Leaves: Gathered from Household Words* (New York: Harper & Bros., 1860), pp. 252-53. "The Police and the Thieves," *Quarterly Review*, XCIX, 166.

30. MEPOL 8/3 (30 Sept. 1867). MEPOL 7/131 (12 Aug. 1852). MEPOL 7/20 (15 Dec. 1859). *P.P.* 1868-69 (185), LI, p. 495.

31. MEPOL 7/30 (16 Jan. 1868).

32. Silver, "The Demand for Order," pp. 13-14.

33. *London Quarterly Review*, 1870, quoted in Silver, "The Demand for Order," pp. 13-14.

34. *P.P.* 1852 (41), XLI, pp. 484-89. *P.P.* 1867 (513), LVII, p. 817. MEPOL 2/ 5801 (1863), Rept. from Mayne to Sir George Grey.

35. "The Police System of London," *Edinburgh Review*, XCVI, 9.

36. MEPOL 8/2 *Instruction Book*, 1871. *P.P.* 1856 (42), L, p. 661.

37. Royal Commission, 1855, q. 6666. MEPOL 7/14 (20 July 1849), memorandum. MEPOL 7/14 (27 Oct. 1848). Wills, "The Metropolitan Protectives," p. 253.

38. "Custos," *The Police Force of the Metropolis in 1868* (London: William Ridgway, 1868), p. 20.

39. Ibid., p. 22.

40. Quoted in Reith, *New Study*, p. 146. *P.P.* 1834 (600), XVI, q. 128.

41. Ascoli, *The Queen's Peace*, p. 150.

42. University College, London, Chadwick MSS 2/86, 1831. "The Police and the Thieves," *Quarterly Review*, XCIX, 170.

43. Clarkson and Richardson, *Police!* p. 73. *P.P.* 1852-53 (71), XXXVI, *Second Report from the Select Committee on Police*, qs. 2870, 2872. *P.P.* 1834 (600), XVI, qs. 53-55.

44. "The Police of London," *Quarterly Review*, CXXIX, 98. Royal Commission, 1855.

45. *P.P.* 1873 (839), XXXI, *Report of the Commissioner*, p. 310.

46. H. Llewellyn Smith, "Influx of Population," in *Life and Labour of the People in London*, 1st ser., ed. by Charles Booth (London: Macmillan and Co., Ltd., 1902), III, 85-87. G.E. Arkell in Booth, 2d ser., IV, 52.

47. Raymond B. Fosdick, *European Police Systems*, Patterson Smith Reprint Series (Montclair, N.J.: Patterson Smith, [1915] 1969), p. 210.

48. Richardson, *New York Police*, pp. 49-50.

49. Royal Commission, 1855, qs. 6668-70.

50. Robert A. Fuller, *Recollections of a Detective* (London: John Long, Ltd., 1912), p. 21.

51. *P.P.* 1834 (600), XVI, q. 128. *P.P.* 1860 (212), XL, Returns, pp. 87-91. Moylan, *Scotland Yard*, p. 35.

52. *P.P.* 1873 (839), XXXI, Report of the Commissioner, p. 310. Booth, *Life and Labour*, 2d ser., IV, 52. Fosdick, *European Police Systems*, Chapter 6.

53. "Police and the Thieves," *Quarterly Review*, XCIX, 170.

54. MEPOL 8/2, p. 8. *P.P.* 1830 (505), XXIII, p. 408.

55. Cavanagh, *Scotland Yard*, pp. 54, 92, 121. *P.P.* 1871 (358), XXVIII. George Dilnot, *Scotland Yard: its History and Organization* (Boston: Houghton Mifflin Co., 1927), p. 332 n. 42.

56. Browne, *Rise of Scotland Yard*, p. 133. Martin and Wilson, *The Police*, p. 15. E.J.

Hobsbawm, *Industry and Empire* (Baltimore, Md.: Penguin Books, 1969), p. 160. A man in the preparatory class would receive only ten shillings a week. Married men were given a money allowance of four pence a week instead of coal. *P.P.* 1870 (150), XXXVI, p. 42, Appendix C. *P.P.* 1860 (212), XL, p. 92. *P.P.* 1867 (154), LVII, p. 798. Martin and Wilson, *The Police*, pp. 13, 16.

57. Royal Commission, 1855, testimony of Mayne, q. 6607.

58. *P.P.* 1830 (505), XXIII, p. 413. *P.P.* 1833 (718), q. 1142.

59. *P.P.* 1860 (212), XL, *Returns*, p. 89. H.O. 65/8 (25 May 1868 and 13 March 1869).

60. MEPOL 7/14 (19 Dec. 1849).

61. MEPOL 7/19 (1857-58); 7/21 (1860).

62. *P.P.* 1834 (600) XVI, qs. 107-8, 534. MEPOL 7/19 (21 Dec. 1858). This same order was repeated year after year around the same time. Cavanagh, *Scotland Yard*, pp. 78-80.

63. MEPOL 7/20 (6 Jan. 1859). MEPOL 7/19 (May 1858). MEPOL 7/23 (Dec. 1862). MEPOL 7/29 (April and Aug. 1867). Other figures are: April 1867, 11 of 30; Aug. 1867, 7 of 27. In some cases no reason is given for a dismissal. Besides fines, reductions in rank were also imposed, so that the statistics tell only part of the story.

64. Martin and Wilson, *The Police*, pp. 21, 23-24.

65. Miller, *Cops and Bobbies*, pp. 9, 106-9.

66. Browne, *The Rise of Scotland Yard*, p. 138.

67. Great Britain, Bishopsgate Institute, Howell Collection, Reform League Papers, *Hyde Park Cases, 1866, Report of the Sub-Committee* No. 45.

68. *Hansard*, Vol. 106 (3 July 1849), col. 1260.

69. Ibid., Vol. 129 (2 Aug. 1853), cols. 1163-66. *P.P.* 1852-53 (71), XXXVI, q. 3662.

70. *Spectator*, XXVIII (30 April 1864), p. 496.

71. George Jacob Holyoake, *Sixty Years of an Agitator's Life* (London: T. Fisher Unwin, 1892), II, 135.

72. *Reynolds' Newspaper* (25 Oct. 1863), p. 4. Henry Mayhew, *London Labour and the London Poor* (London: Frank Cass & Co., Ltd., 1967), I, 16, 20.

73. Mayhew, *London Labour*, II, 370.

74. *P.P.* 1834 (600), XVI, q. 4326. William Ballantine, *Some Experiences of a Barrister's Life* (London: Richard Bentley & Son, 1882), II, 28-29.

75. Cited in Fosdick, *European Police Systems*, pp. 372-73.

76. J.M. Ludlow to the Editor, *Spectator* (4 Aug. 1866), pp. 857-58. *P.P.* 1834 (600), XVI, q. 4379.

77. Robert Storch, "The Plague of Blue Locusts: Police Reform and Popular Resistance in Northern England, 1840-1857," *International Review of Social History*, XX (1975), 84.

78. Miller, *Cops and Bobbies*, p. 138.

79. "The Police System of London," *Edinburgh Review*, XCVI, 25.

80. "The Police and the Thieves," *Quarterly Review*, XCIX (June 1856), 163-64.

81. E.H. Carr, *The Romantic Exiles* (Middlesex, U.K.: Penguin Books, 1968), p. 121. "London Police Duty," *Leisure Hour* (May 1879), p. 279.

82. "The Police of London," *Quarterly Review*, CXXIX, 128-29.

3   "Human Moles": Detection and Surveillance

There was no question in the minds of the founders of the police that the constables were not to act as any army of spies; their mission was to prevent crime. This preventive idea, whatever its subsequent weaknesses, was the basic theory behind the force. In 1822 we find Robert Peel saying: "God forbid that [I] should mean to countenance a system of espionage." What he wanted was a "vigorous preventive police, consistent with the free principles of our free constitution." This meant in practice having a uniformed body of constables, clearly visible, walking their beats to scare away wrongdoers. The public could at least see the police doing their jobs and take confidence in that presence. Such a philosophy of policing, if translated into practice would appear to preclude detectives. Such was not to be. Detectives and other policemen in plain clothes, men colorfully described by the *Quarterly Review* as "those human moles who work without casting up the earth lest their course should be discovered," were soon an integral part of the force.[1]

THE DETECTIVE DEPARTMENT

Secrecy is necessary for much of police work, and the London police found that they could not ignore the clandestine aspects of their job. The small detective force set up in 1842 was the lineal descendant of the thief-takers from earlier centuries who had operated like private detectives. By the eighteenth century the Bow Street Runners and other detectives attached to the police courts received some pay from the government, thus making them semi-private detectives. But the Detective Department, set up in 1842 directly under Rowan and Mayne, was the first full-time, fully salaried corps of detectives.

With only a handful of detectives, supplemented by men put into plain clothes for temporary duty, and aided by informers, the London police never had in the nineteenth century a system of detection and surveillance anywhere close in scope to those of Continental Europe. In fact the Commissioners distrusted detection on principle and limited the detectives in the way they operated; they tried to keep them from consorting closely with criminals, which was necessary in an age with almost no scientific aids for detection.

Although there were some talented and intelligent detectives, detection and surveillance were not strong areas with the Metropolitan Police. Chapters on aliens and on the Irish Fenians will bring out clearly the problems connected with this "other side" of policing.

Being separate from the Metropolitan Police, the City of London detective force had been established in 1840 or 1841 as part of the reserves, and originally consisted of 9 men, easily recognized by their police trousers and unglazed top hats.[2] Although detectives were officially added some thirteen years after the formation of the Metropolitan Police, it is clear that their use predated 1842. Policemen in "colored clothing" (plain clothes) had been used to trap pickpockets in the act, and to attend union meetings or political gatherings; this practice may well have dated from the foundation of the force. In 1833 Superintendent Andrew McLean testified that regular policemen were put in plain clothes for specific duties, and that some of the men were out of uniform for as long as a year at a time. In his testimony before the same Select Committee of Parliament, Mayne admitted that both Peel and his successor as Home Secretary, Lord Melbourne, had approved the practice.

At first there was no full-time force of men trained specifically for detection because there seemed no obvious need for such, given that the Bow Street Runners and other officers attached to the police offices (magistrates' courts) could act as detectives. It was after 1839 with the abolition of the Runners and the court constables that the need for detectives was felt. This was especially so after one particularly brutal murder in 1842 when police ineptitude almost allowed the murderer to go undetected. There is no evidence that Chartist activity had anything to do with the formation of the detectives.

Few details are known about the founding of the Scotland Yard detectives except for a letter from Mayne to the Home Office recommending that two inspectors and six sergeants be selected for "their abilities and general qualifications for those peculiar duties." The new band of detectives, freed from jurisdictional restraints, investigated crimes of a more serious nature. They were sometimes dispatched to other parts of the country or even abroad.

The detectives were placed directly under the control of the Commissioners and worked out of a small office at Scotland Yard headquarters. They remained 8 in number, apparently until 1856 when an extra inspector and a sergeant were added, making 10 men. In 1865 the total was raised to 11, and in 1867 there were 4 inspectors and 11 sergeants, for a total of 15, though some of the men were assigned on a probationary basis.[3]

It had long been obvious, and pressingly so in the face of Fenian outrages, that the detective force was numerically inadequate. "The Commissioners will no doubt see that this [fifteen] is but a very small number of men to carry on the numerous and yearly increasing duties which the Detective Department is called upon to perform." By April 1869, with Edmund Henderson as the new Commissioner, the force was increased to a total of 33 men, led by its superintendent Adolphus Frederick Williamson. All were paid more than uniformed policemen.[4]

Charles Dickens was respectful of the police and took a particular interest in the detectives, who were portrayed favorably in his novels. On one occasion in 1850 he invited several detectives to the office of *Household Words* and interviewed them. He described them as "respectable" looking men, "of perfectly good deportment and unusual intelligence, with nothing lounging or slinking in their manners." Their features showed "traces more or less marked of habitually leading lives of strong mental excitement."[5]

FORERUNNERS OF THE DETECTIVES

The Scotland Yard detective may have been a new creation but he was the lineal descendant of the old seventeenth- and eighteenth-century thief-taker, a much reviled but necessary part of the legal system of those earlier ages. Detection was a private matter that grew in the murky area where the machinery of law did not provide any effective way of returning stolen goods. We expect detectives today to investigate a host of crimes and catch the wrongdoer and perhaps get stolen property returned. In previous centuries there was simply no official agency for doing this. The citizen who suffered a loss and could not identify the guilty party and immediately have him brought to court would have to hire (if he could afford to) a thief-taker, in essence a private detective, to get his property returned. The victim's interest in recovering his property took precedence over any public interest in apprehending and punishing the criminal.

Thief-taking had never been considered a public responsibility, although for certain crimes rewards might be offered by the Treasury. Also, since the state assumed the responsibility of prosecuting only a few serious crimes, it was up to the private citizen to bear the cost of prosecution for most crimes. Justice depended much on the pocketbook of the plaintiff and his determination to subject himself and the suspect to the caprice of the law.

The thief-taker, whose methods and reputation stood him on a par with the bounty hunter of the American West, earned the reward money and other perquisites offered by the victim, and also by the government or local authorities for the successful prosecution of criminals. Operating on the principle that it takes a thief to catch one, he frequently consorted with thieves, and in some cases crimes were conveniently arranged, the thief-taker and the thief splitting the reward money. This sordid and despised business could be very profitable, but at times dangerous. William Payne, a London thief-taker of Bell Yard, new Temple Bar (by trade a carpenter), was instrumental in securing sixty-nine prosecutions in London between 1768 and 1771. This obviously left little time for carpentry. He was beaten up several times and twice someone tried to burn down his workshop.[6]

The most notorious thief-taker of them all was really a professional criminal, Jonathan Wild. Wild, who styled himself "Thief-Taker General of Great Britain and Ireland," was in fact "godfather" of the London underworld from 1715 until he was hanged in 1725. Wild controlled a number of criminal gangs and acted as a receiver for stolen goods, which he was smart enough not to handle personally. In the guise of a thief-taker he became the middleman to arrange the return of stolen property. No questions were asked (no answers would have been given anyway), and Wild afterward would share the reward with his associates. Wild was hardly the typical thief-taker, but the methods used by many humbler and more honest ones put the thief-taker in bad odor with the public.[7]

Detection became "official" in 1749 when the famous Bow Street Runners were set up by Henry Fielding, magistrate at the Bow Street Court. These Runners—the name was not used until years later—were the first London detectives to be salaried public officials directly under control of the magistrates. They were paid at first a guinea (a pound and a shilling) a week as a retainer, but they were not expected to live off that. They made their money from private investigations, from court fees, and from reward money offered after the conviction of criminals.

John Townsend was the most famous of the Runners. With another Runner, he protected the Royal Court. Townsend was also a familiar figure at the Bank of England on Dividend Day when stock dividends were paid out in gold coins. His presence at fashionable balls (announced on the invitations) not only gave the guests confidence to wear their expensive jewelry, but was a deterrent to thieves, many of whom he knew on sight. When he died in 1832 he reportedly left £20,000. Another colleague, Sayer, was worth over £30,000.

When the new police offices were established in London in 1792 each magistrate had a group of detectives assigned to him, so that by the end of the eighteenth century there were fifty or so detectives in eight or nine separate groups. These detectives confined their investigations to their own areas, much like their modern counterparts, investigating crimes in their own divisions. The

Bow Street Runners, being the senior and more experienced group, operated freely over London or elsewhere as their duties required.[8]

All of these detectives worked more like semi-private detectives, and their effectiveness depended on their contacts with and knowledge of the underworld. They operated alone and were reluctant to share information with their colleagues. Given the fact that they also had to consort with the underworld, the opportunities for corruption were obvious. Some detectives no doubt succumbed, but most of the Runners, at least, seem to have been honest public servants.

The methods of the men, nevertheless, raised the question of what should be their proper relationship with thieves. The answers were not obvious because the victim wanted results favorable to him. Was crime to be suppressed and the criminal punished as the primary goal, or was the recovery of property paramount? It was a conflict that became even more pressing when the essentially private thief-taking business became a public service. The taint of corruption and inefficiency that hung over the business of crime detection, not to mention the public sensitivity toward "spies," made the founders of the Metropolitan Police reluctant to have detectives, much less to employ them on a large scale.

The detectives had always been regarded by Rowan and Mayne as an uncomfortable feature within the police. Detectives also removed observational duties from the men on the beat, argued Superintendent Williamson, in a memo to the Commissioner in 1877.[9] In the late 1840s Edwin Chadwick had written: "I know from Sir C. Rowan and Mr. Richard Mayne that they disliked detection on principle, and only yielded to its adoption on what they deemed superior authority."[10] The superior authority was presumably Sir James Graham, Peel's Home Secretary in 1842.

The detectives, notwithstanding some well-publicized successes in crime detection, continued to be regarded with some misgivings. In 1869 when Edmund Henderson put a detective branch in every division he wrote at the same time that the detective system "is viewed with the greatest suspicion and jealousy by the majority of Englishmen and is in fact, entirely foreign to the habits and feelings of the Nation."[11]

THE POPAY INCIDENT

The Commissioners had an early taste of scandal when one zealous constable, Popay, on his own accord infiltrated the ranks of the National Political Union (NPU) in 1832 and vigorously incited the members to violence, denouncing the government and even the police. He was spotted in uniform in a police station by a colleague in the NPU who then accused Popay of being an *agent provo-*

cateur. The Union petitioned the House of Commons and the result was a Select Committee set up the same year to look into the incident. The committee found Popay's conduct reprehensible but cleared the police of direct blame for his actions and even admitted that the limited use of policemen in plain clothes was occasionally acceptable. Popay was subsequently dismissed from the police.[12]

This came at a time when public opinion was still wary of the mere existence of a police force, much less one that apparently condoned the use of spies as a matter of course. It is clear that Rowan and Mayne feared a repeat of the incident, and were cool to the widespread use of plain-clothes policemen until the end of their days. Mayne's attitudes were expressed clearly in official correspondence, and on one occasion in 1854 he wrote to his superintendents, saying that the employment, even temporary, of regular constables in plain clothes violated the police principle of deterring crime by the obvious presence of uniformed officers. Secondly, the public would not have the reassurance of seeing the constable in his proper place. Also, charges might arise that the police were being used as spies "and in other improper ways." Though he said that the disadvantages outweighed the obvious advantages, Mayne was forced to overcome his scruples and use the detectives for sensitive surveillance, though never to the extent his detractors claimed.[13]

In 1859 William Robinson, the Commissioner of the Police of Madras, had written to Mayne for information on setting up a detective force. Mayne advised him to select men of integrity, thrift and perseverance.

No association with thieves or bad characters is allowed except for the purpose of receiving information in a particular case. My practice is to see the detective officers frequently, showing that I repose full confidence in them, while a strict control is maintained.[14]

PLAINCLOTHESMEN

Throughout the early history of the Metropolitan Police, as we have seen, men were employed in plain clothes who were not detectives, strictly speaking, and who were normally used apart from the detective branch. None of the more recent works on the police has clarified the ambiguity; but it is apparent that a few plainclothesmen were used for the prevention of robberies and to keep an eye on those suspected of being about to commit a crime. They were also used to mix with the crowds at political demonstrations and to relay messages back to the uniformed men in reserve, "to give information, if any cause for police interference arises." In this situation the presence of uniformed constables was felt to be provocative.[15] The police and Home Office records are not clear on the use of plainclothesmen, but the police orders of 11 November 1845—"Constables to be employed on additional detective duties"—called for a permanent body of "two intelligent constables of each division" to keep a continual eye on well-known criminals and get to know their habits. Watching pubs would be part of the job. These officers were to be trained by experienced detectives supplied by Scotland Yard and would move among the divisions exchanging information with other constables. Six months later in May 1846 orders were issued that limited the activities of these policemen to their own divisions where their special knowledge would be drawn upon by their own superintendents.[16] No reference was made in either order to clothing, and it seems likely that plain clothing was worn at least part of the time, but more often than the Commissioners intended, since in December 1845, a month after the original order, Rowan issued a verbal warning against the unauthorized wearing of plain clothes. He reiterated that "no man shall disguise himself without particular orders from the superintendent and that this should not be done even by them without some very strong case of necessity being made out." A later order of June 1846 specified that police in plain clothes must make themselves known if they were interfered with in their duty.[17]

The number of non-uniformed men was more clearly revealed in January 1854 when Mayne tried to curb the zeal of his superintendents who were using too many men in plain clothes. He said that 15 sergeants and 55 constables were appointed to such duty permanently and two sergeants and 102 police constables (PCs) temporarily. He complained that the 104 temporaries were actually maintained permanently on this duty against his instructions. The men were apparently rotated, though the total number remained constant, spread unevenly through the divisions. Mayne added that "there is no regulation of the Service authorizing the employment of Police in plain clothes." He demanded that a report be made when plainclothesmen were used, excepting occasions when simple enquiries concerning a crime could better be made by them than by uniformed men, as judged appropriate by the superintendents.[18]

Two years later, in 1856, the *Quarterly Review* estimated that there were about 6 men in each division who acted as detectives when needed, that is, about 108 altogether who would dress according to the character of the work. "Thus, at an agricultural meeting, smock-frocks are worn, or the dress of a small farmer; at a review the habiliments of a decent mechanic in his Sunday best." This claim must be taken with some skepticism: disguises were not usually worn.[19]

The well-publicized garroting incidents ("mugging," in the current jargon) in 1862 prompted the use of more plainclothesmen to augment the uniformed constables on the regular police beats, especially in high crime areas. In August of that year 176 PCs and 17 sergeants were assigned in plain clothes between the hours of 10 P.M. and 2 A.M. to prevent such crimes. Low-class pubs of bad repute were to be visited occasionally to keep known criminals under watch. Each officer was to submit a report of his nightly work.[20] The following year, however, the orders were changed, forbidding plainclothesmen from entering public houses or beerhouses unless in immediate pursuit of a felon inside; and if entry was necessary otherwise, the officer should always be accompanied by a uniformed constable. The same order also called for the rotation of the plainclothesmen, so that "their usefulness for the general duties of constables is thus maintained, and if tempted to become corrupt they have not the same opportunities of being so." It appears that in the 1850s and 1860s men in general were kept on plain-clothes duty a month at a time.[21] There were, however, a number of men whose special duties kept them in plain clothes full-time. PC James Marsh was assigned to the Inland Revenue Service to check cab licenses and had not been in uniform for ten years. Marsh was one of 17 men who were similarly assigned to Inland Revenue. Others were assigned to the palace and the General Post Office.[22]

HENDERSON AND THE DIVISIONAL DETECTIVES

In 1867 Mayne had suggested an increase in the number of detectives and the creation of a body of full-time plain-clothes detectives in the divisions operating under division control. Shortly after Edmund Henderson became the new Commissioner in 1869 such a body was in fact created, called divisional detectives. There were some 189 sergeants and constables drawn into this unit, enjoying salaries slightly above those of regular constables. They had received no special training. These new detectives were concerned mainly with watching thieves and pickpockets in their areas only. They were a separate body from the regular Scotland Yard detectives, though it was intended that both forces would work together closely; however, coordination between the two often proved to be poor.[23]

Even though Mayne had stressed the need for using only the better constables as plainclothesmen, this turned out not to be the case. While those regular detectives attached to Scotland Yard headquarters were generally capable and intelligent, the divisional detectives left something to be desired. Keeping men in close contact with the criminal classes for a prolonged period created problems. Many officers objected to the long and irregular hours, the often unpleasant work, the isolation, the limited promotion opportunities, and the degrading contacts: consequently, they preferred uniformed work.

In the late 1860s Inspector Williamson (head of the detectives and later superintendent) complained that although the men were often experienced in the habits of thieves, they were mostly illiterate and ignorant "with but very little knowledge of the world or mankind outside the circle in which [they] moved."[24] In 1871 in response to a recommendation that divisional detectives should keep a written diary as a way of supervising their movements, Williamson said that many of the men, "for want of education, find it impossible to make a daily comprehensible report of their proceedings. This would keep out from the detective service many useful men."[25]

Detective Robert A. Fuller later recalled that the detectives he knew in the 1870s, especially in the rough districts, "seemed destitute of everything but a certain amount of low cunning, a smattering of thieves' slang, and the knack of making believe they knew every evil-doer in London."[26]

THE C.I.D., 1878

A further reorganization of the detectives was undertaken in 1878 in the wake of a sensational scandal that tied in three of the four detective chief inspectors with an international swindling racket. A Criminal Investigation Department was set up under a barrister named Howard Vincent, who had studied the Paris detectives. This reorganization at least had the virtue of placing all the detectives under one head and eliminating the conflicts of jurisdiction and lack of centralized coordination that had characterized the divisional detectives. Within six years he had increased the size of the C.I.D. from 250 to 800. They received higher pay than uniformed policemen. He also improved training. Vincent delivered his own harsh assessment of the old divisional detectives, saying that they were mostly illiterate men, "many of whom had been put into plain clothes to screen personal defects which marred their smart appearance in uniform." They were inefficient and did very little, living "a life unprofitable to themselves, discreditable to the service, useless to the public."[27]

It was one thing to call for the performance of special skills; it was another to find, to train, and to keep men capable of carrying out the duties effectively. Given the state of police training and the rudimentary scientific aids to detection, the Victorian detective was very much on his own, depending on his intuition and a good memory to be effective. Whatever problems remained with the detective, he was still locked into a web of interaction with the criminal world that could not be avoided, bringing with it some potential for corruption. The modern policeman at least has the advantage of sophisticated investigative and communication devices so that even in undercover work he can distance himself from his suspects, an advantage his Victorian forebears, however honest, did not have.

As we have already seen, the limitations placed on the Metropolitan Police detectives were rooted in public attitudes, too. We can see these attitudes as symbolic of the prejudices and mentality of the age that took a dim view of secret police work. On more than one occasion the police found themselves caught between the need for adequate intelligence from a well-trained plainclothes investigative body and the misgivings of the authorities and the public about such a body. Unlike Continental police forces who employed large numbers of detectives, wielding far more extensive police powers, the London police had to make do with relatively few men in plain clothes. Their roles were limited in England, though important.

CONSTRAINTS ON DETECTIVES

The wearing of plain clothes and the following of suspects were unavoidable aspects of Victorian policing, too. Even though the detective force and the plainclothesmen were few in number, there was no extensive use of spies and informers to make up the deficiency. That there was some spying on private citizens and refugees, as well as on suspected criminals, was obvious at the time, and even led to complaints from the articulate public; but it was not extensive or "professional" to the degree found in European police forces. The London police often had to draw intelligence haphazardly from a variety of external sources: volunteer informers, alarmed citizens or government officials, outside police agencies, or simply paranoid cranks. Surveillance, nevertheless, was a fact of life in the Metropolitan Police and played an important part in mid-Victorian security.

Where there are detectives one might think of disguises. But the police orders and correspondence tell us little about the use of disguises or how often and under what conditions detectives wore them. It seems likely that disguises, when used, were relatively simple and were not the exotic costumes portrayed in literature. Detective Inspector Charles Field—the model for Dickens's Inspector Bucket in *Bleak House*—was well known by the public at large and was fond of disguises. Field originally wanted to be an actor, but poverty drove him into police work (the commonest inducement for police recruits), where he found his métier in detection. Field's costumes were probably more a matter of self-indulgence than professional necessity.[28]

Sir Richard Mayne, like his late colleague Rowan, took a dim view of disguises and insisted on more or less conventional clothing for his detectives and plainclothesmen. In 1864 he forbade the use of "disguises" for policemen entering pubs to check on illegal trading. Those policemen entering pubs for that reason were to be in uniform, to enter by the main doors and accept no drinks. Besides keeping the constables sober, which was always a problem, the "high visibility" would lessen complaints that the police were spying. Mayne's emphasis on openness was clearly revealed in a curious incident in 1851. Through a newspaper account of a court case, he read that a constable hid behind a tree to watch "indecent acts" being committed in Hyde Park. The constable arrested the parties only afterward, instead of preventing the liaison. Mayne was annoyed with the constable and wrote in the police orders: "The commissioners wholly disapprove of such a step & the police are directed never to do so." His insistence on the obvious presence of a policeman beforehand was certainly consistent with the idea of a "preventive police." A police order of 1850 had said that policemen attending Chartist meetings were to be in uniform, and if the superintendent on a particular occasion thought this inappropriate, a report had to be made to the Commissioner.[29]

Complaints by private citizens that they were being followed and watched by policemen are recorded among the Home Office papers, and in numerous instances the Home Office requested an explanation from the Commissioner. It does not appear that such surveillance was done on a large scale, even though many of the complaints were valid. Some detectives found it convenient to pick up extra money by making unofficial private enquiries or by putting pressure on debtors, a practice that reminds us of the private origin of detection. Mayne condemned this as "exceedingly improper and dangerous" and threatened severe discipline for violators.[30]

The Fenian alarms of the 1860s (to be discussed in Chapter Nine) put a strain on the small detective force which was now required to investigate, among other things, the numerous rumors of incendiaries and plots that came flooding in from an alarmed public. The police of Ireland and of some of the provincial cities had proved more efficient in ferreting out Fenians than the Metropolitan force, which came to be criticized by the press and by prominent officials. Now the sentiments were reversed and the police were criticized for doing too little in the area of surveillance.

The Clerkenwell explosion in late 1867 brought a new outcry against the seeming inadequacy of the police. Lord Derby wrote to the Queen that the police "are especially deficient, however, as a detective force, which is at this time urgently required."[31] He also wrote to Disraeli complaining of the inefficiency of the detectives, and the unwillingness of Mayne to employ men for "peculiar duties." The "peculiar duties" had included among other things, having detectives make secret enquiries in France, though Mayne and the Home Secretary had reservations about the wisdom (or usefulness) of such a course, fearing that the French would find out and take it as a license to use their own detectives more extensively in England. In spite of the reservations, English detectives still operated in France following Fenians.[32]

SPIES AND INFORMERS

As adjuncts to police activity the spy and the informer must find their places in police history. Far from being "un-English" both enjoyed a time-honored status that had made them useful to English governments for centuries. Certainly both, particularly the informer, were a regular part of police activity in the eighteenth and early nineteenth centuries. Their employment was expedient and even inevitable in an age before a professional police force made them less essential. It is difficult to distinguish between spies and informers since the terms were often used interchangeably. A spy was presumably employed by the police or the Home Office on a deliberate, regular basis. To the subjects of surveillance, however, such a distinction was irrelevant. Spies were indeed used by the Home Office in the Chartist period, and even after; but they never constituted what could be called a spy "system." Like informers they were usually drawn from the ranks of local talent, and hoped to be handsomely rewarded for their information.

Public opinion came increasingly to regard informers with disdain. Patrick Colquhoun, the leading exponent of a "preventive" police force, was careful not to attack the usefulness of informers. Bentham had extolled their civic usefulness and had bitterly denounced the hypocritical and ungrateful attitude with which the public viewed them. With the establishment of the Metropolitan Police in 1829 came the increased expectation that informers would no longer be needed, since the laws could now be enforced more easily. Hitherto, the authorities often had had to rely on the inducement of rewards to informers for the solving of crimes. The 1839 Metropolitan Police Courts Act reduced the profitability of informing somewhat, by allowing magistrates to deny or reduce a reward offered. Nevertheless, the informer still held his own in the law machinery, but was still hated.[33]

Even though much of the impetus for the use of informers came from local authorities, the Home Office frequently reimbursed informers for their expenses from the Secret Service Fund. Free pardons, perhaps coupled with a reward, were often tendered as bait to get law-breakers to turn Queen's evidence against their former associates.[34]

As it had been difficult to recruit informers and spies (who might be afraid to testify later) for Chartist meetings in the 1830s and 1840s, newspaper reporters often provided much information. One, P.B. Templeton, a reporter for the Chartist paper the *Northern Star*, boasted that he covered nearly every Chartist meeting in Lancashire and Yorkshire, and asked £40 for each report. The Home Office also often imported shorthand writers from afar to attend meetings. In 1867 £21.4 was ordered disbursed by the Home Office to pay the expenses of shorthand writers at Reform League meetings. Uniformed policemen were frequently in attendance at London political gatherings in the 1850s and 1860s, conspicuously taking notes. Such a practice appears to have been more common in London, at least, than the use of paid informers.[35]

Although the fears inspired by organized Chartism had died down after 1848, the Chartist tradition was still strong, especially in London. Chartist meetings continued to be held in the 1850s, and in 1853 Palmerston, as Home Secretary, gave orders for the police to watch an upcoming three-day meeting, a normal procedure on previous occasions. In addition, the term "Chartist" was transmuted into a convenient label of abuse to be applied to any suspected dissident or revolutionary of whatever political complexion.[36]

In spite of Richard Mayne's reservations about detectives, he did not seem to disapprove of the use of informers. In one confidential letter to the Home Office, in which he recommended money for one informer, he said, "I think it greatly for the public benefit that liberal rewards should be given to encourage others to give information." In 1858 "S" volunteered to spy on London aliens for £2 a week. Mayne refused, saying that such an allowance could not be made, but that "compensation will be made" for any really important information.[37]

Although the Irish authorities employed them more than did the London police, spies and informers were used during the Fenian alarms of the late 1860s. In 1867 Mayne paid £5 to one unnamed informer but would pay only £200 more when a prisoner was clearly identified.[38] The information tendered was not always satisfactory. In April 1867 Mayne wrote to the Earl of Belmore complaining that one informer, a Mr. Pickford, who had submitted his bill for services, was probably a fraud. "He had not given me a particle of information, nor shewn that he had any knowledge of dangerous Fenians which he professed, and his statements respecting them were not trustworthy." On one occasion this same Pickford had pointed out an Irish policeman on duty in London "as a dangerous Fenian whom he had known in New York."[39]

Spies and informers in general were used relatively little in the period treated in this paper, and the police relied on their own usual investigative procedures or on unsolicited warnings from anxious citizens, often government officials themselves. Reports of plots or suspicious activity, criminal or otherwise, poured into the Home Office or Scotland Yard daily. That much of it was obviously grossly exaggerated or simply false did not relieve the police of the obligation of making enquiries where appropriate. Fears of the designs of the large numbers of post-1848 refugees coming into Britain, when combined with the recrudescence of anti-Catholic feeling in the early 1850s, added more anxiety to the age. In 1848 a Customs House official at Folkstone was alarmed at the numbers of foreigners landing daily, some of whom had ideas that appeared "to coincide with the views of the Chartists." He said he would keep his eyes open and pass along any useful information.[40] Another man named Breslau warned of foreign plotters in London and turned over to the police some unsigned (and thus illegal) political handbills in French and German. Mayne wanted to question Breslau further and paid his cab fare to Scotland Yard. The Commissioner also wrote to the Home Office saying that there was more talk than action with men such as Breslau. Mayne sarcastically dismissed the rhetoric of the London *émigrés* as the work of "only a few noisy & violent men among them who make all this nonsense."[41]

Joseph Blareau offered to supply the police with information about the aims and activities of foreign political gatherings in London for thirty shillings a week, "which said salary might be augmented in proportion to the importance of my information, and according to the expenses I shall be at [*sic*] in attending the various clubs."[42] Mayne did not reply.

GEORGE GRAHAM, JOHN PATERSON, AND IGNATIUS POLLAKY

The Great Exhibition in Hyde Park in 1851 brought forth a strident crop of dire warnings to the authorities. George Graham, an "aeronaut" (balloonist), provided the police with a colorful scenario of the evils that lay in store for the Realm. His long letter addressed to Home Secretary Sir George Grey, and transmitted to Mayne, warned of 90,000 foreigners, 150,000 Irishmen and 60,000 Irishwomen, and assorted Chartists who were ready to join forces, and at a signal rise up and kill as many English as possible. Guns were being landed on the coast. Certain houses and shops were marked for firing; gunpowder to assist the conflagration was to be blown under the cracks of the doors by means of long tubes. Taking a page from the Gordon Riots, Graham warned that the fire brigades would be impeded in their work and the men killed. While the fires were raging thousands of people—he estimated 20,000—would rush the Bank of England and other public buildings. In the year of "Papal Aggression" Catholics were certainly not forgotten. Thousands of "these wretched individuals" (many being orange venders and match sellers) were ready to rise, supposedly aided by high-placed Englishmen. Then the "destruction of the Empire" would occur and the Roman Church would take over. Graham did not forget to add that all of this useful information from a "thinking man" should be worth some money from the Secret Service Fund, for "deflating the plans of those enemies to our country and religion."[43] He was to be disappointed.

Mayne did send out a policeman to question Graham at length as to his sources and received the report that Graham was studying stained-glass coloring—and was in need of money—that he was sane, though not reliable, and that his information was taken indiscriminately from his friends.[44]

Graham's letter, while more fanciful than most, is typical of the types with which the police had to deal. It would perhaps be of more interest today for psychological speculation than for the police at the time. Nevertheless, there was probably more pure humbug than mental derangement with such men, and their morsels of information to entice the police, coupled with the inevitable appeals for money, remind us that such solicitation was merely one more aspect of London's enormous casual labor market.

From 1848 the informer John Paterson kept up a running correspondence with the police and other officials for a period of five years, resulting in a thick folder of letters preserved in the Public Record Office.[45] Paterson warned of subversive meetings, often enclosing posters and newspaper clippings. According to him, the Chartists were in league with destitute Hungarian and Polish refugees and also in contact with such French radicals as Ledru-Rollin. All were supported by the Jesuits! Mayne rarely answered and was usually vague when he did; on one occasion he thanked Paterson for the offer of information on "the movements of the Chartists." Paterson kept up his flurry of sometimes incoherent letters and even badgered the Commissioner into a personal meeting. At various times Paterson asked for money for his information, or Mayne's recommendation for a government post, or simply a good word that his reports were useful, should a reward be offered. Paterson's last letter to Mayne was dated 26 May 1853, in which he sought assurance that his information had been valuable. "I do not presume nor solicit favor of any kind at your hands, as you tell me you never interfere in such matters." Mayne assured him that his information was useful.[46]

While it is true that Paterson wanted money and a recommendation from Mayne, these seem to have been secondary to him. More important was the feeling of importance that he and others of his type—the supply was plentiful—received from a "confidential" relationship with public figures, carried on at an almost familiar, but obsequious level. The information offered was usually predictable and could almost write itself: the times are out of joint; a subversive group is ready to rise up; but it might not be too late if only the police will take heed and act.

Another figure the police heard from, this time for a year and a half, was Ignatius Pollaky, who styled himself "Superintendent of the Foreign Department" with his offices in the "Foreign Department Bureau of Sûreté, Temple." A letter of his bearing that grandiloquent title, and sent to the police chief in Rotterdam, came to the attention of the alarmed Foreign Office and the Home Office who asked Mayne to investigate. It appeared that Pollaky was trying to drum up business for his private detective agency. From his newly styled "Private (Continental) Inquiry Office," 14 George St., Mansion House, he started sending Mayne regular "confidential" letters dealing with domestic or foreign matters. Among other things he accused the City Police Commissioner Harvey of pocketing gratuity money of £700, and of using his own police abroad for personal purposes. Mayne ignored the information but had Pollaky investigated again. Pollaky did not give up easily and even talked with Horatio Waddington at the Home Office, and finally with a reluctant Mayne himself. Pollaky, it turned out, hoped to make himself as helpful as possible to the authorities in order to be naturalized a British subject. Mayne would only say that the information was "interesting to me," but nothing else.[47]

Men such as Paterson and Pollaky were always ready to present themselves. The sporadic information derived from such informers, if it had any validity, was often all the Metropolitan Police could draw on. The fact that there were regular police detectives did not, as we have seen, obviate the need for informers, however unreliable they might have been.

Intelligence gathering remained one of the weaker aspects of the police, as evidenced when they tried to meet the challenges of Irish Fenianism in the late 1860s. Although in the face of this there were calls to increase the detectives or augment their powers, it was not certain what could be done, or even if the public would truly wish to broaden police powers. Criticism, therefore, fell on the head of Mayne, and in the short run, replacing him seemed to be the cry most often heard.

The reluctance to expand the detectives beyond a handful of men, plus the plainclothesmen, was consistent with the philosophy of "preventive" policing. Of course expansion would lessen the possibility of a repeat of the Popay incident and alarm the more liberally minded public. Although the formation of the Detective Department marked the first time in England that detectives were full-time, fully salaried members of the police, they could not wholly abandon the old ways. The Commissioners tried to keep them from mixing intimately with criminals, in the pious hope that detectives could thereby avoid the odor of corruption that had marked the early thief-takers. This policy may have been made to promote honesty and accountability, but since the means of detection were crude at best, there was no way in the nineteenth century to eliminate the unholy but necessary alliance between the detectives and their subjects, an intimacy that modern detectives can avoid to some extent with scientific aids and communication devices. Much of a detective's work still lay in the shadows.

Of course, calling for specialized skills within the police, and getting those skills, were two different things. There were some highly capable detectives with proficiency in foreign languages who proved very useful in watching aliens, and whose information helped shape official policy toward refugees in England. But their successes depended much on individual initiative and talents. That the Metropolitan Police never developed a "Continental" detective or spy network attests not so much to the shortcomings of the men themselves, but to the strong philosophical and political constraints in which the police operated.

NOTES

1. "The Police and the Thieves," *Quarterly Review*, XCIX, 169.

2. Donald Rumbelow, *I Spy Blue*, p. 175.

3. *P.P.* 1833 (627), XIII, qs. 1090-97, 4001. H.O. 45/292, (4 June, 23 Aug. 1842). Reith, *New Study*, p. 231. MEPOL 2/134 (20 Feb. 1869), memo from Insp. Williamson.

4. MEPOL 2/134 (20 Feb. 1869), memo from Insp. Williamson. H.O. 65/8 (20 April 1869). The Police Orders for 15 May 1869 (MEPOL 7/132) list only 14 second class sergeants. I have chosen the higher figure which probably included probationary detectives.

5. Charles Dickens, "The Detective Police," in *The Uncommercial Traveller and Reprinted Pieces, etc.* (London: Oxford University Press, 1968), p. 487.

6. John Brewer, "An Ungovernable People? Law and Disorder in Stuart and Hanoverian England," *History Today*, XXX (Jan. 1980), 25-26.

7. Jonathan Wild is portrayed in many books, one of the more recent being Gerald Howson, *Thief-Taker General: The Rise and Fall of Jonathan Wild* (London: Hutchinson and Co., Ltd., 1970). I have used mainly the accounts in J.J. Tobias, *Crime and Police*, pp. 13-15, and Christopher Hibbert, *The Roots of Evil: A Social History of Crime and Punishment* (London: Penguin Books, Ltd., 1966), pp. 47-49.

8. Tobias, *Crime and Police*, pp. 46-49. Henry Goddard, *Memoirs of a Bow Street Runner* (London: Museum Press, Ltd., 1956), p. xii.

9. MEPOL 2/134 (4 Sept. 1877).

10. Quoted in Reith, *New Study*, pp. 221-22.

11. *P.P.* 1870 (150), XXXVI, *Report of the Commissioner*, p.3.

12. Hibbert, *Roots of Evil*, p. 319.

13. MEPOL 2/28 (23 Jan. 1854).

14. MEPOL l/46 (30 June 1859).

15. MEPOL 7/20 (30 July 1859).

16. MEPOL 7/11 (11 Nov. 1845). Ibid. (10 Dec. 1845).

17. MEPOL 7/11 (10 Dec. 1845, 26 June 1846).

18. MEPOL 2/28 (23 Jan. 1854). MEPOL 7/13l (23 Jan. 1854).

19. "The Police and the Thieves," *Quarterly Review*, XCIX, 174.

20. MEPOL 7/132 (Aug. 1862).

21. MEPOL 7/24 (25 May 1863). MEPOL 2/134 (l Sept. 1877).

22. Royal Commission, 1855, qs. 8229-32. *P.P.* 1857-58 (384), XLVII, p. 654.

23. H.O. 65/8 (2 June 1869).

24. MEPOL 2/134 (22 Oct. 1880).

25. Ibid. (20 Nov. 1871).

26. Fuller, *Recollections*, p. 12.

27. *P.P.* 1878-79 (2413), XXXIII, p. 433. MEPOL 2/134 (2 Oct. 1880). Tobias, *Crime and Police*, p. 113.

28. Philip Collins, *Dickens and Crime* (2d ed.; London: Macmillan and Co., Ltd., 1965), pp. 210-11.

29. MEPOL 7/25 (18 Feb. 1864). MEPOL 7/15 (27 Nov. 1851).

30. H.O. 65/20 (7 Sept. 1855). MEPOL 7/25 (12 March 1864).

31. G.E. Buckle, ed., *The Letters of Queen Victoria*, 2d ser. (London: John Murray, 1926), I, 479 (19 Dec. 1867).

32. Leon Ó Broin, *Fenian Fever: An Anglo-American Dilemma* (London: Chatto & Windus, 1971), p. 216. MEPOL l/47 (6 Dec. 1886, 10 Dec. 1866, 19 July 1867).

33. Sir Leon Radzinowicz, *A History of English Criminal Law and Its Administration from 1750* (London: Stevens, 1956), II, 153-55.

34. Mather, *Public Order*, pp. 203, 217.

35. Ibid., p. 19l. H.O. 65/8 (26 Sept. 1867).

36. H.O. 65/19 (29 July 1853), Waddington to Mayne.

37. MEPOL l/46 (31 May 1850). Ibid., 3/25 (6 March 1858), "S" to Mayne.

38. Ibid., 1/47 (15 July 1867), Mayne to Naas.

39. Ibid. (11 April 1867), Mayne to Belmore.

40. Ibid., 2/43 (7 June 1848), Faulkner to Grey.

41. Ibid. (9 May 1851).

42. Ibid. (10 May 1851).

43. Ibid. (5 April 1851).

44. Ibid. (May 1851).

45. Ibid., 2/62 (1848-53). See also MEPOL 1/46 (6 Dec. 1851) and H.O. 65/18 (24 May 1852).

46. MEPOL 2/62 (26 May 1853).

47. H.O. 65/23 (19 July 1861). MEPOL 2/130 (July 1862).

4 The Alien Question: The Metropolitan Police and Continental Refugees

There were many Englishmen who began to notice after 1848 that the streets of London seemed to be filled with foreigners. The Duke of Beaufort also noticed, and was worried because they included some of the "worst characters" from France. The Marquess of Lansdowne heard it on good authority that there were perhaps 50,000 aliens ready to overturn the British government and dismember the Empire. Lansdowne, like Beaufort and others, called for a law that would allow for the expulsion of undesirable aliens. The "problem" they and others perceived was the influx into England of European refugees after the revolutions of 1848. London provided a convenient home for the exiles.

The flow continued into the early 1850s, although at a slower rate, with the Great Exhibition of 1851 temporarily drawing thousands more foreigners to England. Before the Exhibition opened in May 1851 anxiety ran high in the minds of many Englishmen, that the wrong types might be attracted, the kind Lord Brougham called "good specimens of Socialists and men of Red Colour," or in the words of Richard Mayne, men of "extreme democratic revolutionary principles," not to mention thieves and other undesirables.[1]

The worst did not, of course, materialize, and the Crystal Palace Exhibition was a rousing success and demonstrated to the admiring multitudes British industrial supremacy and the blessings of liberalism and free trade. Afterward, foreigners came to be taken more for granted in the public mind. But in the political and diplomatic sphere, often beyond the gaze of the average Englishman, the refugees posed some delicate problems for the government during the 1850s.

Britain's policy of not expelling political refugees who plotted against their former countries caused some acute diplomatic problems. Faced with weak laws governing refugees, British attempts to control and to supervise the aliens were minimal, and police surveillance of refugees was limited. The police did, however, become engaged in administering a government policy of paying refugees to leave England for New York, a scheme kept as secret as possible, which resulted in the voluntary emigration of almost 1,500 refugees. None was expelled, and the policy of asylum remained until the early twentieth century.

REFUGEE FACTIONS IN LONDON

At various times in its history, England has been the point of arrival for refugees. In the summer of 1831, some 2,500 Frenchmen arrived in London and so did a few Spanish and Portuguese. In the two or three years after the European revolutions of 1848 several thousand refugees arrived from various European countries, mainly from France and Germany. Louis Napoleon's coup against the French Republic in November 1851 prompted the flight of more French refugees, whose numbers rose to well over 4,000. By March 1853 most of the French had returned home, leaving 1,000 in London. It seems likely that in March 1853 there were about 4,260 refugees from various nations living in Britain, with about 1,900 of that total living elsewhere than London. This represented a considerable drop from two years before. Like those of 1831 the figures for 1848 and after were derived from police reports which may well be inspired guesses at best, but are nonetheless about the most accurate we are likely to find.[2] If those numbers seem to us less than overwhelming they were sufficient to excite many Englishmen. The fact that these were political exiles who were potentially troublesome to their home governments as well as to England meant that they could not be ignored. Few British officials were ready to look upon the refugees as calmly as did the Russian *émigré* and revolutionary Alexander Herzen who said: "Expect nothing of *them*; they are dead men burying their dead." Though the majority of the refugees were politically passive, some were openly revolutionary, wishing to combine a democratic regime at home with socialism.[3]

Some of the groups loudly and openly advertised for funds and volunteers to carry out revolutions against their respective countries. A band of French refugees, after hearing of Napoleon's coup in 1851, published a proclamation circulated in the papers calling the French people to arms. Many *ad hoc* organizations were created after 1848, such as the Central National Italian Committee, the Central Committee of Hungarian Refugees, and the Central Committee of European Democracy, the latter being founded with the expectation that it would coordinate the activities of the Continental democratic exiles.[4]

Inevitably the factions looked to prominent refugees for leadership. The Hungarians acknowledged the leadership of Louis Kossuth, the Poles of Stanislaw Worcell the French were divided between Louis Blanc and Ledru-Rollin. Alexander Herzen appeared in London in 1852 and came to represent the Russians.

The Germans were as divided as Germany itself. Its most famous exile, Karl Marx, joined a political organization called the German Workers' Educational Association, a branch of which was dedicated to providing aid to German *émigrés*. Its meetings on Great Windmill Street were usually watched by Prussian spies.[5]

The Italians had a somewhat easier time of it in England than did most other foreigners. Divided though they were into the Cavour or Mazzini factions, they could still benefit from the lingering Italophilia that was part of the cultural terrain of educated upper-class Englishmen, which would smooth their paths into English life. Being somewhat better bred than other refugees, they were more easily accepted as tutors or as marriage partners. While the subtleties of Italian politics may have escaped most Englishmen, if they were at least sympathetic to the principle of Italian unification and some measure of liberalism, they could assume a posture of simply being "pro-Italian" without choosing one faction over another.

In general the refugees' social class determined the degree of acceptance by Englishmen. "Respectable" *émigrés* were less inclined to espouse socialism and were thus more likely to benefit from both English sympathy and charity than were purely working-class ones. Antonio Panizzi, the Principal Librarian of the British Museum and a Cavour admirer, had views that were tame enough to allow him to mix in the society of Gladstone, Palmerston, and Lord John Russell. A knighthood eventually came his way. Some prominent Englishmen also took an interest in the more staid refugee organizations. Lord Dudley Stuart had been a founder of the Literary Association of the Friends of Poland in 1832 and remained active in it through the 1850s.[6]

BRITISH POLICY TOWARD REFUGEES

The position of the various British governments toward the refugees had been relatively consistent, in that domestic tranquility was to be preserved and foreign allies were not to be embarrassed (if possible) by plots hatched in England. There was little in the law that could effectively curb refugee plotting. A Registration Act of 1830 ordered aliens to have passports and declare their business in England, but it was ineffective and difficult to enforce. Then there was the Foreign Enlistment Act which could be invoked to suppress mercenary operations against friendly foreign powers by aliens in England. The law was virtually a dead letter, easy to circumvent, and little hindrance to the recruitment and fundraising of mercenaries in England.

The immediate response to the influx of 1848 refugees was an act that would give the Home Secretary the power to order out of the country aliens of less than a year's residence in England who were involved in misdeeds. This was nothing new: there had been an Alien Act passed in 1793 which was renewed annually for thirty-three years, permitting the arbitrary expulsion of aliens. The 1848 Alien Act was passed with large majorities in both houses of Parliament—

despite spirited opposition from radical MPs like John Bright—and received the Royal assent on 9 June 1848. The law expired at the end of 1850, but was not renewed; no one had been expelled.[7]

The British government was being pressured by foreign states to curb the activities of the *émigrés*, or preferably, to expel them. In France where refugee threats were a constant preoccupation with the government, the secret police were kept busy. Since police links between France and Britain were relatively weak, the French hoped that diplomatic persuasion would inspire a tougher British line on exiles. In 1851 Jules Baroche, Minister of Foreign Affairs, importuned London for more stringent controls over refugees and for prosecution of the leaders of the Central Committee of European Democracy.

The Austrian government also raised questions about refugees, namely Marx, Engels, and others whose discussions touched on regicide. Home Secretary Sir George Grey replied that talk of regicide, unless against Queen Victoria, was no cause for arrest as long as it remained talk. Grey had already assured the House of Commons that the principal exiles were being "closely observed" by the London police.[8]

Irritated by Louis Kossuth's warm reception in 1851 the Austrians wrote to the new Foreign Secretary, Lord Granville, to remind him that he had promised to watch the conduct of refugees. Similar assurances had been given to France, Prussia, the Diet of the German Confederation, and Russia. Count Nesselrode wrote to Granville that Russia took note of this assurance and awaited "with confidence the realization of this promise." With the case of the Austrians assurances seemed insufficient, especially after an attempt on the life of the Austrian emperor in 1853 by a refugee who had come from London. This further aroused the Austrians against the British policy of asylum.[9]

Beyond watching the refugees there was little that the British government could or would do in actually attempting to control aliens, who had some sympathy—or at least toleration—from the English middle classes. As Foreign Secretary in the Derby cabinet, Lord Malmesbury wrote to his ambassador in Vienna in 1852, saying that there could still be no question of expelling the refugees, especially if they obeyed the English laws and did not give their conspiracies a "practical form." "You must be aware that no Government which complied with such demands [expulsion] could exist a month in England."[10] A year later Malmesbury made the same assertion to the Emperor Napoleon, while dining at the Tuileries. When warned by Napoleon that the refugees would inevitably provoke diplomatic storms, the Foreign Secretary admitted that "half of them were rascals," whom he would willingly see deported if that were possible.

"Every country had its subjects on which no cession could be made. The Holy Places in the East was that of Russia, the Refugees was ours, and it was useless to torment us about an impossibility, for no English minister could alter the law at present." [11]

The basic position of the British government as expressed in diplomatic circles was that asylum could not be selective. Accepting some applications for asylum and rejecting others at the behest of other countries would force the British government to make subtle, perhaps unpalatable, distinctions among refugees. Also, foreign governments were wasting their time trying to get the English to change the laws on asylum, public opinion not being favorable to any such alteration. In spite of this, England's position was an awkward one. The long-winded, self-conscious debates in Parliament made it clear that few British politicians enjoyed their country's growing reputation as a haven for alien plotters who were threatening diplomatic stability in what was anyway a very difficult period. On the other hand no one wanted to appear to truckle to the demands of foreign governments and expel aliens who obeyed the English laws. [12]

Foreigners were for the most part regarded with indifference by the British. They were tolerated, not out of love, but on the humanitarian principle of asylum, and because of the English disapproval of the despotic regimes that had forced the flight of exiles.

Paradoxically, England's open-arms policy to refugees was built on a heavy degree of xenophobia, stemming from middle-class liberalism. The Victorian period had brought the middle classes not only unparalleled economic prosperity, but also confidence and a sense of "progress." If liberalism was taken as the shedding of archaic restrictions and the unfolding of various "freedoms," then liberty in all forms was the result. Did not capitalism and free trade encourage economic growth? Would not political liberalism and free speech encourage an open healthy government capable of holding its own in an otherwise hostile world? Capitalism and liberalism thus shaped Queen Victoria's world which stood on its o.vn and was its own best defense. The English middle-class liberal was convinced of the manifest superiority of British institutions, so that a few wild-talking foreigners were little worse than nuisances even when they hatched conspiracies against their own countries. They could not be a real threat to Britain.

Having little experience with plots, assassinations, and political conspiracies, the English naively underestimated their potency and assumed that their own institutions were immune from the cancer of subversion. A large dose of luck helped too. If the refugees mostly stayed out of English domestic politics, it was partly because they directed their efforts towards their own countries, but also partly because their previous political education left them with an abiding fear that the asylum so freely granted could easily be revoked.

The differences between England and her Continental neighbors on this question involved more than just refugees; they involved an economic imbalance more pronounced than ever before, as well as critical internal constitutional differences. If the British felt "better," or at least different, this attitude resulted in more disapproval of other countries than at almost any other period in history. The British resented being told what to do about aliens, because the aliens themselves were created by despotic governments whose practices affronted liberal Victorian sensibilities. European complaints about British toleration of refugee activities and opinions were in effect criticism of the British government and its policies. Having to accept refugees, thought the British, was no flaw in policy, but the fault of the illiberal and backward governments in Europe.[13]

The strains over exiles did not really last much longer than the early 1850s, after which time the anxieties on both sides of the Channel seemed to subside. The Orsini conspiracy against the life of the French emperor in January 1858, however, created another period of stress, but only with France; other countries did not seem too bothered.

WATCHING ALIENS

If expulsion was out of the question, police surveillance was not. The London police had long made a habit of keeping a watchful eye on foreigners, although some of the spotty and casual observation would scarcely deserve the name of surveillance. In an age of less social mobility than today, observation then was comparatively easy. Even in a sprawling city like London, each area had its particular flavor, a local identity which became even more defined, and its characteristic trades with appropriate dress, making personal identification of the residents relatively easy for the constables who walked the beats.

In attempting to enforce the Registration Act of 1830 the police checked the certificates of recent immigrants, and in 1831 the superintendent of S Division recommended that the certificates be kept on file by the local police who would then get to know the new arrivals, their "pursuits, character and habits. . . . By this means also, their numbers would be known, and it would be a check upon any movement that might be contemplated." While reporting that there were only about 150 foreigners in the Camden Town and Somers Town areas, mostly Spaniards and Portuguese, the police obviously looked around and reported that "there was not [a] weapon seen in any of their apartments, nor was there any thing observed to occasion any suspicion of malpractices."[14]

In 1848, having been tipped off by the French Ambassador about a number of "republicans" landing in England, Police Commissioner Mayne sent word to Superintendent May to keep an eye on a "low class" of foreigners, probably French, who would most likely settle in Whitechapel. Other police reports came in to Scotland Yard of aliens settling in Leicester Square, Finsbury Square, Blackfriars, Leadenhall Street, and in hotels and lodging houses elsewhere.[15]

THE POLICE AND LOUIS KOSSUTH

The question of surveillance was mooted in Parliament in 1853 in regard to the refugee Louis Kossuth, the Magyar nationalist. In April the police raided a house in Rotherhithe, which they had been watching for at least ten days, and found a quantity of rockets and other weapons and 260 pounds of gunpowder. The house was owned by a Mr. Hain, an arms manufacturer of radical sympathies, who was a friend of Kossuth's. Kossuth was in Manchester at the time. The police had got wind of Hain's activities and had assumed that the weapons were meant for Kossuth and his followers in Hungary, to start a revolution against Austria. *The Times* picked up the story of Hain's arrest (for having gunpowder in excess of what his license allowed) and reported the incident as if Kossuth himself had been making weapons in a house in Rotherhithe. The newspaper proceeded to work up a campaign against subversive aliens in England.[16]

In Parliament radicals jumped to Kossuth's defense, and the Home Secretary, Lord Palmerston, was pressed to dissociate Kossuth from the events, since he could not be charged for violating the Explosives Act and was not linked to the Hain arrest in any overt way. Palmerston refused to do this, and was vague in answering questions about the circumstances of the incident, though he did take responsibility for the raid. He was asked by Sir Joshua Walmsley whether police were watching Kossuth. Palmerston answered vaguely that it was the duty of the police to watch "proceedings of any person suspected rightly or wrongly of a breach of the laws of England—whether British or foreign.... Neither the house of M. Kossuth, nor of any political refugee in this country, can be exempted from those ordinary precautions which may be taken with regard to any individual, whether he be a British subject or a foreigner."[17] John Bright tried to pin him down further as to what evidence linked Kossuth with the house, since Kossuth's name was still publicly blackened by the incident. Palmerston equivocated and said that further investigation on this matter would be necessary. Richard Cobden insisted on knowing what information had led Palmerston to set police to spy on the house, as it had been widely stated in the press that the police had been watching the Rotherhithe house and all who entered. "What I want to know is this, are the boastings of this country that we are different from Austria, that we are not like the French, with or without foundation?"[18] Lord Dudley Coutts Stuart said that Palmerston had admitted that "some of these refugees were subject to that which could not be expressed in English—a system of police surveillance." The radical Stuart, a friend of Kossuth's, claimed that police acted as spies and disguised themselves as servants, haunting everyone who came to the Hain house. Such practices, he felt, could as easily be applied to Englishmen as well as foreigners. "But would Englishmen, when they knew it, be long content to live under such a system as this?" Palmerston did not deny that police were watching the Rotherhithe house but said that he gave no "special directions" to have the house watched by the police before the raid. He was asked sarcastically if the expenses were to be borne by police rates, the British government or by Austria. Palmerston assured his colleagues that his government would pay.[19]

Palmerston's critics were correct when they said that Kossuth's house, like Hain's, was watched, but how this was done was not made public. In March, while Kossuth was in the process of moving into a new residence at 21 Alpha Road, Regent's Park, a rug fitter gave the key to the constable on the beat to keep an eye on the house at night. The police were most happy to oblige and looked around inside the partially furnished house. Three days later PC Brown got himself hired as a furniture mover and assisted as suspiciously heavy wardrobe cases were moved into the house while Kossuth was there. Did they contain guns or rockets? Brown did his best to watch as they were opened, but this was done out of his sight.[20]

Palmerston earlier had emphatically denied that surveillance of foreign refugees in Britain was carried out upon the request of foreign governments.[21] The parliamentary Radicals were alarmed further when T.S. Duncombe quoted a passage from a Frankfurt, Germany, newspaper that said that the Prussian police were "most efficiently assisted in the late political arrests at Berlin and elsewhere by repeated communications from the police at London, without which many of their disclosures might not have been made." The article went on to say that the English government had promised to keep watch over the refugees. The paper quoted "other sources" as saying that the London police kept a list of fugitives residing there "and [watched] over their communications with the Continent." Palmerston earlier had said that no letters of refugees were being opened. He and others no doubt recalled the furor in the 1840s when it was revealed that Mazzini's letters had been opened by order of the Home Secretary.[22]

Palmerston's own enthusiasm for Kossuth—which in 1851 had contributed to his removal as Foreign Secretary—stopped short of turning a blind eye to the revolutionary preparations Kossuth and others were making in England. As a lukewarm supporter of radicals—abroad—Palmerston remained fairly consistent in his attitude. Before Kossuth's arrival in England in 1851, he solicited the opinion of J.A. Blackwell on Kossuth and may well have taken to heart Blackwell's answer. "There is probably no man in Europe more capable of awakening popular sympathy for any cause he may choose to advocate. But if we are to remain at peace [with Russia], he ought, in my humble opinion, to be crushed" to save England any embarrassment.[23] Lord John Russell backed Palmerston's views in being prepared to welcome exiles to English shores as long as they did not conspire to make war against other countries who were allied with England.

The public was left in little doubt that plain-clothes policemen were watching Kossuth and other refugees and had been doing so for quite some time. This should have been no surprise, since Home Secretary Sir George Grey had stated in Parliament in 1851 that the movements of the principal refugees were "closely observed" by the police. Palmerston's refusal to state the specifics of the case seemed a sufficient answer to the radicals, whose fears were confirmed. Walmsley vowed to convene a committee of enquiry if necessary to look into the question of spies. This did not take place.[24]

The question of Louis Kossuth and the police came up once again in Parliament eight years later, in 1861, when the Austrian government sued Kossuth in Chancery Court to cease printing what Austria considered to be counterfeit money. It was money Kossuth planned to issue as the official currency after a hoped-for revolution. Someone had apparently run off a sample of the money being printed by Messrs. Day, Lithographers, and mailed it to the London police. Or it could have been that a London policeman got himself employed by the printer. Parliamentary Radicals, especially T.S. Duncombe of Finsbury, took up the hue and cry of police spying once again. After repeated questions about how the police obtained the money, the Home Secretary, Sir George Cornewall Lewis, refused to say what the police role was. Said Duncombe, "There ought to be no equivocation shown in this matter, because if there is anything more repugnant to the feelings of this country than another it was the spy system."[25] Sir George remained evasive on the issue and his parliamentary antagonists believed that his obstinacy merely made the point for them. To the rest of the MPs, it no doubt appeared that the police were merely exercising vigilance in doing their duty.[26]

DETECTIVE JOHN H. SANDERS

In the early 1850s police surveillance of foreigners—or for that matter anyone else—became for the first time what could be called "professional," thanks

largely to one young detective who made his mark, and who was described by
Lord Clarendon as "worth all the French police agents and spies put together."
John Hitchens Sanders, one of the forgotten worthies of the Metropolitan Police,
would have been more than a match for Dickens's Inspector Bucket. No biography of Sanders has ever been written, and none probably ever will be, as very
little is known about him. He was not a well-known figure to the public like
Inspector Charles Frederich Field, who was the model for Inspector Bucket.
Sanders joined the police in August 1850, left,but rejoined in January 1851 as
a detective in A (Whitehall) Division. In November 1851 he was promoted to
sergeant at age 26, and inspector at age 31 in January 1856. Police papers record
his death of "apoplexy" in August 1859.

His brief career seems to have been devoted to political refugees, an area
where his intelligence and discretion were well used, and his fluency in French
crucial. He may have had a French background, and apparently married a French-
woman since his marriage certificate of 3 May 1855 gave his residence as
Boulogne-sur-Mer.

The numerous reports from Sanders, today found among the police and Home
Office papers, show a tact and a sophisticated, at times sympathetic, understanding of refugee politics. He was able to distinguish between wild talk and action.
Sanders came to be considered indispensable, and was the government's most
trustworthy source of information on refugees and virtually the only credible
source on the subject. His observations shaped official policy to an unusual
degree. In response to French anxiety over plots in 1851, Palmerston suggested
that the French send over some sharp "detectors" of their own, as "our police
are good for nothing [sic] little for such purposes, and besides they are not
linguists."[27]

By 1851 the police reports show that Sanders and his colleagues were busy
at work. Altogether there were some 50 houses used as cafes in London where
political meetings would be held. In a report that went to Palmerston Sanders
described refugee meetings around London, especially at 10 Little Compton
Street in Soho, where 20 to 30 Frenchmen talked politics and made "rambling
speeches." Occasionally one person, inflamed with drink, would shout a slogan,
but would be hushed up by the others. He also listed the "chiefs" who included
Louis Blanc and Ledru-Rollin. Sanders saw no particular reason for alarm. Most
of his subjects of observation were very poor.

In April he reported watching a house owned by a Marcus Breslau. He talked
to the postman and followed visitors to the house. German refugees, meeting
every Friday at the Cranborne Hotel in Soho, also caught Sanders' eye. He

observed that Marx and Engels were excluded from the meetings since they were deemed "violent and intriguing men."[28]

If the government was less alarmist about refugees, that attitude was due in part to Sanders. In his reports he always gave the benefit of doubt to the refugees and saw most of them for what they were—poor, lonely, and largely quiescent. In this sense Sanders was probably the refugees' best friend. Commissioner Mayne also took a more benign view of the exiles, but he had the official obligation of trying to allay the fears of others. Discounting persistent rumors of subversive doings by the foreigners, as "either wholly untrue or so exaggerated as to amount to misrepresentation," he told the Foreign Secretary that the German refugees "are in extreme poverty, living in a most wretched manner."[29]

THE GREAT EXHIBITION AND FOREIGN POLICE

The mid-Victorian age was symbolically ushered in by the Great Exhibition of 1851, a fitting temple to the industrial supremacy of Britain and the triumph of free trade and progress. For five months the Crystal Palace in London's Hyde Park was the focus of activity and the mecca for swarms of people attending from all parts of the globe. As might be expected great opposition was raised. Clergymen fulminated against the pride and folly of the undertaking, and *The Times* worked itself up with the fear that foreigners would rent houses near the Park to use as brothels, foreigners apparently being prone to such enterprises.[30] Doctors warned that the alien visitors would bring the plague and venereal diseases, and the Exhibition was expected to provide an unparalleled opportunity for the "swell mobs" (well-dressed pickpockets) and other assorted criminals to ply their trade. Lord Brougham warned of some 70,000 to 80,000 of the vagrant classes making their way to London. And as for foreigners, they would have "some good specimens of Socialists and men of Red colour, whose object it would be to ferment the mass."[31]

In November 1850 Police Commissioner Mayne vented his own fears (probably to justify the request to add 1,000 new policemen) by pointing out that many refugees from abroad were of "extreme democratic revolutionary principles.... Attempts may be made by those parties to create disturbance by holding public meetings & in other ways to create mischief or alarm [;] large & continuing demands on the police would be thus occasioned for measures of observation & precaution."[32]

There were over 1,000 police inside and outside the Crystal Palace. Their ranks were augmented by the presence of some 35 policemen from different countries and 24 from other British cities. Their mission was to keep an eye on well-known criminals from their respective areas. The idea of inviting foreign police to the Exhibition may possibly have been Palmerston's. Palmerston had worked out an arrangement with the French police whereby Britain would pay them and defray their traveling expenses. The British provincial police received double pay and a shilling a night for lodging. There were other countries whose police were not invited but who hated to pass up the opportunity of surveillance in London and sent men anyway. The British Embassy in St. Petersburg wrote that a Russian police agent had already been sent to London. The Viennese police, who may not have been invited, sent two officers and paid their own way. The British Consul at Dresden wrote to Palmerston and asked that he invite Mr. Eberhardt, the head of the police of Saxony, who was very knowledgeable about German criminals.[33]

An invitation also went out to major cities in the United States to send over men "to point out the persons known to them as criminal and dangerous characters who should be kept under observation by the Metropolitan Police." Mayne also indicated to the Home Secretary, Grey, that a notice in *Reynolds' Newspaper* had revealed that a number of American "democrats" would "act as propagandists of their principles" during the Exhibition. The British Consul in Washington also warned: "It is not improbable that if the [filibustering] movement against Cuba be deferred or abandoned, many other useless individuals who would have taken part in that expedition as being disposed to seek adventure & fortune by any means will now proceed to London." New York by itself sent over three officers, Captains Leonard and Hopkins and Officer Robert Bowyer, Bowyer being an experienced detective.[34]

Colonel Brown of the Dublin police offered to send some of his own men. After conferring with Grey, Mayne declined the offer, saying that great objections would be raised in Parliament, "and perhaps excitement of the Public raised against it. . . . It is very satisfying to hear that Ireland is in a condition to admit of giving police aid to us." Mayne's letter to Brown only reminds us that 1851 was also the year of "No Popery" and "Papal Aggression." Mayne apparently reversed this decision, because other documents show that Dublin did send two men, later recalling one.[35]

There is no question that the foreign governments were all too happy to have this unique opportunity to keep an eye on not only their own thieves and pickpockets, but on their political refugees, that is to say, to do openly what they had already been doing secretly. The Berlin police were concerned primarily with German dissidents in London and sent over two high-ranking officers whose efforts were "directed to political objects for their own country" and who did not "detect crime." Previous to their arrival the Berlin authorities sent to Scotland Yard a list of names and data on thirty-one "suspicious political characters" who had obtained passes to proceed to London.[36]

The following list shows the numbers of foreign and provincial police at the opening of the Great Exhibition. Many of them left after a month or so.[37]

Foreign Police		*Provincial Police*	
Brussels	5	Dublin	2
Berlin	2	Edinburgh	2
Lyons	2	Hull	2
Marseilles	2	Leeds	2
Breslau	2	Sheffield	2
Cologne	2	Newcastle	2
Carlsruhe	2	Cambridge	2
Paris	8		
Frankfurt	2		
Magdeburg	1		
Rouen	2		
New York	3		
Vienna	2		

Sir George Grey questioned the expense of maintaining all the invited police and did in fact make cuts later, after the Exhibition was well under way. Mayne assured Grey that the guest officers had certainly discouraged revolutionaries and criminals from abroad; and in light of this he was amenable to reducing the foreign police numbers. Some rivalry must have existed among the various police agencies. For example, the Paris police could not see why Lyons and Marseilles had sent officers.[38]

The daily routine for the visiting policemen was for one or more of the officers to be inside the Crystal Palace during the day looking over the crowds from the galleries and pointing out to the Metropolitan officers criminals they recognized. Colleagues would observe the arrivals of excursion trains at the stations, and of boats at the London docks. All of the police contingents had to file daily reports which were read by Mayne.

The reports of the New York police officers, Leonard, Hopkins, and Bowyer, give an idea of these duties. Having arrived late, their first report was filed on 30 May, almost a month after the Exhibition opened. Bowyer positioned himself at the north entrance of the Exhibition to point out any suspicious characters he might know. He recognized no one and left at 6:00 P.M. Leonard and Hopkins went around London and to the docks and railway stations, ''as they deemed most likely to meet with suspicious characters from America.'' They saw no familiar faces. Their first day was not completely uneventful. That night as the weary officers walked back to their hotel a man rushed past them on Westminster Bridge and flung himself over the side to his death.[39]

On 3 June Officer Bowyer accompanied Superintendent May to the races at Ascot, and ''saw a number of pickpockets, but only recognized one as being from New York.'' Two days later Capt. Leonard was also taken to Ascot and recorded his impressions in tortured prose. ''During the day I saw a great number of pickpockets attempting to follow their avocation; but we did not succede in catching any of them in committing a fellony but saw several of them attempting to do so without they were caught in the act.'' On 19 June, inside the Crystal Palace, Capt. Leonard recognized two men from New York who had been engaged in the first Cuban filibustering expedition. The British Consul's earlier warning turned out to be true.[40] Shortly after this, two of the officers returned to New York, seeing no real reason to stay; the third remained until the close of the Exhibition.

The Brussels police arrived at least ten days before the opening of the Exhibition and wasted no time in exploring London. Besides checking docks and train stations, they visited the Red Lion Pub in Windmill Street and listened to the conversations of some Belgians and Germans. Nothing of importance was heard. On 29 April they went into a private house at 46 Rathbone Place and, apparently posing as Englishmen, asked if any English were present; they were told no. They stayed and heard talk against the French government (but not against England's) and of the coming socialism.[41] Unfortunately, their reports do not give details of just how they conducted this investigation. On 6 May they again visited the house on Rathbone Place, which was owned by a Frenchman named Poitier, but were refused admittance ''*parce qu'il y avait séance secrète.*'' The report caught the eye of Mayne, who scribbled on the back, ''Let them observe parties who go there & report if they know any of them.'' He directed that the French police be advised of this as well.

On 9 May the Brussels police again visited the house, which must have been well known as a refugee gathering place, and were again refused entry because, as they reported, a secret meeting was still in progress. They tried to get names, but were unsuccessful. On 20 May they recorded that the French ''demagogues'' had a dispute with the owner of the house and chose another location to meet.[42]

Also prowling about London were the Paris police whose reports include references to watching ''democrats.''[43] They noted that one pub in Great Windmill Street near Picadilly Circus was a hangout for German and Polish revolutionaries whose meetings were closed to outsiders. The German police were notified of this. The Paris officers also noted that another "low class" pub had a mixture of all nationalities, poor men whom they considered potential revolutionaries "*on aura l'oeil sur cette maison.*" They also watched 46 Rathbone Place, as their report from 12 May indicates. On 27 June the Paris report included a notice that a M. Gros, a "violent republican" had moved into the house.[44]

The Rouen police were not inactive either, and their reports—in English—show that they watched a French house on Compton [Street?]. They also followed a man called Letellier from Oxford Street north to Rathbone Place. Letellier was described as a "*saboteur*" from Rouen and "a very warm red republican . . . under a condemnation for publishing an article in a Democratical paper tending to excite the citizens against one another." A month later they observed Poitier, the owner of the house at 46 Rathbone Place, greet seven Frenchmen, whose names were unknown, and escort them to his house.[45]

The police of Marseilles and Lyons also joined the legions of those watching 46 Rathbone Place—and probably each other—which by now must have been by far the best policed building in London. The Marseilles police reported that Poitier received groups of French "socialists" or those of the same opinion.[46] Presumably the detectives watching the house had been introduced to each other to avoid any embarrassment. Their presence in the narrow street, if only intermittent, must have been conspicuous to the visitors to the house.

Verbal communication between the police of the various countries and the London police had indeed been something of a problem. At the opening of the Exhibition a party of Metropolitan detectives mingling with the crowds on the floor saw several foreigners acting suspiciously. They arrested the foreigners who protested vehemently in "very good French," but who turned out to be Belgian police.[47] The foreign police were often accompanied by London officers, but even this arrangement had its problems. Complaining that he was being impeded by not being understood by his English counterpart, the Brussels police leader recommended that they both speak the same language. The Metropolitan Police and Exhibition officials had attempted to avoid such difficulties by employing a number of interpreters; but these appeared to have been kept busy mainly in answering questions by foreign tourists.[48]

THE LONDON POLICE AND FOREIGN GOVERNMENTS

By the time the Exhibition closed in the fall of 1851 there seems to have been a collective sigh of relief and a lessening of the fears that the refugees posed any real threat to the British government beyond diplomatic embarrassment.

What connection did the foreign police detectives and informers in London have with the Metropolitan Police at times other than during the Great Exhibition? Although there seems to have been some unofficial liaison in the form of information exchange between the London and the Paris police, for example, it was never extensive. The same was true with other foreign police forces where communication with London was minimal. Liaison became even more limited after a major flap in 1844 when it was publicly revealed that Home Secretary Sir James Graham had authorized the opening of letters to and from Giuseppe Mazzini and other refugees and passing the information to foreign governments. The British ended the practice in the face of public indignation and upon the recommendation of secret parliamentary committees. Henceforth the opening of letters of resident aliens was stopped.[49]

If the flow of information between British and foreign police was but a trickle, it nonetheless continued. The English, however, insisted that requests for information come through diplomatic channels and not direct to Scotland Yard. In fact many tips from abroad came through the Foreign Office, often from British diplomatic officials. This was not a one-way flow: there is ample evidence to suggest that British police information was sent abroad through embassies. This was a touchy situation, since such information was usually considered fit for British eyes only. There were qualitative problems with the information. The British often regarded foreign police intelligence to be sensational, especially about Socialist conspiracies and assassination plots. The Europeans considered the English smugly naive and their information disappointingly bland.

We can see evidence of the information exchange in the Home Office letter books and other documents where there are terse messages to the police, instructing them to send up reports on certain immigrants to the Foreign Office, to be passed on to other governments. In 1851, acting on a tip from the Paris police, the Home Office ordered the London police to have a coffee house and its clientele "carefully watched." It was apparently run by a German Socialist. In 1852, upon the request of the Austrian authorities, the police were ordered to check "privately ... the character and connections" of Julius Lipmann, a Bavarian refugee.[50]

Mazzini had been the subject of continual surveillance when he was traveling around in England, but in 1844 the police had some trouble keeping up with him, though he apparently made no effort to evade them. In June and July 1860, while trying to recruit volunteers in England for Garibaldi's army, Mazzini again was followed, with some difficulty. As late as 1865 the police were transmitting material on Mazzini, but only through official channels. Assistant Commissioner Labalmondiere punctiliously reminded a foreign official that he could not provide police reports on Mazzini's movements unless application came through the "ordinary official channels of government."[51]

While on a diplomatic mission to Louis Napoleon in 1852, Lord Malmesbury's cousin and private secretary, George Harris, relayed to Napoleon information gleaned from Sanders and other policemen that Louis Kossuth might land on the south coast of France. Never short of rumors himself, Napoleon said he had heard that Mazzini and Kossuth might land in Algeria, "corrupt" two regiments there and use them to "revolutionize all Italy," but this did not unduly alarm him. Napoleon was more concerned with assassination.[52]

THE EMIGRATION SCHEME

If alien watching left much to be desired, and if expulsion was legally out of the question, there was yet another acceptable alternative: assisted emigration. This was nothing new, for the government had aided with emigration to South Africa in the 1820s. Also, under the terms of the New Poor Law the counties had borne the expense of sending off paupers to relieve chronic unemployment. Colonies such as Australia paid for all, and later half, of the expenses of bringing over settlers. Various private emigration societies in England helped sponsor the departure of individuals who met their qualifications. At some point it occurred to the government that "shoveling out" aliens might be a useful practice as well.

The possibility of providing government money to pay for passage abroad for those refugees who wished to emigrate was raised in Parliament by Lord Ashley in 1848. Lord John Russell answered that it could be done, but that the money for such a thing was very limited. Limited government and private charity was about all the refugees could count on anyway.[53] In spite of some parliamentary opposition, funds had been voted through as aid to destitute refugees in England. For instance, in the fiscal year ending 31 March 1848, £11,000 was spent on relief for Polish and Spanish refugees. How the money was used is not mentioned. Although aid money from the Exchequer was increased in some years, the general trend was a reduction in funds, the largest amounts going to the Poles, but lesser portions going to various French groups. By 1860 the total for all was £3,353, scarcely a princely sum when spread out among hundreds of people. We can get an idea of individual amounts in 1855-1856: most Poles got charity of five shillings, threepence a week, and the highest "field officers" got fifteen shillings a week, what an unskilled manual laborer might make, and which for a family, was at poverty level. Private charity was paltry and even harder to come by.[54]

Much of this subsistence money was given in direct aid for the refugees in

England, but it was given grudgingly and not to the most recent arrivals. It was but a short step from providing such relief to providing aid in the form of passage money to allow refugees to emigrate. Before 1851 it was normal to commute pensions granted by Parliament to Poles who preferred taking their money in a lump sum to permit them to emigrate. Direct aid for emigration was extended by the government to a group of Poles from Malta who had landed at Southampton. In March 1851 some 250 Polish and Hungarian political exiles who had been staying in Turkey also landed at Southampton. Aid was not immediately forthcoming, but many of them later emigrated from England to New York.[55]

A regular but discreet program of assisted emigration for bona fide refugees who were willing to go to New York started in February 1852 and lasted for six years. The British government provided the *émigrés* with money and transportation, amounting to about £10 a person. The exact working of this little known program is not clear, but the police were involved in supervising the physical arrangements for sending the refugees to New York and giving them subsistence money. Throughout the several years of this assisted emigration some 1,500 French, Italian, and Polish emigrants were dispatched from England. The Home Office and Metropolitan Police records provide us with scattered and incomplete reports, tally sheets and memoranda which give us only a skeleton of the process.[56]

Curiously, the program received very little attention at the time and seems to have gone unnoticed by most Englishmen. There was no debate on it in Parliament. This was no mere oversight: the program was intended to be conducted as quietly as possible to avoid any public uproar that aliens were being forcibly packed off to New York, maybe at the behest of foreign governments. Also, the less the United States knew about this the better, to avoid complaints, wrote Lord Clarendon in 1858. "The moment it was known that we were making them our penal settlement there wd. be an uproar & protest from one end of the Union to the other & not a man wd. be permitted to disembark."[57] The funds used for the scheme came not from the refugee aid from the Exchequer as one might assume, but rather from the Secret Service Fund of the Foreign Office, thus avoiding any public accounting of specific expenditures.

The idea for the emigration scheme may have come from Lord Granville, who was Foreign Secretary in 1852. In one letter from the Home Office asking assistance for French refugees, there is an interesting exchange of penciled comments: "How can this be done as to be sure that they go, and yet not incur publicity?" [Granville?] The answer, scribbled on the back, probably by an under-secretary [Addington?] said: "By paying their passage from the SS Fund, to *the Packet* [?] *Agent*. We must first ascertain how many there are and their names; and to what port they wish to go." The answer: "Pray let this be done." In another letter of probably April or May 1852 to Home Secretary Sir George Grey, a Foreign Office official, perhaps Granville again, authorized funds to ship 71 refugees to New York "if he can by means of the police insure their departure, quietly, and without any public notice being taken of the means by which they are sent."[58]

Word was apparently put out in the refugee communities of all nationalities that passage and allowance money would be provided for those who wished to leave for New York. Refugee organizations, such as the Literary Association of the Friends of Poland (headed by Lord Dudley Stuart) also sent to the Home Office or Foreign Office lists of candidates for passage. Politics among the refugees undoubtedly played a part in encouraging certain people to go, as in the case of the young Poles and Hungarians who arrived in Liverpool in 1851. The Polish conservatives and their allies in the Literary Association of the Friends of Poland feared that they would only add to the liberal wing of the *émigrés* and prevailed upon the government to refuse new arrivals funds unless they removed themselves to New York. Some went, but those who stayed in England got no government aid.[59]

As the revolutions of 1848 receded into the past and the existing regimes showed no signs of imminent collapse the disappointed exiles who chose not to make England a permanent home might well have decided to cut the bonds with their old homelands and go to the United States. Those who stayed in England, whose own respectability and acceptance by the British were all-important, increasingly had little use for the recent arrivals with extremist ideas and no appreciation for the punctilio of class distinctions. In a perceptive report in 1853 Sanders noted that the French "Chiefs" like Ledru-Rollin were determined not to meddle in French politics or hatch plots. Where a year before Ledru-Rollin and other leaders discouraged emigration by countrymen useful to them, they now hoped to get rid of low-class troublemakers and thereby make themselves look tame enough to return to France. Kossuth and his followers, wrote Sanders, were the only really dangerous ones.[60]

It is not clear how much, if any, real pressure was applied by the government to encourage emigration, but the letters to the Home Office and police from aliens themselves requesting passage money indicate that the numbers willing to go were plentiful. Forcible removal would only have resulted in public exposure of the program and embarrassment.

The police function appears to have been to investigate the legitimacy of private requests for emigration aid, to see that the individuals were indeed refugees, and to get the Foreign Office's approval of the lists of names; then the police would arrange for groups to be transported in a body to the ships departing from London or other ports, and give the emigrants subsistence money and utensils aboard ship. Passage was £5 a head, with approximately £5 being given to each person for clothing, food, and utensils. The Foreign Office periodically reimbursed the police Receiver—the official in charge of police finances—for the funds already expended.[61]

In the middle of all of this, as we might expect, was Detective Sanders, along with two other French-speaking policemen. The head of this trio was Superintendent Douglas Labalmondiere, who later became an assistant police commissioner. There was also Constable Adolphus ("Dolly") Williamson who became chief of detectives in 1869 and was perhaps the most famous detective in the 1870s and 1880s. Williamson had joined the police in 1850 (as did Sanders), following in the footsteps of his father who was already a superintendent. Williamson acquired his French from a tutor in the French colony in Leicester Square, and learned German at age forty.[62]

Concerning the numbers and identities of the emigrants, the miscellaneous and sometimes contradictory fragments in the Metropolitan Police papers do not give coherent statistics, so that a clear picture of exactly who was sent and when cannot be made. The largest number left between March and October 26, 1852. There were 613 emigrants, costing a total of £5,525.6.2, which would average about £9 a head. From January 1853 up through 1854 about 395 more were sent, 280 of them being French; Hungarians, Poles, and a few Italians made up the rest.[63]

Requests for passage continued to come in from individuals as well as from refugee organizations. In 1853 the Home Office forwarded to Mayne letters from Joseph Guiriot and Joseph Antoine Ducantou "who state that they are political refugees." Eugene Aubin, referred to as a French political refugee, made a similar request, as did the ex-secretary to Kossuth. Also in that year General Mészáros, a Hungarian ex-Minister of War, importuned Palmerston, then Home Secretary, in a flowery letter requesting passage from "that world where I have lost all, except honour and conscience," to go to America to become a "plain *homo virgilianus*." He also sought money for his friend, Colonel Bodrowitz, a "future associate in husbandry," and one other man. Enjoying their social status to the last Mészáros and friends refused to sail, but insisted on taking a steamer from Liverpool. Their wishes were granted, costing the government almost £74, including first-class rail fare from London.[64]

The largest number of Poles left in 1852 and 1853. On 9 July 1852 Mayne wrote to the Foreign Office that he had been in touch with Count Janowski— an *émigré* leader—and would send 200 Poles to New York. Mayne said that he had only 50 names but wanted all 200 sent, otherwise "it will give rise to dissatisfaction and complaint." In 1853 the Literary Association of the Friends of Poland requested that 200 be granted passage; presumably the previous group of 200 had already left. Lord Malmesbury consented to this. During 1855, 139 Poles left the country for Turkey and France, but we have no indication whether government money was used for this.[65]

For the poverty-stricken Poles the government largess provided more temptation to spend it than Sanders and his colleagues wished. In 1853 Sanders made it a policy of giving them their clothes and other provisions on board ship so that they would not pawn them for drink. "The Poles," he wrote, "more particularly are inclined to sell their things."[66]

Foreign governments were aware of the emigration and were no doubt pleased, especially when the English seemed to heed their wishes about deporting aliens. On one occasion in late 1857 Mayne sent the prefect of the Paris police the papers of a "French political refugee" who applied to Lord Clarendon for free passage to New York. Clarendon asked Mayne to enquire whether the French wanted the person "removed from England."[67]

SANDERS AND THE REFUGEES ON JERSEY

For some time after 1848 the English authorities had been viewing with jaundiced eyes the roughly 126 aliens, some Polish, but most French, who had settled in the Channel Islands, particularly Jersey, which was under British rule. Being close to the French coast, and with an Anglo-French ambiance, Jersey was a convenient haven for French refugees. Napoleon's coup in late 1851 had caused their numbers to swell with republican exiles, among whom was Victor Hugo. Much to the distress of the French and British, Jersey soon became a center for republican propaganda, and a point of concern for the two governments.

Sergeant Sanders was in the thick of all this and was dispatched to Jersey at Malmesbury's request, for "making the enquiries about the emigrants, and effecting all the arrangements for sending them off." Groups of French, and some Poles, were being sent from Jersey to New York as part of the emigration scheme. For discharging what Home Secretary Spencer Walpole admiringly described as "a delicate & difficult duty," Sanders was given a gratuity of one pound, "the mark of approbation [being] valued more than the actual amount," Mayne wrote. Sanders's most important duty, however, had been to circulate among the refugees and report on their plans and movements.[68]

For Major-General Sir Frederick Love, the Lieutenant Governor of Jersey, the refugees, especially Victor Hugo, were dangerous nuisances preaching "socialism, communism, and atheism.'' Love wanted nothing better than to get rid of them all, but until that happy day of deliverance he had to make do with surveillance, using Sanders—whom he depended on completely—as his main source of information. Unlike Love, Sanders thought Hugo no threat; the more dangerous ones, he reported, were the frequenters of low-class pubs, but even they did not plot against France.[69]

Sanders visited Jersey at least six times between October 1852 and November 1855, staying days or months, as ordered. There was practically a tug-of-war between Love and the police and Home Office for his services. Love continually asked for the detective, claiming that he could not otherwise find out what the exiles were up to, and that no one else knew as much about them as Sanders did, which was certainly true.[70] By 1853 the numbers of Jersey refugees had dropped from around 120 to 84, but they still met regularly, sometimes furtively on horseback.

With all the references to Sanders so far, one can only wonder exactly how he operated. His reports read as if he were present at some of the meetings, and he may well have been. He probably used many informers among the exiles so as not to make himself too obvious. Nevertheless, his movements back and forth between Jersey and London must have aroused some notice, especially if he ran into the same people in both places. In the emigration scheme, and in 1858 when he followed the trail of the Orsini conspirators, his official position was obvious. Still, in August 1855 after some ''material'' was seized from the Jersey exiles, Sanders apparently decided to lie low for several days, so that he could ''prove'' that he was not out to watch them. He would have to have been discreet in not asking too many questions; that alone would arouse suspicion. Certainly, the refugees could not have been naive about their own anonymity, and must have assumed—correctly—that some of their numbers were spies. It may have been that Sanders simply passed himself off as a French refugee, although not actually wearing disguises, which were officially frowned upon. Perhaps, and quite likely, he said he was a traveling businessman. Unfortunately, we shall probably never know.[71] There were, of course, foreign agents on Jersey, but there was no contact between them and Sanders.

The French had managed to buy the services of John Sullivan, a quartermaster in the Jersey Militia, to spy on refugees. In 1853 at the urging of General Love, Sanders watched him carefully, and was even kept on Jersey longer than he would have been for that purpose. In 1855 an unpaid Jersey constable who was in league with the refugees somehow impeded Sanders in his investigations, although Sanders does not say how. Sanders by then had too many friends among the refugees, and said that "nothing can now take place here without my knowing it."[72]

Sanders was not the only Metropolitan policeman sent to Jersey. In the spring of 1854 a plain-clothes constable from G Division, named Larindon, who was not a detective, was sent to Jersey at Palmerston's request. Larindon's main qualification seemed to have been some experience in watching foreigners during the days of Chartist activity. Perhaps his visit had something to do with investigating a murder which had occurred on Jersey the previous October; the records do not say. Whatever Larindon's duties, General Love asked that he be recalled as he was no longer needed. He was not, in the words of a police official, the "style of man" that Sanders was.[73]

It was clear that the government felt that one Sanders was not enough. Palmerston advised the police to try to recruit one or two other police officers who knew French like Sanders, and who could perform the "special duties" that he usually did.

From time to time refugees were sent off from Jersey. In May 1854 Mayne wrote to Love: "The political refugees will be deported as soon as passage to New York can be provided and communication will be made to them when they should come here from Jersey. I am very glad you are to be relieved from such troublesome subjects." Money and passage to New York had been arranged for those "dangerous" refugees on Jersey who were willing to leave. Love would like to have had all the exiles shipped off, but the Foreign Secretary, Lord Clarendon, felt obliged to inform him that only "dangerous characters are sent away."[74]

Back in England in late May 1854 Sanders reported that the London émigrés were corresponding with those on Jersey and "drawing up manifestoes and revolutionary pamphlets, which are sent to Jersey to be printed, but I cannot hear of any plotting on their part." In July he attended a French meeting at Great Chapel Street, at which the participants discussed ways of trying to keep their "best men" from leaving England or applying to leave. Sanders's work was obviously worth enough to earn him a gratuity of £50.[75]

THE EXPULSIONS FROM JERSEY

Later in 1855, with France and England staunch allies in the Crimean War, the refugee situation on Jersey appeared more irritating for the English government, which was hardly prepared to look sympathetically at the openly revolutionary statements and flood of printed propaganda directed at France.

In October 1855 three men, Pyat, Rongée, and Jourdan, were expelled from Jersey under martial law by General Love, for publishing a letter in the Jersey refugee paper *L'Homme*, in which they used particularly colorful language to decry Queen Victoria's friendliness toward Napoleon III. "You have sacrificed all—queenly dignity, feminine scruples, aristocratic pride, English feeling, rank, race, chastity, all, even the sense of modesty, for the sake of the great ally." What was intended as Gallic hyperbole was an assault on the sensibilities of the more literal-minded Anglo-Saxon: an indignant Jersey mob wrecked the offices of the paper.[76] Palmerston, on good terms with Napoleon, was furious with the exiles and wrote to Home Secretary Sir George Grey, calling for the immediate expulsion of all the refugees from Jersey. "I think they ought all and every one without any exception to be sent out, and that the misconduct of their Fellow Refugees should be assigned as the reason." The British government could not allow Napoleon III to be plotted against by a "knot of his mortal enemies . . . when we have the power of sending them away from thence. . . . True they will pass over into England. Never mind; they can do less mischief to Napoleon and to us, in England, than in the Channel Islands." He also wanted to prosecute *L'Homme*, if possible. If the evidence for that was not adequate, then "a good watch on the proceedings of these people might soon furnish proper materials." Events soon overtook Palmerston, when a protest petition signed by thirty-six men against the expulsion of the three letter-writers gave Palmerston and Love the opportunity they were looking for. With martial authority and with the backing of Palmerston's government Love then expelled the 36 signers of the petition—who included Victor Hugo and his two sons—on the pretext that they were endangering the Anglo-French alliance. Most went to nearby Guernsey.[77]

This was the government's most dramatic victory against the refugees, and the most drastic action taken in the century, but as a victory it was more symbolic than concrete. There were no more expulsions beyond the 39, although more were being considered. This depended on the behavior of the rest of the exiles—who were, as we might expect, being observed again by Sanders. He noted that the denunciations of Napoleon were very violent, and that the refugees' conduct was "infamous in the extreme." This, for Sanders, was strong language.[78]

THE ORSINI PLOT

Napoleon had ample reason to be more concerned with assassination attempts on his own life than with any inflammatory newspaper articles or even any military or political maneuvres the exiles could make. In 1853 he complained to Lord Malmesbury that three armed men had been arrested within yards of him and that "these men all came straight from England, and had not been twelve hours in France. Your police should have known it and given me notice." Napoleon conceded that Malmesbury had often notified him, but complained that Malmesbury's successors did not give him warnings.[79]

In 1857 Mayne wrote to the French Ambassador that an enquiry in London had failed to turn up a suspected assassination plot. Later Mazzini and his associates in England were being carefully watched as well for their possible involvement in a suspected plot against Napoleon, though no solid information of this could be adduced.[80]

Finally on 14 January 1858 a bomb attempt in front of the Paris Opera was made on Napoleon's life by Felix Orsini and three others, disgruntled with French policy in Italy. The attempt failed, though bystanders were killed by the blasts. Since the conspirators had hatched the plot in England, where they had been living, the outcry against the British government for harboring assassins reached a new peak. The percussion grenades used had been manufactured in Birmingham by another refugee, Dr. Simon Bernard; the pistols carried by the men were of English make. Orsini held a British passport issued in the name of Allsop, and his accomplice, Pieri, had English money with him.[81]

Sanders, now an inspector, and Labalmondiere were assigned to investigate the movements of the conspirators in England, Belgium and France, and also to gather evidence for prosecution of Simon Bernard in England for his part in the conspiracy. While Labalmondiere went to Paris, Sanders visited various clubs in Belgium, with the knowledge of the Belgian police, and followed a man named Pianciani to get his address. The latter had been expelled from Jersey in 1855.[82]

The police were especially eager to keep a closer eye on the London aliens for news of further plots that would embarrass the government. Hammond of the Foreign Office wrote Mayne: "Surely by a little money you can get some of these Italians to tell all they know. You may spend it if required." Sanders, back in England, visited refugee houses in London and reported that the French refugees were excited and wanted more information about the Orsini attempt. They were generally sorry the attempt had failed. He got little information from the Italians as they "were very quiet and conversed but little." It was also widely suspected that Orsini's loose association with the Mazzinian faction in London made them privy to the plot. The astonished Mazzinians, however, disavowed any connection, and Sanders was convinced that there was none. Orsini had not been popular with them, having quarreled with Mazzini himself, but it was likely that he timed his bomb attack to coincide with a military move by the Mazzinian forces in Italy.[83]

Not all of the London exiles were happy with such lethal plots, which could only raise suspicion and hostility against themselves. Members of the conservative Italian National League, hoping to put as much distance between themselves and the conspirators as possible, passed a resolution at their March meeting expressing their "utter abhorrence of the recent attempt made by one or more of their countrymen on the life of the Emperor of France." They also condemned the silence of the other exiles over the bombing. Advance notice of this meeting of these tamest of exiles caused consternation in government circles before its purpose became clear, and Bowyer, in Parliament, questioned allowing the gathering to take place. But more important, he was alarmed at the inability of the police to "discover and suppress" conspiracies—proof, he believed, that the police were defective.[84]

Frequenting such popular London meeting places as the Café Suisse in Tichbourne Street, Sanders and other detectives kept their eyes open. Mayne and quite possibly the Foreign Office may have paid extra agents to move among the exiles, though the evidence is extremely slim. In 1858 a Miguel Carbonel wrote to "M. Le Comte" (presumably Earl Cowley, the British ambassador in Paris), telling him that he had been making enquiries in London among the Italians and thought another attempt on Napoleon would be made; if so he would keep the police posted. He continued: "Believe me that I will not fail to transmit to you any information which may in any way affect H.I. Majesty [Napoleon]." Carbonel may well have volunteered his information gratis, however.

In August, Mayne wrote to the Foreign Office, referring to the "great anxiety to get information both as to the past & what might still be going on amongst the refugees—after the attempt of Jan'y 14." The curious part of the letter is the statement, "I have many reasons to believe that the persons employed were the best that could be procured. Their information was useful and the payments reasonable."[85]

STRAINS IN ANGLO-FRENCH RELATIONS

At the diplomatic level the conspiracy caused a storm of protest by the French against the British government for allowing England to be used as a haven for assassins. The French Foreign Minister demanded that something be done about the "sect of foreigners which, in its publications and its meetings elevates assassination to doctrine, and which in the space of six years, has sent into France not less than eight assassins to strike a blow at the Emperor." The Emperor's anxieties were hardly assuaged any by the public notice made by the aged and eccentric poet Walter Savage Landor, that he would give £100 to anyone who would kill Napoleon. In Paris a group of French colonels petitioned Napoleon to allow them to come to England and destroy the "assassins' " den.[86] Napoleon apologized for the widely-publicized petition, confident that Whitehall had got the message. Malmesbury was certain that war would be inevitable if one more attempt on Napoleon's life were made. While war may have been unlikely, Napoleon told his ambassador in London that a diplomatic break would ensue—was it a bluff?—if England did not pass some sort of alien act. Napoleon was in a difficult position, since a break would have wrecked the Anglo-French alliance that was one of the cornerstones of his foreign policy. Palmerston agreed that the government had to act, but dismissed as opinions held by the "ignorant and vulgar" the charge that England harbored revolutionaries and assassins to weaken France.[87]

The British were stung by the barrage of criticism from France, and this coincided with a growing anti-French mood of the country, which rose to a panic when it was discovered that Napoleon had built a new harbor at Cherbourg for his steam-driven ships. At the same time the writer Montalembert was charged with sedition in France for having contrasted the French government unfavorably with the British one. Both events heightened anti-French sentiments in England.

Palmerston had been consistent in his attitude toward political refugees: Britain could give them asylum but must not let them plot against their own or any other country. He had adopted this attitude toward Italian and Hungarian refugees against Austrian rule, even when Britain and Austria were on cordial terms. Likewise, he would certainly uphold his policy after the Orsini Affair.[88] In 1849 when Austria was demanding the return of Kossuth and the Hungarian refugees who had taken refuge in Turkey (and later came to England), Palmerston opposed surrendering them to Austria. Unless a treaty specified such a return, "the law of hospitality, the dictates of humanity, the general feelings of mankind, forbid such surrenders." Governments who would do that are disgraceful. On the other hand, he said, refugees who wish to leave Britain voluntarily should be given free passage to Europe.[89]

Nevertheless, it was also clear that by 1858 Palmerston's attitude toward plotting aliens had hardened. A few days after the Orsini attempt Palmerston circulated among his cabinet a proposal to allow the Secretary of State to expel aliens suspected of being involved in some conspiracy against a foreign state or sovereign. This would remove doubt about the power of the law to deal with conspiracies to commit offenses abroad as well as at home. The other aspect of the proposal was to elevate conspiracy to murder from a misdemeanor to a felony. To spare England from having to apply such a law, if passed, Palmerston tartly added that France might do well to spend money to send its political dissidents directly to the United States, rather than to let them filter into Britain, the difference being that ''the longer passage would be a little more expensive.'' The comments of the cabinet members, preserved among the Broadlands papers, make illuminating reading. All but Clanricarde and Panmure were opposed to Palmerston's proposed law, for one reason or another. Palmerston wisely dropped the expulsion part and proceeded to introduce a Conspiracy to Murder bill that would have made it a felony for anyone in England, British or foreign, to conspire to murder someone in another country. Even this watered-down bill was too much. Although it had gone through easily on the first reading, the rising tide of francophobia caused the conservatives to desert it on its second reading ten days later. The Conspiracy bill went down to defeat, bringing with it the Palmerston government. The bill was tame enough, but the timing was off, and Palmerston paid the price for misreading the mood of the House. The public would have no part of any law that would appear to capitulate to foreign ultimata.[90]

In this same atmosphere the government tried Dr. Simon Bernard for his part in the Orsini conspiracy, and to no one's surprise he was acquitted by a sympathetic jury, against the backdrop of jubilant crowd scenes.

This trial attempt and Palmerston's failed bill at least had the effect of mollifying the French, who saw the British government taking symbolic steps— about the most France could expect. It made it easier for diplomatic fences to be mended.

THE WANING OF THE ALIEN PROBLEM

Nevertheless, the temperament of the time did not lessen official cooperation between the two governments. Britain's policy of paid emigration was still going on, and it appears that the French were helping to pay some of the expenses. In 1858 Hammond, at the Foreign Office, informed Mayne that the French government would publish ''a list of those whom they are most anxious to have sent [to America] and the entire expense of sending whom they are prepared to bear; while as regard those whom we may send on our own information they will bear half the expense.... We cannot send any against their own will, and that it would not be prudent to urge any to go.'' Lord Cowley in Paris was directed to make this clear to the French. ''Lord Malmesbury would not be disinclined to send even as many as three hundred, supposing, of which I presume there is no doubt, there are as many really dangerous men who would wish to emigrate.''[91] Just as expected, two lists came from France, one of Italians, one of French. The titles of the lists left nothing in doubt: ''*Français que le gouvernement de l'Empereur verrait avec plaisir s'éloigner de Londres et gagner les États-Unis.''* There were some nineteen names on the French list including Felix Pyat and Ledru-Rollin. The other list substituted the word "Italians" for "French" in the title and had thirty-seven names on it, including Mazzini's.[92] The eventual outcome of this particular arrangement is not clear; but the nineteen rough tally sheets of emigrants sent abroad show that some 200 French and Italian emigrants were dispatched to New York between 2 February and 28 August 1858. No Poles were on these lists, but the May Report of the Literary Association of the Friends of Poland shows that 29 Poles had left for America, Poland, and other places. There is no indication that the emigration scheme continued after 1858. In those eight years that it existed passage was granted to 960 men, 305 women, and 233 children. The majority of them were probably French. By 1858 London's refugee population had indeed dropped to 2,210.[93]

From England's standpoint refugees were ceasing to be considered a problem, and if we must pick a watershed date for this change of attitude it would probably be 1851, not 1858, because after the closing of the Great Exhibition virtually nothing was heard inside Britain of refugee threats to the British government; it was then hard to float rumors. Magazines like *Punch* and *Household Words* ridiculed gossip of conspiracies for years after. Although the average Englishman could sleep more soundly the diplomats and the police could not, but by the end of the 1850s the diplomatic storms over harboring political refugees had been weathered, and there had been no erosion of England's traditional readiness to accept exiles.[94] Palmerston's difficulties in 1858 proved the futility of trying to expel aliens. The public had put pressure on the government to leave well enough alone, and no one was interested in pushing the issue again. In the 1860s and 1870s there was little bother about aliens, and for the rest of the century the right of asylum remained a hallowed practice. Indeed, it was only in 1905 in the face of immigration from Eastern Europe that the law was changed to allow selectivity in accepting refugees. It remains a fact that between 1823 and 1906 no alien was either blocked from entry or thrown out of Britain.[95]

In complying with foreign demands for control of the aliens, the British took steps that could only be regarded as minimal. Police surveillance was, as we have noted, very limited and involved a few officers on an intermittent basis. There was not a forcible shovelling out of undesirables. Limited as the emigration scheme was, its political and diplomatic usefulness cannot be taken lightly, because it showed foreign powers that the British were doing something. Certainly the recipients of the aid had no cause for complaint and applauded the program. Any appearance, however, that Britain was cooperating with the wishes of foreign governments, especially of France, in a matter as delicate as emigration, would no doubt have caused a public outcry. This cooperation, which included some liaison with Paris on intelligence matters was, as we have seen, more intimate than anyone outside of the appropriate government circles knew. Nevertheless, such cooperation on intelligence matters may well have helped keep France and England from a diplomatic break in the late 1850s.

NOTES

1. *Hansard*, Vol. 112 (4 July 1850), col. 870. MEPOL 2/90 (5 Nov. 1850). See Chapter 5 for a discussion of the Exhibition.

2. MEPOL 2/43 (8 Nov. 1831), S Div. Rpt. MEPOL 2/43 (June 1848). MEPOL 2/43 (30 Dec. 1851). Ibid. (4 March 1853). Bernard Porter, *The Refugee Question in Mid-Victorian Politics* (Cambridge: Cambridge University Press, 1979), p. 16.

3. E.H. Carr, *Romantic Exiles*, p. 119. A.R. Schoyen, *The Chartist Challenge: A Portrait of George Julian Harney* (London: William Heinemann, Ltd., 1958), p. 133.

4. *Hansard*, Vol. 115 (27 March 1851), cols. 621-29. Great Britain, Parliament, *Sessional Papers* (House of Lords), Vol. XVI, 1852, "Accounts and Papers," Granville's Dispatch, p. 40. Peter Brock, "Polish Democrats and English Radicals, 1832-1862: A Chapter in the History of Anglo-Polish Relations," *Journal of Modern History*, XXV (June 1953), 152, n. 34.

5. Carr, *Romantic Exiles*, pp. 119, 123. David McLellan, *Karl Marx, His Life and Thought* (New York: Harper & Row, 1973), pp. 229-31.

6. Jasper Ridley, *Lord Palmerston*, (London: Granada Publishing, Ltd, 1972) p. 702. Brock, "Polish Democrats," p. 142 n. 11. Derek Beales, *England and Italy, 1859-60* (London: Thomas Nelson and Sons, Ltd., 1961), pp. 32-33.

7. *Hansard*, Vol. 98 (13 April 1848), col. 266.

8. *Hansard*, Vol. 115 (1 April 1851), col. 885. McLellan, *Karl Marx*, p. 231.

9. *Sessional Papers* (House of Lords), Vol. XVI, 1852, "Accounts and Papers," pp. 36-37. Earl of Malmesbury, *Memoirs of an Ex-Minister. An Autobiography* (London: Longmans, Green, and Co., 1884), I, pp. 385-86.

10. Malmesbury, *Memoirs*, I, p. 314 (8 March 1852).

11. Ibid., pp. 391-92 (20 March 1853).

12. P.R.O. Foreign Office (F.O.) 27/924 (13 Jan. 1852). *Hansard*, Vol. 120 (1 April 1852), cols. 477-526; Vol. 124 (4 March 1853). For a general discussion of French refugee activities see Howard C. Payne, *The Police State of Louis Napoleon Bonaparte, 1851-60* (Seattle: University of Washington Press, 1966).

13. Porter, *Refugee Question*, passim.

14. MEPOL 2/43 (30 Oct. 1831, 8 Nov. 1831).

15. Ibid. (15 April 1848, 13 Jun. 1848).

16. Ridley, *Lord Palmerston*, pp. 555-57.

17. *Hansard*, Vol. 126 (29 April 1853), cols. 796-97. H.O. 45/4816, Rept. Supt. Evans, Thames Div., 4 April 1853.

18. *Hansard*, Vol. 126 (29 April 1853), col. 801.

19. Ibid., col. 804. Ibid. (5 May 1853), col. 1158.

20. H.O. 45/4816, D Div. Rept. 24 March 1853.

21. *Hansard*, Vol. 125 (15 April 1853), col. 1210. This was not true.

22. Ibid., Vol. 126 (5 May 1853), col. 1148. Ibid. (3 May 1853), col. 1045.

23. Broadlands MSS, GC/BL5 (7 Nov. 1851), Blackwell to Palmerston.

24. *Hansard*, Vol. 115 (1 April 1851), col. 885. Ibid., Vol. 126 (5 May 1853), col. 1167.

25. *The Times* (London), 26 March 1861. *Hansard*, Vol. 161 (14 March 1861), cols. 1976-77.

26. *Hansard*, Vol. 161 (14 March 1861), cols. 1978-79. *Hansard*, Vol. 162 (22 March 1861), col. 1217; (8 April 1861), col. 260. Thomas H. Duncombe, *The Life and Correspondence of Thomas Slingsby Duncombe* (London: Hurst and Blackett, 1868), II, 158-59.

27. Porter, *Refugee Question*, pp. 150-51, 156-57. MEPOL 4/2 (26 Aug. 1859).

28. MEPOL 2/43 (23, 24 April 1851). H.O. 45/3518 (5 Aug. 1851). Alvin R. Calman, *Ledru-Rollin après 1848 et les proscrits français en Angleterre* (Paris: F. Reider & Cie., Éditeurs, 1921), pp. 175-76.

29. MEPOL 2/43 (March 1852) Sanders to Mayne. Porter, *Refugee Question*, pp. 154-57. MEPOL 1/46 (5 June 1852), Mayne to Malmesbury.

30. Eric de Maré, *London, 1851: The Year of the Great Exhibition* (London: The Folio Press: J.M. Dent, Ltd., 1973), n.p. Christopher Hobhouse, *1851 and the Crystal Palace* (London: John Murray, 1950), pp. 12-20.

31. *Hansard*, Vol. 112 (4 July 1850), col. 870.

32. MEPOL 2/90 (5 Nov. 1850), Mayne to H.O.

33. MEPOL 1/53/1295 (2 June 1851), Mayne to H.O. Ibid., 2/92 (June 1851). Ibid., 1/53 (21 May 1851). H.O. 65/17 (22 May 1851). H.O. 45/3518 (23 April 1851), Forbes to Palmerston. C.R. Fay, *Palace of Industry, 1851: A Study of the Great Exhibition and its Future* (Cambridge: Cambridge University Press, 1951), p. 8.

34. MEPOL 1/53/1204 (31 March 1851), Mayne to H.O. Ibid., 2/192 (19 May 1851), Bulwer to Palmerston.

35. Ibid., 1/46 (15 Jan. 1851), Mayne to Col. Brown. Ibid., 2/92 (June 1851).

36. Ibid., 2/99 (22 May 1851). Ibid., 2/92 (June 1851).

37. Ibid., 2/92 (June 1851).

38. Ibid.

39. Ibid., 2/93 (30 May 1851), N.Y. Police rept.

40. Ibid., (3, 19 June 1851).

41. Ibid., 2/94 (20 April 1851).

42. Ibid., 2/94 (6, 9, 20 May 1851).

43. Ibid., 2/95.

44. Ibid., 2/95 (8, 12 May, 27 June 1851), Galbi's rept.

45. Ibid., 2/97 (7 May, 4 June 1851), Harivel's repts.

46. Ibid., 2/96 (21 May, 8 June 1851), Marseilles repts.

47. "The Police and the Thieves," *Quarterly Review*, XCIX, 182-83.

48. MEPOL 2/94 (4, 5 July 1851). Ibid., 2/105.

49. The episode is described in Howard Robinson, *The British Post Office: A History* (Princeton, N.J.: Princeton University Press, 1948), pp. 337-51.

50. H.O. 65/17 (14 April 1851); 65/18 (20 Dec. 1852); 65/24 (22 June 1862).

51. H.O. 65/23 (29 June 1860, 4, 6, 13 July 1860), H.O. to Mayne. MEPOL 1/47 (25 May 1865), Labalmondiere to Count Maffei.

52. Malmesbury, *Memoirs*, I, p. 356, Harris to Malmesbury (25 Sept. 1852).

53. *Hansard*, Vol. 102 (19 Feb. 1849), cols. 872-74. Vol. 100 (7 Aug. 1848), col. 1172.

54. *Hansard*, Vol. 134 (3 July 1854), "Civil Service Supply Estimates." Vol. 141 (14 April 1856). Vol. 146 (13 July 1857). Vol. 160 (17 Aug. 1860). *P.P.* 1849 (268-vi), XXX, p. 467. *P.P.* 1850 (256-vi), XXXIV, pp. 452-53. *Reports of the Twenty-Third and Twenty-Fourth Annual Meeting of the Literary Association of the Friends of Poland* (London: E. Detkins, 1855, 1856).

55. Porter, *Refugee Question*, pp. 82, 160. Brock, "Polish Democrats," p. 152 n. 35. *Sessional Papers* (House of Lords), Vol. XVI (1852), pp. 223-60. W.J. Linton, *Memories* (London: Lawrence & Bullen, 1895), pp. 138-41.

56. MEPOL 2/43. H.O. 4302.

57. From the Clarendon Papers (3 Feb. 1858), quoted in Porter, *Refugee Question*, p. 161.

58. H.O. 45/4302 (6 Jan. 1852, April-May [?] 1852.) Ibid., (19 Jan. 1852), F.O. to H.O. Few modern historians record the program. Calman, writing in 1921, and Schoyen, writing in 1958, used the Home Office papers, but not the police records. Porter has used all of these records and has written the most complete account to date. Not having seen the Home Office letters cited above until 1978, the present author revised the account in his 1976 doctoral dissertation concerning the source of money (p. 136), in which he suggested that while Foreign Office or Home Office funds could have been used, the money probably came from the refugee funds voted by Parliament. That F.O. Secret Service funds were used is now beyond question. See also Porter, *Refugee Question*, pp. 160-61.

59. Linton, *Memories*, pp. 138-41. Brock, *Polish Democrats*, p. 152 n. 35. Schoyen, *Chartist Challenge*, p. 229.

60. H.O. 45/4816 (5 March 1853).

61. H.O. 45/4302 (6 May 1852) MEPOL 2/43. H.O. 65/18 (3 May 1852).

62. Cavanagh, *Scotland Yard*, p. 41. Prothero, *History of the C.I.D.*, p. 60.

63. MEPOL 2/43. H.O. 45/4302 (23 April 1852).

64. H.O. 65/19 (12-19 Aug. 1853, 7 Sept. 1853). MEPOL 2/43 (Aug. 1853).

65. MEPOL 1/46 (9 July 1852), Mayne to Addington. *Reports of the Twenty-First, Twenty-Second, and Twenty-Third Annual Meetings of the Literary Association of the Friends of Poland*, 1853, 1854, 1855.

66. MEPOL 2/43 (1853), Sanders' Rept.

67. MEPOL 1/46 (12 Nov. 1857), Mayne to Pieri.

68. MEPOL 1/46 (1 Nov. 1852), Mayne to F.O. H.O. 65/18 (18 Oct. 1852). Payne, *Police State*, p. 156.

69. H.O. 45/4816 (8-10 Nov. 1853), rept.

70. H.O. 45/6188/4. H.O. 45/4816 (19 Oct. 1853). H.O. 65/19 (19 Sept. 1853, 22 Sept. 1853, 20 Oct. 1853).

71. H.O. 45/6188 (5 Aug., 5 Oct. 1855). H.O. 45/4816 (13 Sept. 1853).

72. H.O. 45/4816 (13 Sept. 1853), rept. H.O. 45/6188 (5 Oct. 1855).

73. H.O. 45/5180 (n.d.) Yardley to F.O. H.O. 65/19 (18 April 1854), H.O. to Mayne. MEPOL 2/43 (29 March, 16 May 1854), Mayne to H.O.

74. H.O. 65/19 (16 Jan. 1855). H.O. 65/20 (19 March 1855). H.O. 45/5180.

75. H.O. letters (25 May, 3 July 1854), quoted in Calman, *Ledru-Rollin*, pp. 175-76. MEPOL 2/43 (21 Aug. 1854).

76. Howard Payne and Henry Grosshans, "The Exiled Revolutionaries and the French Political Police in the 1850s," *American Historical Review*, LXVIII, No. 4 (1963), 965. Duncombe, *Life*, II, p. 306. H.O. 45/6333 (13 Oct. 1859), Love to H.O.

77. British Museum, Palmerston Papers, ADD MSS 48579 (12 Oct. 1855), Palmerston to Grey. H.O. 45/6333 (13 Oct. 1859), Love to H.O. Certain individuals were allowed to return to Jersey in 1859.

78. H.O. 45/6188 (5 Oct. 1855), rept. Porter, *Refugee Question*, p. 168.

79. Malmesbury, *Memoirs*, I, p. 392 (20 March 1853).

80. MEPOL 1/46 (15 April 26 Nov. 1857).

81. Ibid., 3/25, for details of the plot. Ibid., (15 Feb. 1858).

82. Ibid., 3/22 (26 March 1858).

83. Ibid., 3/24 (16, 17, 18 Jan. 1858), Hammond to Mayne and other reports. Ibid., 3/22 (8, 25 Jan. 1858), Sanders' report.

84. Ibid., 3/25 (10 March 1858). *Hansard*, Vol. 148 (8 Feb. 1858), col. 946-47.

85. MEPOL 3/25 (20 Feb. 1858). Ibid., 1/46 (20 Aug. 1858), Mayne to Hammond.

86. *P.P.*, 1857-58 (180), LX, pp. 124-25 (11 March 1858), Walewski to Malmesbury. MEPOL 3/25 (20 Feb. 1858), Carbonel to Cowley. Spencer Walpole, *The History of Twenty-Five Years* (London: Longmans, Green, and Co., 1904), I, 117.

87. H. Hearder, "Napoleon III's Threat to Break Off Diplomatic Relations With England During the Crisis Over the Orsini Attempt in 1858," *English Historical Review*, LXXI (1957), 479-81. Malmesbury, *Memoirs*, II, 105 (13 March 1858). Broadlands MSS CAB/A/89 (21 Jan. 1858), Cabinet proposal.

88. Ridley, *Lord Palmerston*, pp. 645-51.

89. Broadlands MSS, MM/TU/39/2 (1849), Palmerston to Lord Ponsonby. MM/TU/41 (6 Oct. 1849), Palmerston to Schwarzenberg.

90. Broadlands CAB/A/89 (21 Jan. 1858), Palmerston to Cabinet. Ibid., CAB/A/91-101 (21 Jan. 1858). Porter, *Refugee Question*, p. 175.

91. MEPOL 2/43 (24 April 1858), Hammond to Mayne.

92. Ibid. (n.d.).

93. *Reports of the Twenty-Sixth, Twenty-Seventh Annual Meetings of the Literary Association of the Friends of Poland* (13 May 1858), pp. 7-8; (7 July 1859), p. 7. MEPOL 2/43 (n.d.). F.O. 27/1233 (21 Jan. 1858), F.O. to Lord Cowley.

94. *Household Words*, III, No. 57 (26 April 1851), 103. *Punch*, January-June, 1851, p. 104.

95. Porter, *Refugee Question*, pp. 1, 88, 209.

5 Public Order and Crowd Control

The Metropolitan Police was intended to be a civil police agency that could deter crime and keep the streets orderly. It was not supposed to look like or act like a branch of the military. From their very beginning the police had to face crowds and prove themselves. Although the police were not designed to be an anti-riot force, and they were not specifically trained in crowd control, they learned by experience how to deal with unruly crowds. It was apparent that an organized, disciplined body of men armed only with truncheons was more than a match for a much larger crowd. Although the police overreacted in Hyde Park in 1855, as we shall see in the chapter following this, their behavior in controlling crowds was usually characterized by restraint. The Commissioners realized that it was important for the constables not to be provocative at the outset, which might cause violence. When the police had to intervene with force, they should do so with minimum violence but with sufficient numbers to avoid being overwhelmed and disgraced.

Ironically, public approval of the police in the early years increased most noticeably not because of routine law enforcement on the beats, but from their successful confrontation with mobs at Coldbath Fields in 1833. Police success in facing down the last large Chartist demonstration in London in 1848, and the efficient and courteous management of millions of visitors to the Crystal Palace Exhibition in 1851 proved to be further milestones that strengthened the confidence of the propertied classes of London in the police, a confidence that remained, although somewhat eroded by the Reform Bill demonstrations in Hyde Park in the 1860s.

EIGHTEENTH-CENTURY DISORDER

Eighteenth-century England, like Old Regime France, abounded in a variety of collective actions. As we have already seen, popular violence on a limited scale had long been a feature of English society. In county districts and market towns, food prices, enclosures, toll gates, turnpikes, poaching, or workhouses were likely subjects of popular disturbance. In London, while food riots were rare, violence often broke out in response to threats to the livelihood of craftsmen, shopkeepers, or workers; or against the importation of foreign goods and workers, as in the Calico Riots in Spitalfields in 1719-20, and in the later anti-Irish riots. Political splits of the time often took the form of disturbances: among Whigs, Tories, and radicals; between the government and the opposition; or between the City of Westminster and the City of London. Such divisions were reflected in riots over, for example, gin, excise taxes, the War of Jenkins' Ear, John Wilkes, and Catholic relief, the last named provoking the most serious disturbance of the century, the Gordon Riot in 1780. Many of these modes of action were directed toward immediate goals and for a limited "audience." Quite often these events, particularly rural ones, had ritualized and exotic touches, such as costumes, disguises, displays of effigies, and mock trials.[1]

Since rioting in the eighteenth century was the only time-honored avenue for working-class protest, the propertied classes lived with it uneasily, provided it was not unduly destructive or radically threatening to the social order. When things got out of hand as with the Gordon Riot, brutal suppression of the disturbance followed by exemplary hangings usually got things back to normal. Limited disorders were almost expected and not wholly denounced as a means of achieving limited goals. Such forms of violence were, in Allan Silver's words "part of an articulate system of demands and responses, in which needs and obligations are reasonably clear to each party."[2]

As the pre-industrial polity gave way to the modern age and as industrial capitalism developed, the urban economy became more complex. It was increasingly vulnerable to disruption in its many parts. In fact, the long-term impact of disorder could not be ignored, and even the London stock market prices were sensitive to the instability resulting from both riots and violent suppression.

THE DEMAND FOR ORDER

The nineteenth-century world of professional bureaucrats and professional police forces was also a world that saw the prevailing methods of collective action change. The message was now put across in different ways: by banners, signs, handbills, pamphlets, and badges.

Even the term riot was only slowly losing its earlier connotation of revelry and mirth, emerging in the early nineteenth century into its current usage. By the mid-Victorian years, the frequent employment of the word demonstration betrays the changes that had come about as economic, social and political groups found their voices in collective organizations created to apply systematic pressure on the body politic. Local sporadic resistance as a political tool was becoming a thing of the past. With the breakdown of local authority and the waning of the influence of guilds and churches, more power came to be vested in the national state. The expansion of electoral politics not only increased the number of active participants in the political culture but also rewarded certain forms of collective action, such as the election rally, and even the protest, the demonstration, and the strike. The response was mutual: the state drew its mandate from a wider, better organized constituency, but it had to make concessions in return. The setting in the nineteenth century was a broader one, and the give and take of politics was played out on a much larger stage before a national audience.[3]

One should not assume from the foregoing that the changes in the style and type of popular volatility represented a kind of evolutionary determinism, that the ''new'' replaced the ''old'' as part of some dialectical process. History shows us nothing of the sort, and the older forms of collective action coexisted with the modern ones. ''Primitive'' violence never disappeared; it simply became less prevalent. Election violence did not disappear at all, but remained common throughout the Victorian age. The apprentices who demonstrated and shouted ''Wilkes and Liberty!'' in the 1760s did not automatically evolve into the membership of the tamer political associations of the 1860s.[4]

In dealing with public demonstrations the police had to weigh the demands of freedom of assembly and speech on the one hand, and the preservation of the peace on the other. That crowd control had fundamental political implications was obvious, and the Commissioners tried to minimize the impact of such actions on the public by using restraint. The ''law'' of public order was necessarily a compromise. Questions of public order were rarely raised to the highest constitutional levels. Many were simply resolved in the magistrates' courts as ''obstructing the police,'' ''abusive language,'' ''causing an affray,'' etc. Control of public n.eetings in parks was usually provided for in local acts or bylaws, and such rules were difficult to challenge in the courts.[5]

LAWS ON PUBLIC ORDER

The English legal system could counter public disorder with one of a number of laws, most notoriously the ''Riot Act'' of 1714. By the late nineteenth century a riot was interpreted as being a display of force or violence by at least three people having a common purpose in mind at the outset. The violence and terror engendered were supposed to be ''sufficient to alarm people of reasonable firmness and courage.'' After having the Riot Act read to them, persons who remained in the area were rendered felons if they did not depart within an hour. An "unlawful assembly," unlike a riot, did not require the conspirators to put their plan into effect, but only to show the common intent to commit a crime of violence. Perhaps the most practicable category to apply was that of affray. An affray was fighting by two or more persons to the terror of British subjects. There did not have to be a common purpose for the disturbance. The latitude of this law made it a convenient one to apply in the courts.[6]

The Metropolitan Police Commissioner had been empowered by Section 52 of the Police Act of 1839 to make regulations for preventing obstruction of thoroughfares, and to give specific directions to the constables to keep order and avoid obstructions. This act also gave the Commissioner the authority to ban demonstrations that would block a thoroughfare. By the Trafalgar Square Act of 1844, that area was considered a thoroughfare; thus the police were legally entitled to block demonstrations there without raising some of the legal questions that surrounded Hyde Park demonstrations.[7]

POLICE CROWD CONTROL TACTICS

Since their foundation the Metropolitan Police attempted to improve their technique of controlling disorderly mobs, by minimizing the use of force and by adding some degree of science to crowd psychology. The public at large would no longer tolerate the use of armed troops against mobs—invariably after damage had already been done—when police units, by their timely intervention, could have prevented the disorder in the first place, and with few injuries. The police had been successful in meeting the challenges of crowd control without the direct intervention of the military, until the Reform demonstration of 1866. In theory policemen armed only with wooden staves (truncheons) were bound to provoke crowds less than would the presence of armed troops. Controlling police violence and substituting moral force for physical force were necessary to win public support.

This preventive ability of the police impressed such reformers as Edwin Chadwick, who pointed out in 1839 with undeniable clarity that the armed soldier had to rely on lethal force while the truncheon-wielding constable was able to take his prisoner with his free hand. Soldiers, unlike police, were ill-equipped to act continuously in small dispersed units in civilian society, whereas the police were, though it was also true that the police adopted military drill movements and acted in concert when confronting crowds. The infrequency with which they confronted crowds as a group, however, meant that they were not always very effective. Still, police organizational flexibility proved to be an asset.[8]

The very earliest crowd control tactics put the police in an entirely defensive role, that is, standing their ground and letting the crowds attack them before hitting back with their staves. It was soon obvious that such a posture was unsatisfactory and the concept of the "baton charge" was introduced, reputedly from an unlikely quarter. The moderate radical Francis Place had befriended Police Inspector Thomas and tendered the advice to him that the police should not wait to be attacked by a threatening mob. Rather, they should move into the mob quickly and "thrash those who composed the mob with their staves as long as any of them remained together, but to take none into custody; and that if this were done once or twice, there would be no more such mobs." The advice was taken to heart and soon put to good use in 1830 against a mob that came rushing out from the City during disturbances at the Lord Mayor's show.[9]

A similar tactic was employed at Coldbath Fields in Westminster in 1833, but the results were mixed. It was the most serious confrontation the police had had with crowds to date and reflected intense anti-police hostility by the 3,000 or so people who had gathered, ostensibly for a political meeting. The meeting was probably illegal, but the police (operating with ambiguous orders from the Home Office) only intervened when an orator invited the crowds to march on Whitehall and hang the Cabinet "from as many lamp-posts as were necessary." Under the command of Commissioner Rowan the police advanced into a shower of brickbats, stones and lumps of pig-iron ballast. The rioters were dispersed with truncheons, but some of the constables in their zeal pursued individual rioters for considerable distances. When the mêlée ended one constable lay dead on the street and two others had been wounded by knives. No rioters had been hurt. A public enquiry exonerated the police from blame, and from this time public opinion turned decisively in favor of the police.[10]

Police conduct in controlling mobs was generally restrained and good-natured throughout the period under consideration, and the only serious deviation from this pattern of behavior led to a Royal Commission in 1855 to investigate their actions.

Police orders and other records make it clear that the Commissioners were chary of using the police to intervene in civil disorders, unless they were on the spot in sufficient strength to prevent a "defeat" or any humiliation. The Trafalgar Square demonstration of 6 and 7 March 1848 protesting the income tax was illegal—being within a mile of a sitting Parliament and thus a violation of the Seditious Meetings Act of 1817—and was initially confronted by a police force of only about twenty or thirty men facing a crowd of some 15,000. They were unable to operate until aided by strong reinforcements.[11] This no doubt strengthened the Commissioners' resolve not to let it happen again. On 12 July 1855 after the Sunday Trading Riots, Mayne wrote to the Home Office that the police should not resist a riotous mob unless they were numerous enough to do so. A failure by them would only encourage rioters "to oppose the police with force and the consequences might be most serious." Mayne had good reason to feel so since, eleven days before, his own men had failed to control the crowds in Hyde Park protesting Lord Robert Grosvenor's Sunday Trading Bill. It was precisely on this issue that the Royal Commission found the police deficient. "If the attempt [to disperse the crowds] had been made by an adequate force it seems to us that the people might have been moved without resorting to the use of staves; but the attempts made with inadequate force produced much of the violence which cannot be justified."[12]

In 1864 Mayne reprimanded Superintendent Loxton for unwarrantably dispersing a Garibaldi meeting on Primrose Hill. Mayne was embarrassed by Loxton's action, and particularly so because Loxton did not have enough men present had there been resistance; fortunately there was none.[13]

It was normal procedure that when the police got notice of a political meeting that was about to take place, and where a breach of the peace was likely, an investigation of the meeting had to be made beforehand and a full report sent to the Commissioner. It was on this basis that Mayne decided the numbers of constables to be present near the meeting, and the arrangements for regulating traffic and preventing the obstruction of thoroughfares. The police were always cautioned to ignore taunts and never to interfere with a meeting unless an actual breach of the peace took place.[14] Bringing together large numbers of constables at a minute's notice was never an easy thing in the pre-telegraph age. When Mayne was asked how many men he could have assembled on 24 July 1855, the first day of the Sunday Trading disturbances, he estimated that on a Sunday (with men away) he could have called up about 1,000 within about three hours, allowing for communication to various stations and for the inspectors and superintendents to go to the men's houses and round them up.[15]

Timing was important in dispersing a meeting if there was disorder, and in this the Metropolitan Police gained some expertise. A careful watch was made on large assemblies, usually by a few plain-clothes constables in the crowd who would relay information back to the strong detachments of police scattered about the area in convenient, discreet locations, so as not to provoke the crowds. In meetings in Hyde Park the detachments, except for scattered officers standing away from the crowds, were invariably kept at the police stations and other buildings very close to the park, but not in view of the assemblies. Plain-clothes policemen would mix with the crowds to relay messages back to the commanders.

With a careful watch being kept on the meeting, the police would be able to move quickly if disorder broke out, and to disperse the crowds.

In cases of serious disturbances special constables could be sworn in for a limited time to help keep the peace, their expenses being defrayed by the local authorities. In London special constables were sworn in by magistrates in the parish halls and were normally used in filling the absence of the usual police in their areas.

The 1839 Police Act allowed special constables to have "all the powers, privileges and duties" of Metropolitan constables, within the area for which they were sworn. The most notable example of their use was during the large Chartist demonstration at Kennington Common in 1848, during which 170,000 special constables, armed with staves, were employed, including the future Napoleon III of France. Their zeal in volunteering was inflamed not only by the Chartist threat but also by the specter of European revolutions, which, many were convinced, would engulf England itself. In 1852 over sixty special constables were sworn in, several of them especially for the funeral of the Duke of Wellington. In 1867, when the government made a last-minute effort to recruit special constables to head off trouble during the Reform Bill demonstration, there was a less enthusiastic turn-out of volunteer constables than in 1848.[16]

By law (1 & 2 William IV, c. 41 and 5 & 6 William IV, c. 43) any able-bodied man could be pressed into service as a special constable; but the government was reluctant to invoke such a drastic measure, and never did. Volunteers were always sufficient.[17]

USE OF TROOPS

Troops were also available to support the London police in keeping the peace. Under the *Queen's Regulations and Orders* a magistrate (for example, the Police Commissioner) could call up troops; but in all cases he had to accompany and direct the soldiers. Home secretaries, who had the ultimate authority, were reluctant to give rural magistrates a free hand in directing troops, because they distrusted the magistrates' judgment. Aside from the possibility of bloodshed, the misuse of soldiers by a nervous magistrate might worsen the situation and ultimately discredit the government. There were also temptations to deploy the troops incorrectly in small detachments or they might simply be worn out from continuous duty. Soldiers dispersed among the people in small units might arouse the sympathy of the people among whom they were quartered. Also, the troops hated being put in the position of having to coerce civilians, much less firing into crowds, and the public for its part took a dim view of unarmed citizens being confronted with armed soldiers. These situations did not arise in London, since the existence of the Metropolitan Police there meant that troops, when called up as in 1866, were only used as a back-up and never had to resort to lethal force.[18]

POLICE AND WEAPONS

One of the most admired features of the British police is the fact that they have ordinarily been unarmed, a policy that continues and is supported overwhelmingly by both the police and the public today. There had been no consideration of arming them in 1829, just as there had been no inducement to arm the parish officials before them. Although the Bow Street Mounted and Dismounted Patrols were armed with pistols and sabers, given the dangers of patrolling the dark and isolated roads on the outskirts of London, the New Police as a whole did not take up the practice. Inspectors were, however, issued pocket pistols, and constables in some of the country districts were issued sabers and, from the 1850s, pistols if there was felt to be some danger, most likely from armed bands of poachers. Side arms have been available in the police stations since 1829 for emergency use, but it seems unlikely that more than a few constables received any training in their use. Little reference was made to firearms in the police records, and pistol practice was not recorded as being part of "basic" training.

The Fenian alarms of 1867-1868, however, forced the police to start taking revolver drill seriously. In late December 1867, several constables from each division were sent to Wormwood Scrubs for pistol practice. This was done on a rotating basis. The police orders show that from August 1868, Adam's breechloading revolvers were being sent to each police station to replace the old single-shot pistols. They were kept under lock and key and were the responsibility of the superintendents. By 19 November 1868 four hundred of these pistols had been received. The issue of revolvers had obviously begun before 1868, since in October 1867 the City of London Police Commissioner mentioned that the Metropolitan Police were getting arms. He wanted weapons as well and got one hundred pistols to be kept in the several City police stations.[19]

IDENTIFICATION

Another aspect of police work that aided police in preventing disorders was knowing the people with whom they dealt. The police were instructed to get to know by sight as many people as possible on their beats. Individuals who were likely to be recognized would presumably be careful before participating in crowd violence. On a more prosaic level, personal recognition of residents aided the police in making arrests. For example, policemen were cautioned that in the case of street affrays it was better not to take the participants into custody if their names and addresses were known. This would lessen assaults on police who tried to break up an affray. A warrant could then be taken out and the subjects arrested in their lodgings, presumably after they had had time to calm down or sober up, or both.[20]

Only rudimentary records of past offenders were kept, and it was only after the "Habitual Criminal Act" in 1869 and the "Prevention of Crimes Act" of 1871 that a register of persons with two felony convictions was kept in the Commissioner's office at Scotland Yard. The information was taken from prison files. Information on convicted criminals was also kept in the appropriate police stations. Even this proved to be insufficient, and a police memorandum of 1872 complained that the register was not being used enough by police officials in checking past offenders.[21]

Photography was used to a limited degree in this period. Its adaptation to police purposes could be said to have begun in 1854 when the governor of Bristol jail began to make daguerreotype pictures of prisoners. In 1868 upon Mayne's recommendation the Home Secretary approved of setting up photographic equipment in Scotland Yard. However, only "notable" criminals were to be photographed and only with the Commissioner's permission. From 1868 "Fenian prisoners of note" were to be photographed as well.[22]

PUBLIC CONFIDENCE IN THE POLICE, THE 1850s

The increasingly policed society of the nineteenth century allowed the government to control the population with potential force and to concentrate that force in small discretionary ways if need be. In the midst of disturbances the police had the uncomfortable task of trying to contain or disperse violence while actually being violent themselves to a limited extent. Nevertheless, from early on their careful organization and control gave the police an advantage over mob numbers, a phenomenon that impressed contemporaries. In 1870 the *Quarterly Review* wrote,

A comparatively small number of honest, steady men—compact and well organized— acting under the direction of skilled and experienced officers, will always have an immense advantage over the heterogeneous mass of roughs, thieves, and desperate characters which constitute the scoundrelism of great cities.[23]

The last point of the quotation reminds us that the very diversity of London, its shifting population and disparate interests—not yet welded into more sophisticated, interrelated pressure groups capable of waging sustained strikes and widespread demonstrations—gave police organization an advantage, an advantage that at times would be increasingly strained in the last part of the century. Also London's economy was based on a large number of trades, thus obviating the discontent and impact from massive layoffs that would face a community dependent on any one trade which had collapsed.

In 1856 the *Quarterly Review* said that even with a population of about two and a half million, with at least fifty thousand of those belonging to the "dangerous classes," the police would ultimately be superior, because "the capital is so wide that its different sections are totally unknown to each other." The article goes on to say that a London mob is "wholly without cohesion.... They would immediately break up before the determined attack of a band of well-trained men who know and have confidence in each other."[24] Some believed that the turning point in crowd control had been at Kennington Common in 1848 when the police, with a massive show of strength, blocked the bridges to Westminster. It was the last major Chartist demonstration, after which time police supremacy over disorderly crowds was considered inevitable. It also strengthened greatly the public's confidence in the police. In a memorandum to Palmerston in 1863 Mayne wrote: "It has been stated by a high financial authority, that the quiet decisive suppression of the meeting of April 10, 1848, was of greater importance than the victory of Waterloo." Mayne no doubt shared this view to a great extent.[25]

A further measure of public confidence in the police in dealing with crowds came after the Great Exhibition in 1851. Mayne added a thousand men for the occasion, which allowed him to form a new X Division, made up of experienced constables, most of them from Whitehall Division.[26]

Mayne made provision for mob violence by having police reserve units located around the park. They were backed up by some 10,000 of Wellington's troops stationed around London, and even bivouacked in Hyde Park. New gates were also added to the park fence to allow the cavalry to enter if need be. If a riot broke out it would happen suddenly, having a ready-formed mob who "will act on a sudden excitement of feeling, and will have to be removed and dispersed from its vicinity."[27] If a crowd ascembled in another part of London, the places threatened, besides the Crystal Palace, would probably be the royal palaces and

Whitehall. If such an attack originated south of the Thames, "nothing need be added to the police and military precautions taken in 1848." Confidence in the police had been bolstered by their successful confrontation with the Chartists at Kennington Common in 1848. If an attack came from north of the Thames the police would act quickly to block the streets in the Westminster area. A tele-graph—fitting symbol for the occasion—connected the east, west, and south entrances to the Exhibition with Mayne's office, and was used to notify him of emergencies or when the crowds inside the Exhibition reached 50,000, after which time the doors would be closed until the numbers diminished.[28]

The numbers of people attending were considerable. *The Times* estimated that on 30 April alone about 50,000 were present. Altogether millions of visitors attended over the five months the Exhibition was open, many of them attending several times, as did Queen Victoria. The orderly, good-natured crowds were a pleasant surprise for Englishmen. Also, the unwonted casual social mixing on "shilling day" between the "classes" and the "masses" invoked a mutual class curiosity.[29]

In a sense the Great Exhibition could be considered another significant mile-stone for the Metropolitan Police, following their successful confrontation with the Chartists in 1848. It strengthened their reputation with property owners and shopkeepers, giving a vivid demonstration that public order could be maintained. The pessimists who had feared that Hyde Park would become a magnet for hordes of riffraff, revolutionaries, and criminals were proved wrong. As we saw in the previous chapter, after 1851 it became difficult for Englishmen to get worked up over the prospect of revolution spearheaded by the political exiles.

DOUBTS: THE 1860s

Nevertheless, in the face of the uncertainties of the later 1860s, the post-Reform Bill era, doubts were expressed about the government's being able to insure public order. Sensitive writers such as Matthew Arnold and Frederic Harrison, who were alarmed at the fall of the railings at Hyde Park in 1866, felt acutely the thinness of the veneer of civilized society. In a perceptive essay—which bears quoting—written shortly after the passage of the Reform Bill in 1867, the Positivist Frederic Harrison said:

Governments are plainly unable to keep a mob in check, and are afraid to try unless they have twenty-thousand shopkeepers as special constables to back them.... A centralized bureaucratic system gives a great resisting force to the hand that commands the Executive. Our Executive has nothing to fall back upon. There are practically no reserves. The few bayonets and sabres here and there are perfectly powerless before the masses, if the people really took it into their heads to move; beside which it is an instrument that they dare not in practice rely on. A few redcoats may be called on to suppress a vulgar riot; but the first blood of the people shed by troops in a really popular cause would, as we all know, make the Briton boil in a very ugly manner.... Men with heads on their shoulders know that an appeal to force would be the end of English society; and what is even more to the purpose, that there is no force to appeal to.[30]

He also felt that the police were no match for the mobs. With Harrison there was no smug confidence in repression, and in this attitude he was not alone. In the past (for example the 1830s and 1840s) magistrates over England as a whole had frequently been caught between the need to act quickly to quell disturbances by reading the Riot Act or calling up the militia, on the one hand, or not acting at all, or belatedly. In either case they incurred personal responsibility (and possibly some sort of retaliation) and ran the real risk of facing prosecution for the blood shed by the troops or for the damages done by the mobs.

From a tactical consideration Harrison underestimated the power of the authorities to apply rational police force over heterogeneous crowds. He also did not consider the fact that in the Hyde Park Reform Bill demonstrations in 1866 (see Chapter eight) the government failed to amass sufficient force and also use it in the right place. But Harrison was talking on another level. His gloom was not that the force applied was inadequate, but that extra force would probably have been unjustified. He did not call for suppression of that which he acknowledged was only a manifestation of the wider reform movement, and which was beyond the power of the police to suppress anyway. Harrison perceived the limits of power and realized the inadequacy of force beyond that point. Certainly those who call for and use force in a planned way feel that its use is justified and that their own careers and consciences are secure.

We have looked at the basic apparatus of public order, and we have seen how the crowd control functions of the police were developed in the light of experience. In dealing with a wide range of disturbances the police had an advantage over their adversaries because of their organization and discipline. Their work in crowd control was also facilitated by the diversity of London and its heterogeneous population. That the tactics were generally restrained was a significant contribution to moderating some of the tensions created in this age which was transitional between a pre-industrial society and the emergence of industrial capitalism and urbanization. Since the Victorian bureaucratic state, of which the police were simply one element, drew its mandate from a wider constituency than in previous centuries, its responses to pressures from below had to be made with an eye toward accommodating more segments of society. Just as the police response to collective violence was becoming "institutionalized" so too were the methods of collective action: at least the means were changing. Election rallies, petitions, unions, demonstrations, strikes, and the like were all being used to apply more systematic pressure on the prevailing institutions of authority.

By the mid-Victorian years revolution was not a realistic possibility, but disorders of lesser magnitude—the kinds perhaps tolerated in earlier times— were potentially disruptive to the complex urban economy of London, and had to be controlled in some way.

The police were the first rampart in the edifice of public order, but they could be assisted by the military and by special constables, as happened in 1848, in the late 1860s, and later in the century. Although the institutional framework of order may have seemed shakier than it actually was to pessimistic observers like Matthew Arnold, the strongest fortification was the flexibility and good sense of the rulers and the ruled to make mutual accommodation, however belatedly or grudgingly.

NOTES

1. Charles Tilly, "The Web of Contention in Eighteenth-Century Cities," in *Class Conflict and Collective Action*, ed. by Louise Tilly and Charles Tilly (Beverly Hills, Calif.: Sage, 1981), pp. 19-20. George Rudé, *Hanoverian London: 1714-1808* (London: Seeker & Warburg, 1971), pp. 183-85.

2. Silver, "The Demand for Order," p. 19.

3. Tilly, "Web of Contention," pp. 20-22.

4. Donald Richter, "The Role of Mob Riot in Victorian Elections, 1865-1885," *Victorian Studies*, XV, No. 1 (1971), 25.

5. David Williams, *Keeping the Peace: The Police and Public Order* (London: Hutchinson of London, 1967), pp. 9, 66.

6. Ibid., pp. 38, 236.

7. Ibid., p. 68.

8. *P.P.* 1839 (169), XIX, cited in Mather, *Public Order*, pp. 101-02.

9. Graham Wallas, *The Life of Francis Place, 1771-1854* (London: George Allen & Unwin, Ltd., 1918), p. 248, n.3.

10. Tobias, *Crime and Police*, pp. 89-90. Lisa Keller, "Public Order in Victorian London: The Interaction Between the Metropolitan Police, the Government, the Urban Crowd, and the Law" (Ph.D. diss., Cambridge University, 1976), pp. 12-13.

11. Mather, *Public Order*, p. 100.

12. MEPOL 1/46 (12 July 1855), Mayne to Ellis. Royal Commission, 1855, *Report*, p. xii.

13. MEPOL 7/25 (7 May 1864).

14. Ibid., 8/3 (1867), p. 142.

15. Royal Commission, 1855, q. 6367.

16. Mather, *Public Order*, p. 84. MEPOL 4/4.

17. H.O. 45/7799/1572, pouch 7 (18 Jan. 1868), Lord Thring to H.O.

18. Ibid., 45/7799/1577 (18 Jan. 1868), legal opinion: Selwyn and Karslake. Stevenson, "Social Control," p. 35.

19. Miller, *Cops and Bobbies*, pp. 49-50. *P.P.* 1828 (533), VI, p. 329, *Select Committee on the Police*. *P.P.* 1834 (600), XVI, qs. 179-80. MEPOL 7/29 (20 Dec. 1867). MEPOL 7/30 (28 Aug. 1868). MEPOL 7/133 (12 Jan. 1832). City of London, Guildhall Record Office, the Guildhall, *Police Committee Minutes*, Vol. 21 (23 Oct. 1867).

20. MEPOL 7/27 (22 Jan. 1868).

21. *Public General Statutes. P.P.* 1871 (358), XXVIII. MEPOL 8/3 (1 May 1872).

22. Lee, *History of Police*, p. 359. MEPOL 7/30 (3 April 1868).

23. "The Police of London," *Quarterly Review*, CXXIX, 91.

24. "Police and the Thieves," *Quarterly Review*, XCIX, 173.

25. Broadlands MSS, PM/C/14 (1863), Mayne to Palmerston.

26. MEPOL 1/53/1155 (21 Feb. 1851), Mayne to H.O.

27. Ibid., 2/91 (15 April 1851), rept. by Mayne.

28. Ibid., (April 1851), rept. by Labalmondiere. Ibid., 7/115 (25 May 1851).

29. *The Times* (London), 1 May, 8 Oct. 1851.

30. Frederic Harrison, *Order and Progress* (London: Longmans, Green, and Co., 1875), pp. 182-85.

6 The Police and the Crowds: The Sunday Trading Disturbances, 1855

"Do not think we are exaggerating in saying that the English Revolution began yesterday in Hyde Park," said Karl Marx on 25 June 1855. *The People's Paper* on 7 July made a similar observation: "The men of London have accomplished a successful revolution." *The Times* was as dramatic in saying that "Hyde Park on Sunday was the Champ-de-Mars of the English race."

SABBATARIANISM AND SUNDAY LEGISLATION

The series of weekly demonstrations, particularly the one on 1 July, that provoked such comments were the immediate result of an attempt by Lord Robert Grosvenor to secure passage of a bill in Parliament that would severely limit or prohibit selling on Sundays. The resulting demonstrations in Hyde Park epitomized an unhappy dilemma in which the police seemed to be the upholders of unpopular legislation that threatened to break the fragile bond of support from the working classes, a bond that the Commissioners were assiduously trying to strengthen. Since the police were attempting to be impartial agents of the law, having to enforce unpopular legislation would undermine not only their impartiality but also the nonpartisan image they tried to project.[1]

Police failures to control the crowds in the park on successive Sundays and brutality by individual constables won for the police a further measure of ill will from the working classes in particular. Also, police behavior made the police the issue and eventually prompted a Royal Commission to study their behavior in Hyde Park on 1 July 1855.

To many, especially among the working classes, the bill limiting Sunday trading was regarded as another odious encroachment of Evangelical and sabbatarian legislation into the lives of ordinary Englishmen. Sabbatarian pressure had already resulted in the Wilson-Patten Act the previous year that limited drinking hours in public houses on Sunday. The West End clubs, being private, were conspicuously untouched. While Grosvenor's Sunday Trading Bill did not further limit drinking, as many incorrectly believed, its shop-closing provisions seemed a blatant piece of class legislation that would bear down heavily on the working classes, especially since for many people wages were paid on Saturday afternoon, leaving Saturday night or Sunday for shopping. Both bills won for their proponents widespread disfavor for attempting to curtail the Englishman's right to shop and enjoy himself on Sundays. The issue was not strictly one of rich versus poor, but one that divided all classes. Sabbatarianism was not widely popular. Still, class appeared to be the issue: one law for the rich, one for the poor. Grosvenor's bill polarized its critics and admirers into two camps, the Sunday traders and drink sellers versus the sabbatarians and temperance reformers.

Until the 1830s the only comprehensive law that regulated Sunday activity was one passed in the reign of Charles II that prohibited all Sunday labor and trading except for "works of charity or necessity." Over the years Sunday had begun to look less religious and more secular, and the law was virtually a dead letter in many parts of London. By the 1830s, however, Evangelicalism was making itself felt throughout British society, especially among the middle classes, and it would do much to shape the tone of Victorian England.

The "Sunday question" was one of the most persistent and tenaciously fought issues in the Victorian period that brought Evangelical, and more narrowly sabbatarian, pressure to bear against the habits and amusements of the laboring classes.

Although it had aristocratic spokesmen in Parliament like Lord Shaftesbury and Lord Robert Grosvenor, sabbatarian legislation made little headway because of the political opposition which was especially strong in London. London was also the center of working-class radicalism. There was also a reluctance on the part of the upper classes to interfere with the amusements or customs that kept the lower orders contented, and which did not bother them personally. Also some sporting aristocrats shared with the working classes an interest in animal and other sports and a fondness for the conviviality of the public house. For these and other reasons sabbatarians were never able to get all they wanted, but their efforts did result in stricter licensing laws and limited pub hours, the closing of museums and galleries on Sundays, and even the discontinuance of Sunday military band concerts in the parks. The high water mark of sabbatarianism came in 1855 with Grosvenor's Sunday Trading Bill.

POLICE ATTITUDES

Against this backdrop we must place the attitudes of the police. Since 1829 Rowan and Mayne had been clear in their objections to the passage of Sunday laws whose enforcement was likely to provoke widespread public resistance and hostility toward the police. Working-class sentiment against interference with familiar customs was such that the police were prudently liable to ignore the law of Charles II and leave street venders alone unless there were complaints that the venders' cries disturbed churchgoers.

This is not to say that the police opposed all Sunday laws. Where the cause of public order could be served the Commissioners were favorable to some Sunday legislation, even at the expense of diminished popularity for the police. No Sunday annoyance was more likely to give offense to the respectable than to be going to church and have to walk past pubs as drunks were being turned out, or step over people lying insensible on the pavement. Frequently churchgoers had to endure coarse language or witness the inevitable small riots as policemen dragged drunks off to jail. The situation improved when, upon the recommendation of Mayne, pub closing hours were incorporated into the 1839 Police Act, closing the pubs from Saturday midnight to 1:00 P.M. Sunday. At least tipplers could not drink all night.

The act brought about a definite improvement in public order, but it now imposed on the police the obligation of enforcing the laws. Publicans, especially in slum areas, often tried to evade the law and stay open, and policemen, who found pub inspection an unpleasant duty, were often likely to turn a blind eye to violations. Mayne insisted that his men be in uniform and enter by the front door of pubs. Summonses could only be issued selectively with the prior approval of Scotland Yard. The "open" method of enforcing this law sacrificed efficiency to some extent, but Mayne preferred this to over-zealous enforcement of the Sunday laws which would provoke even more evasion and hostility. Since good order could be secured with limited pub hours and flexible enforcement, why nullify the results so far obtained with further legislation?

But matters did not stand there. Much to Mayne's distress the Wilson-Patten Act was passed in 1854 that allowed pubs to remain open only five and a half hours on Sunday: they were henceforth to be open only from 1:00 P.M. to 2:30 P.M. and from 6:00 P.M. to 10:00 P.M. Since Sunday afternoon excursion trains often returned to London at 10:00 P.M. thirsty travelers were incensed to find that they could not get a drink. This caused enough of an outcry, but when Parliament almost passed Grosvenor's bill to disallow all Sunday trading, riots in Hyde Park ensued.

THE DEMONSTRATION OF 24 JUNE

If any time of the year is likely for riots, or even revolutions, summer is it. The Gordon Riots began in the heat of the summer of 1780, and the Reform demonstration of July 1866 also took place in the heat. The summer of 1855 was relatively hot and dry with temperatures averaging 74°F between 22 June and 11 July. Hunger also may well have played an indirect part in aggravating the situation. High grain prices had provoked serious bread riots in Liverpool and in London's East End in February. Prices were even higher in May and June and stayed high through the fall.[2]

The first hint of trouble came when a protest meeting against Lord Robert Grosvenor's bill was advertised for Sunday, 24 June, in Hyde Park. A crowd assembled in the early afternoon on the north bank of the Serpentine, "to see how religiously the aristocracy observed the Sabbath." The police had seen the posters and ordered one inspector, two sergeants and thirty constables to be at Triumphal Arch (Wellington Arch at the top of Constitution Hill), with only a few constables scattered near the Serpentine "so as to avoid observation." Those attempting to address the meeting were told by the police that they could not.[3] Soon the crowds began to heckle the riders in carriages or on horseback along the carriageway, shouting at them, "Go to Church!" One man began to speak against the bill, but was soon interrupted by a police inspector who informed him that he could not hold a public meeting, as it was not a public park: it was Crown property. Other attempts to speak were also thwarted by the police. The crowd then dispersed but thousands remained in the park and yelled and hooted at riders who were taking their usual Sunday airing. Lord and Lady Wilton, Lady Granville, and the Duke and Duchess of Beaufort were so frightened that they got out of their carriages at the demand of the crowd and walked. This only inflamed the throngs more.[4] Mayne was himself walking through Hyde Park with his daughter, on the way to church, and was surprised to see the disturbances, which he had not anticipated. Hearing the shouting and seeing frightened horses running away, he called up about 200 police reinforcements, some to be held in reserve out of the way. Detachments of police marched at intervals up and down the carriageway between the lines of jeering demonstrators. The crowds took up the chant—in marching cadence—"Where are the geese? Ask the police!" in reference to a recent well publicized theft of geese by a constable in Clerkenwell. The disturbances lasted about three hours and finally died away. Four or five arrests were made for picking pockets.[5]

THE DEMONSTRATION OF 1 JULY

This was only a prelude to the demonstration that was now called for the following Sunday, 1 July. Police reports from various divisions predicted that the meeting would be large. Articles in the *Weekly Dispatch* and *Reynolds'*

Newspaper, as well as a number of placards, also convinced Mayne that the demonstration would be serious. One placard read:

Hyde Park.——On Sunday, the open air fête and monster concert, under the patronage of the "Leave-us-alone" club, will be repeated on Sunday next. The "private property" . . . will be open to the public on the occasion. Hot water for parties supplied by Lord Robert Grosvenor, who is in plenty of it.[6]

At the Home Secretary's urging Mayne decided that the meeting should be banned. By virtue of his status as a magistrate, Mayne issued a proclamation to that effect which was reprinted in some Saturday newspapers, and which was distributed around London and put on the gates of Hyde Park. The notice said:

No such meeting or assemblage of persons in large numbers will be allowed to take place; and all well disposed persons are hereby cautioned and requested to abstain from joining or attending any such meeting or assemblage; and notice is further given, that all necessary measures will be adopted to prevent any such meeting or assemblage, and effectually to preserve the public peace, and to suppress any attempt at the disturbance thereof.[7]

Orders went out to the police to enforce the printed notices strictly and to caution anyone who began a meeting, or who made noises calculated to frighten horses. Four superintendents, 6 inspectors, and 250 constables were to be in the park at 2:00 P.M. divided into several groups of about 25 men each and all under the supervision of senior Superintendent Samuel Hughes. The men were spread along the length of the carriage drive from the Achilles statue near Hyde Park Corner to the Magazine. At each end of the line was stationed a reserve force of about 50 men. The men were told to sit or lie on the grass and not to interfere with the crowds unless necessary. Mayne instructed Superintendent Hughes that those hooting at the riders on the carriage drive were to be driven back thirty or forty yards behind the drive railings on the north side. Other reserves were to assemble at various points near the park: the Triumphal Arch, the Walton Street police station, Lowndes Square, Stanhope Gate, Marble Arch, and the Kensington police station. Mayne stayed in his office, though Karl Marx incorrectly identified him as being among the police "dignitaries" in the park that day. It was probably Hughes whom he saw. Lord Robert Grosvenor's house was also guarded by police, though Grosvenor had prudently scurried out of London the day before in a hired carriage.[8]

By 2:30 P.M., the police estimated that about 50,000 people—many of them young—had gathered in Hyde Park. *The Times*, which described them as being

Figure 1. Hyde Park and vicinity, 1850. W. Kelley, *Post Office London Directory.* (Scale: three inches to one mile.)

mostly respectable in their dress, put the figure at 150,000, and Marx, somewhat improbably, guessed 200,000. Marx said they were of every age and social estate, with about two-thirds from the working class and about a third from the middle class.[9] Fewer carriages and riders than the previous week ventured out. The crowds began hissing, booing, and shouting, "Go to church!" and frightening the horses. Police tried to stop the commotion and were themselves booed. They also advanced on a speaker, stopping him from speaking, which incited the crowd to boo and yell "Down with the crushers!" Stones were thrown at constables and some of their hats were knocked off. Arrests were made. The police tried to keep the crowds moving and cleared the carriage drive north of the Serpentine. The crowds now lined both sides of the drive from Apsley House (the late Duke of Wellington's residence) to Kensington.[10]

By late afternoon a total of 538 police were in the park, with a 50-man reserve under Superintendent O'Brien staying by the Stanhope Gate on Park Lane. Crowds gathered near the Serpentine when some boys drew a large eel out of the water and threw it back and forth, and even tried to hand it to the police—who were barely able to control their tempers. Hughes figured the critical time had come and ordered his men to use their clubs to clear the carriage road in earnest. It was time, he said, to let those persons "see that there was a police there to govern them."[11] The constables then advanced along the carriage drive clearing it of people and roughly pushing and striking some. Other police moved down the drive waving their clubs and hitting the rails to drive the people back. As Hughes worded it in his report, the difficulty in dispersing people from the road was "as always is in such cases, not being able to get the respectable portion of the assemblage to separate from the evil disposed."[12] Word was sent to Mayne that "it has been found necessary to disperse them by force several times from the railings." At 4:30 P.M. Mayne gave the order (*de facto*) that the police could "act vigorously in compelling all rioters to move to a distance from the carriage road, and disperse and apprehend rioters." The constables moved back and forth along the drive pushing people back under the single pipe railings and using their truncheons freely. Another group of constables moved between the drive and the Serpentine forcing some of the people ankle-deep into the water. Hughes and his men were trying to force the crowds back from the railings for thirty or forty yards, and made repeated rushes into their midst, being heckled and stoned the whole time. Numerous arrests were made.[13]

The police made no attempt to form lines along the carriage drive; consequently, the people would merely surge back into the drive as soon as the constables moved on. Hughes made himself prominent by shouting and waving his horsewhip at the crowds in positions that he later described as the fifth, sixth, and seventh saber cut positions. Other witnesses, less impressed by such sub-tleties, said that Hughes acted like a madman and struck people indiscriminately.[14]

At about 5:00 P.M. Mayne sent word back by messenger that all shouters and disturbers were to be moved away a distance from the carriage road and that disorderly groups of people anywhere in the park were to be dispersed. His orders were belatedly irrelevant. There was no effort to clear the park, which probably would have required help from the military. From 3:30 P.M. until around 5:30 P.M. "a state of tumult and disturbance prevailed," as the Royal Commission's report later described it. The commotion started to die down around 6:00 P.M., after heavy police reinforcements arrived. But between six and seven o'clock various groups gathered at open areas of the park, only to be dispersed by police rushes.

By 7:30 P.M. some of the police were being removed from the park. By that time the demonstrations consisted mainly of whistling and jeering as the officers took prisoners away in commandeered cabs lined up at the park. At the same time, according to Marx, a group of young Grenadier Guards [actually 20 Foot Guards] joined the demonstrators. They marched up and down the park, cheered by the crowds shouting "Long live the army!" and "Down with the police!" Some of the soldiers scuffled with the police. They were ordered to leave the park and refused, saying they had a right to stay. One Guardsman told a constable that "he should not go away for any damn'd policeman." Military guards soon arrived and took away four soldiers, and a noisy crowd followed them stoning the guards.[15]

Antagonism between the police and the army was nothing new and was, as Marx put it, "as old as the hills in England." Certainly the wartime patriotism for the army and the excesses of the police in Hyde Park would naturally make the soldiers the more popular and even to some extent the upholders of law and order and protectors of the public from the police. This in itself was embarrassing for the government and would, some feared, stiffen Russian resistance in the war and dismay the French allies at what might look like English political instability.[16]

Soon after six o'clock a mob had assembled near the Serpentine, and to cries of "Now to Lord Robert Grosvenor's house," started running out of the Gros-venor Gate toward Grosvenor's house on Park Street, arming themselves with rocks along the way. Superintendent O'Brien and his 54 men, stationed at Stanhope Gate to the south, dashed north in the hope of cutting off the crowd before it got out of the park. They were too late and could only chase the crowd across Park Lane and into Park Street. All of this was witnessed by people watching from their windows, some of whom saw police strike bystanders needlessly.[17]

The figures vary considerably on how many actually assembled before Grosvenor's house: O'Brien guessed about 4,000, and the Royal Commission report, 200 to 400. The assembled mob started shouting and threw stones at Grosvenor's servant who had imprudently made himself briefly visible. O'Brien formed his men into a column of five men across and ten deep and marched toward the crowd to scare them off. The few constables on the spot had already mingled with the people in an effort to persuade them to leave.[18] Some of the crowd fled while others threw rocks at the advancing police. O'Brien shouted for the people to disperse, was tripped up and fell flat, injuring his knee. At that moment and without orders, his men rushed forward into the crowds, truncheons swinging, while O'Brien was left behind on the ground. He later told the Royal Commission that he gave no specific directions to remove the crowd by force, but that his call for the crowd to disperse was interpreted by his men as an order to scatter the "dangerous mob" by truncheons if necessary. The crowds were soon repelled, and O'Brien and his men returned to Stanhope Gate.[19]

At about 9:00 P.M., while there was still light, Hughes formed about 100 men into a line extending north from the Serpentine and advanced them eastward toward Hyde Park Corner and Stanhope Gate. After some seven hours of constant activity, in over 70°F heat, the men were tired and inattentive to Hughes's commands, and he had trouble keeping them in line. The crowds offered little resistance and dispersed from the park, bringing the day's skirmishing to an end. The total arrests were seventy-two, ten of whom would be charged with a felony, and the rest with riotous conduct, or assaults on police. Most of the prisoners came from the East End and south of the river, areas most threatened by the trading bill.[20]

While many in the crowds that day had been youths, quite a few émigrés had been prominent in encouraging the masses, Karl Marx among them. Two Frenchmen had been arrested for assaulting a policeman and for cheering the crowds on with shouts of "Bravo, Englishmen! A republic! A republic!" Captain Paget of the artillery was in the park and heard three or four foreigners say that they could do such things better in their own countries. They would "upset the cabs very soon and make a barricade." The next week, on 8 July, a well-dressed foreigner led a group of boys in breaking windows in Belgravia.[21]

The crowd mood had at first been fairly light-hearted, though much less so than the preceding Sunday of 24 June. Some of the promenaders on 1 July appeared unafraid and had acknowledged the jeers hurled at them by raising their hats or waving, which only further antagonized the crowds. However, as historians of public order have indicated, the festive mood is present in crowd disorders, even in revolutions. Singing, bantering, and horseplay were observed in the French Revolutionary crowds and in the London Reform Riots of 1831. In 1855, therefore, the police attacks on the crowd appeared all the more surprising and provocative, not seeming to "grow logically out of the prevailing emotions." The violent charges by the police seemed in sharp contrast to the antics of the young people in the park seemingly out for a lark.[22] The police discomfort at being jeered at, together with their ill-conducted attempts to keep the throngs back from the carriage drive railing, made violence almost inevitable. Also the police had sustained injuries of their own. Forty-nine were injured with stones or pieces of wood, or simply hit or kicked. Even though numerous demonstrators—as well as people who were not involved—were struck, there were no no broken bones or loss of life.[23]

THE AFTERMATH: COMPLAINTS ABOUT THE POLICE

Soon after the *mêlée* the Home Office and the police were surprised by the storm of protests over police behavior, as letters came in to newspapers and the Home Office complaining of arbitrary brutality by constables who were too free with their truncheons. Radical and working-class papers condemned the police. Said *Lloyd's Weekly*, "As a body they contain among their number ... cowards and ruffians of the most brutal, the most savage temperament; scoundrels who rush like Malays amuk." On the other side of the journalistic scale *The Times* editorialized against the "outrageous conduct of the police and Sir George Grey's mismanagement of the affair." "We most entirely believe that but for the police there would have been no riot at all." The paper excoriated the "unsparing use of their truncheons ... The police made the worst of the bad regulations, and in every way exceeded their duty.... The truth is, that no injury was done to anybody, and therefore it was perfectly absurd to plan against the crowd a campaign of a far more vigorous description than any of which we have yet had notice in the Crimea." *The Times* was not the only paper to make a sarcastic comparison with the Crimean War. Since the government was unable to capture Sebastopol, proclaimed *Reynolds' Newspaper*, it tried to crush public opinion in England instead.[24]

The Times and the other major papers (excepting *Reynolds' Newspaper* and the *People's Paper*) were in the uncomfortable position of seeming to approve of the demonstrations in the park by their condemnation of Grosvenor's bill and of the police excesses. The London papers, while condemning Grosvenor's bill, were generally on the side of public order, and hoped to minimize the class conflict by indicating that the rioters' zeal was misdirected and that the Hyde Park promenaders were not sabbatarians.[25]

In Parliament the next day, Sir George Grey was pressured to hold an inquiry into what Thomas Duncombe of Finsbury called the "illegal and ferocious conduct of the Metropolitan police." Grey said that "monster meetings" that interfered with the public right to enjoy the parks could not be permitted. Furthermore, the police had cleared the carriage road only after it had been obstructed.[26]

Mr. G. Dundas was adamant in defending the police and said they were moderate in driving back the *canaille* from the railings. Those who were hit probably deserved it, he said. It was a sign of changing times that Dundas was roundly condemned by his parliamentary colleagues, and by *The Times*, for saying that "nothing will frighten a mob more than the crash upon the pavement of the trail of a 6-pounder." A statement like that might have gone unchallenged in earlier times when the military was regularly used for riot suppression; but resorting to such measures was rendered obsolete by modern police crowd control methods, however faulty. Dundas backed down, saying that what he really meant was the "moral effect that would be produced by the presence of a military force." Nevertheless, persistent complaints by respectable citizens of brutality by the police forced the hand of the government in appointing a commission of investigation.[27]

Bowyer and Duncombe in the Commons were skeptical of the objectivity of any investigation initiated by the Home Office, and probably relied heavily on the word of the police. Bowyer was particularly upset by having seen soldiers mistreated in the park. Grey assured them that a "full and searching inquiry . . . with regard to the conduct of the police" would be made, not merely a Home Office investigation.[28] Superintendent Hughes in particular was singled out for comment. Of the eighty-six witnesses who later testified before the Royal Commission, twenty of them complained that he was too free with his horsewhip and his language.

The Sunday trading disturbances were by no means over, even though Grosvenor had withdrawn his bill from Parliament, much to the relief of many, including Mayne, who thought it a foolish bill. Now many of the demonstrators wanted nothing more than to take revenge on the police. Like Coldbath Fields in 1833, Hyde Park in 1855 provided an opportunity for working-class police haters to retaliate for police excesses.

MORE DISTURBANCES

More trouble was expected in the park the following Sunday. Mayne was determined not to make the same mistakes in controlling the crowd as the preceding Sunday. He ordered Superintendent Labalmondiere to command the police in the park, with Superintendent May to assist. "Constables of experience and steady conduct are to be selected for this duty, where so much depends on the discretion and good temper of each man." The constables were to patrol in pairs, keeping away from the carriages and the carriage road north of the Serpentine. Reserves, numbering about 100, were to be kept ready at stations near the park, to assist if the patrols were set upon. The latter, if attacked, were to fall back to the Magazine and wait for reinforcements. The police were warned not to notice jeers and hissing. They were also to prevent rioting or harassment of riders, and if the carriage road or railings were to be cleared the police were to move slowly in a body to do so, using their truncheons only if set upon. "They are to bear in mind that their behavior will be watched by many ready to find fault, and after the occurrences of the past week, their own safety even may depend on their obtaining the support of the well disposed amongst the crowds by which they may at a moment be surrounded." In order to keep the police as non-provocative as possible the hundred or so men assembling as reserves at stations near the park were to report to their stations individually rather than being marched there in formation, as would be normal.[29]

There was no lack of well-meaning advice from anxious citizens who feared that subsequent meetings would grow more violent. For novelty Charles Gregory's suggestion to the Home Secretary was perhaps most imaginative. Gregory suggested that several military bands start playing in the park to attract crowds, after which time the bands would march off in different directions, leading the throngs with them and so dispersing them. The music would create "in the minds of the People a soothing kindly feeling particularly in the lower orders who seldom hear any other than street organs."[30]

Few carriages or riders dared venture out into the park on Sunday, 8 July, and the few who did were jeered by stone-throwing youths, as happened the previous two Sundays. The police stayed mostly out of sight and did little to interfere. There was no real crowd activity until just after 4:00 P.M., when a large group of boys ranging in age from twelve to twenty headed toward Marble Arch. They turned south, shouting and throwing rocks at carriages in Park Lane and then moved on down near Hyde Park Corner and surrounded Inspector Durkin and two of his men, hooting and pelting them. Durkin and his associates diplomatically "retired slowly" to Triumphal Arch where Labalmondiere waited. The noisy crowd stayed at Hyde Park Corner. Labalmondiere watched them and decided that they were mainly a clamorous lot, but no particular threat, so he refrained from calling for reserves, which might have provoked them to violence.[31]

Shortly before 5:00 P.M. the crowd of several hundred melted away down

Grosvenor Place. Labalmondiere probably assumed that the crowd, having left Hyde Park and no longer threatening Mayfair, would split up. He was wrong. The mob broke windows in the Hanoverian Legation in Grosvenor Place, turned west into fashionable Belgrave Square, and promptly started smashing windows there as well. Their arrival surprised the several constables in the area who quickly sent for reinforcements. Inspector Cumming and only 6 men from Cottage Road police station caught up with the crowd as it was breaking windows in Eaton Square to the south, and managed to disperse them. Cumming reported that those in Eaton Square consisted of about 150 boys and young men, accompanied by about 300 well-dressed and apparently respectable men, who seemed to have been onlookers.[32]

Meanwhile Labalmondiere, still at Triumphal Arch, heard the report of vandalism and dispatched Inspector Durkin and 26 men to Belgrave Square. Durkin and his constables could not catch up with the rapidly moving mob and were too late anyway, since the damage had already been done. One hundred and forty B Division men under Superintendent Gibbs were called up from Walton Street in Knightsbridge. They did manage to find and disperse the crowd, by now very large, that had reassembled in Pimlico. The time was about 5:30 P.M. Gibbs took no chances and ordered patrols back to guard the various areas of Belgravia. By this time Mayne, at Scotland Yard, sent orders for a group of policemen to guard Buckingham Palace. They did not know where the crowds were likely to head.[33]

The crowds in the Belgravia area seem to have been led, or at least encouraged, by well-dressed adults. When they entered Eaton Square the aged and retired Admiral Seymour saw a mob of boys followed by men. Seymour tried to talk them out of doing mischief, but the young man leading them goaded the others on. Seymour broke his cane on the youth and was himself hit in the head by a stone and knocked down in front of his own house. The police had not yet arrived.[34] Only a few courageous residents ventured out to defend their property. Damage in Belgravia was a total of 749 broken window panes.

Shortly after the Belgravia skirmishes, groups of demonstrators, some with staves, came up Park Street and managed to break windows in Grosvenor's house and in the nearby Grosvenor Square before constables in the area could disperse them. Inspector Webb and other reserves arrived too late to avert damage. Two policemen, with a youth they had arrested, were chased by the mob and had to take refuge in the Mount Street workhouse, which was then stoned. The crowd then spread out eastwards toward Lord Shaftesbury's home (Shaftesbury was an ardent, and currently unpopular, sabbatarian) but were dispersed before any further damage could be done.[35]

More skirmishing took place after dark when about 50 boys broke windows in Chandos House, the Austrian ambassador's residence, before being chased off by Superintendent Hughes and 20 men. The same group (apparently) assembled before the Oriental Club at Hanover Square at about 10:15 P.M. breaking a few panes. They crossed Oxford Street toward Cavendish Square. Meanwhile a group of youths, led by two cane-waving privates of the Grenadier Guards, rushed up Tottenham Court Road breaking lamps and house windows, and continued up the Hampstead Road before being dispersed by police at Albert Road. The total damage for this escapade, which ended at about midnight, was 33 broken street lamps and 343 panes of glass in 84 houses, with one man wounded by a stone. The soldiers and several others were arrested.[36]

All in all the day's activities had been a failure for the police. They had simply been unable to keep up with the mobs and to prevent damage from being done. Also the police had been impeded in getting to the scenes of action by crowds of the curious who followed the window-breakers.[37]

The following Sunday, 15 July, saw further disturbances, though on a lesser scale, consisting mainly of youthful rock throwing and some name calling by small bands of boys. By this time whatever public sympathy had existed for Hyde Park demonstrators had evaporated completely, since the original bill that provoked the riots had been dropped. The *Spectator* described the events of 15 July as "of a contemptible character." "The rioters," it said, "were dirty boys who ran furiously about in order to give the pickpockets opportunities of earning distinction."[38] Class hatreds and a desire to get revenge on the police also motivated the demonstrators, though the demonstrations also were a splendid opportunity for youths to indulge in horseplay and vandalism. Few people were prepared to look kindly at such wanton activities and the police now came under attack for being too soft. *The Times* put it succinctly: "All we know is that the police did far too much one day, and far too little another."[39] Angry letters again poured in to the police, the Home Office and the newspapers. "Are the peace and safety of quiet families to be threatened once a week, and each succeeding Sabbath to be desecrated by the riotous proceedings of the mob?" Other writers urged respectable people to form themselves into bands of special constables. For the propertied classes it was loathsome enough having mob violence take place in Hyde Park; but it was intolerable to allow window-smashing vandals to rampage through surrounding areas. As successive Sundays saw a drop in the respectability of the crowds, public opinion was correspondingly less favorable to the youthful working-class crowds that turned out.[40]

THE ROYAL COMMISSION

Police brutality on one occasion and laxity on another had replaced sabbatarianism as a public obsession. As promised by the Home Secretary, an enquiry was begun by a Royal Commission to investigate the incidents of 1 July only. The other days' disturbances were not considered. The Commission, with three members, met at the Court of Exchequer at Westminster, beginning 17 July, having publicly advertised for plaintiffs to come forward. Eighty-six appeared.[41]

During Mayne's testimony he admitted that he and not Commissioner Hay had complete charge of the police where rioting, disturbances, and large movements of police were concerned. All decisions for the deployment of police were his alone and were made without consultation with his superintendents, a fact that surprised the Royal Commissioners, but was typical of Mayne.[42] Some of the questions directed at Mayne during the examination concerned 24 June 1855, the first Sunday's disturbance. He admitted that the police force in the park that day was inadequate to disperse the hecklers, and that there would have been a delay before sufficient reserves could have been assembled. Mayne hesitated calling for more reserves at first thinking that the disturbances would soon die out. "I really thought that each ten minutes or a quarter of an hour would put an end to it." Finally over 200 reserves were called up.[43]

As for the preparations for 1 July, Mayne made it clear that the distribution of inflammatory leaflets and the appearance of articles in *Reynolds' Newspaper* and the *Weekly Dispatch* were expected to excite people and lead to more severe disturbances. He expressed his own well-known distaste for Lord Robert Grosvenor's bill but felt that opposition to it was played up in the papers, giving the appearance that it was a battle "between the aristocracy and democracy."[44]

The Commission's main concern was to investigate the charges of brutality on 1 July brought up by the 86 plaintiffs who appeared. Mitchell, the barrister for the plaintiffs, blamed Mayne directly for the occurrences of 1 July, saying that he should have been on the spot. Most of the culpability for specific movements, however, was put on the shoulders of Superintendent Samuel Hughes, a twenty-five-year veteran of the police. Hughes was accused of cursing and using his horsewhip on people, as well as ordering the police to use their truncheons unnecessarily and failing to control them properly when they did. According to police rules truncheons were supposed to be used only in self-defense or to prevent the rescue of prisoners.

The report of the Royal Commission which came out in the fall of 1855 censured Hughes for his actions, though absolving him of charges that he personally struck people. The report also said there was no real mass resistance to the police and that Hughes's resorting to violence was unwarranted.[45] The decision to clear the carriage road and the people thirty or forty yards from the railings had originally been a verbal order from Mayne to Hughes before the latter left the station that day. In his own testimony Mayne offered a dubious justification for the "rushes" of police into crowds beyond the railing. This was necessary since the ground rose in elevation on the north side of the drive, "it being very steep, and would require a man to run to it in order to reach the place where the people had assembled."[46] The report criticized the rail-clearing movements as unnecessary and poorly conducted, especially the attempt to move people from the narrow space between the carriage road and the Serpentine. The crux of the matter was that if the police had had sufficient force the road could have been cleared and a line of constables left along the railings to keep the crowds from surging back into the road. As it happened the police moved in a body along the road and periodically pushed the people back from the railings, which meant that the actions were repeated time and time again, accompanied by inevitable violence. The report also criticized the police for dispersing small groups of people in the park in the evening who did not appear to be causing disturbances. *The Times* also reproved the police for not acting sooner with sufficient force, and with better strategy; they termed Hughes's leadership as "incompetent guidance."[47]

Much of the testimony of witnesses was exaggerated or incorrect. There was often difficulty in identifying individual policemen because witnesses did not get their numbers, or if they did they reversed the numbers in their minds. No evidence was adduced to prove that the police struck women and children. The crowds were not armed with weapons, although Thomas Frost, with some exaggeration, later wrote that he saw very few men heading toward the park on 1 July who did not carry staves. Others, he said, had bundles of stout sticks to sell to those unprovided with weapons for use against the police.[48]

It was clear that the majority of the people in the park that day were simply curious bystanders, often very young, hoping (at most) to annoy those riding in the park. The Commission condemned the unnecessary police violence but praised their moderation as a whole. Eight policemen were singled out for special discipline because of their individual brutality, and three of them were indicted on criminal charges.[49]

Public opinion was increasingly intolerant of violence, and a show of force that might have gone unnoticed in an earlier day was now attacked at all levels of society. The police were unsure of themselves that day, were subject to great provocation and were paradoxically trying to contain violence while themselves engaged in it. With deterrence as their main function, only well-controlled large bodies of police concentrated in specific locations could have overawed the crowds and so have prevented the violence.

The Royal Commission also said that a higher-ranking officer should have been on the spot, presumably Mayne. This would have been "preferable to any attempt to direct the proceedings from a distance."[50] Brian Harrison suggests that Mayne stayed in his office so that he could coordinate police activity in the face of a possible violent Chartist disturbance. A warning of this had in fact been transmitted from Paris and reached Scotland Yard on 20 June. The news had been taken from a daily police report to Napoleon which was picked up by the English ambassador in Paris and passed through the Foreign Office, and on to Grey and Waddington at the Home Office, and finally to Mayne. The report warned of a Chartist meeting on 1 July and great scenes of violence and disorder. The principal instigators were allegedly Reynolds of *Reynolds' Newspaper* and Ledru-Rollin and other French refugees. Like the good civil servant that he was, Mayne was willing to remain quiet about this and take personal blame for police arrangements, according to Dr. Harrison.

When we view the actions of the Commissioner over a period of time, however, Mayne's staying in Scotland Yard was normal procedure. Moreover, Home Office correspondence to Mayne after the disturbances made no reference to or criticism of his having remained at his office instead of being in the park.[51] In fact Scotland Yard was felt to be the proper place for the Commissioners at such times. In a memorandum of 1848, concerning the reorganization of the Commissioner's office, Mayne wrote: "In times of actual disturbance the Commissioner must probably remain at his office to receive reports from various quarters, to give directions . . . and also to be within immediate reach for constant communication with the Secretary of State." He recommended that a colleague of slightly lesser rank take the field during disturbances.[52] The recommendation was taken to heart in 1856, since the need to have leaders of higher rank on the spot was obviously one of the considerations that led to the reorganization of the Commissioner's office in that year. Mayne was appointed sole Commissioner, with two Assistant Commissioners under him, one of whom would direct police activities during the deployment of large bodies of police. Again the Commissioner ordinarily stayed at Scotland Yard. Furthermore, during the Fenian alarms of the next decade, Mayne wrote to Major General Lindsay saying that if troops were called out to meet an emergency, Mayne would stay in his office, while the Assistant Commissioners would be elsewhere. In such a case the military could communicate direct to Mayne who could then telegraph instructions to all the police stations.[53]

As we have seen, warnings of civil disorder were not uncommon, and the diplomatic report does not seem to have given the Home Office or the police any excessive anxiety. Before sending the report from Paris on to Mayne, Sir George Grey scribbled on the back of it: "make the necessary arrangements for preserving the peace." No other instructions for the police were issued; but then it was true that personal directives from the Home Secretary were verbal.[54] In any case neither the police orders nor comments during the hearings of the Royal Commission indicate that the police anticipated anything more serious than what was stated about the park riots that did occur. As Dr. Harrison mentions, several Chartists verbally attacked the aristocracy before the meetings started, but there is no proof that they advocated violence. Ernest Jones, one of their number, denounced window breaking. All preferred mutual improvement as a political aim.[55]

No reference was made to the Chartist-alien threat during the hearings of the Royal Commission, but Harrison contends that the counsel for the plaintiffs, Mr. Mitchell, alluded to it when he asked Mayne what conversation took place between the police and the Home Office. At that point one of the Commissioners, Stuart Wortley, intervened to say: "No, I do not think we can enquire into that." This hearing was not about Chartists: the whole line of questioning referred specifically to responsibility for the police violence. Mitchell said clearly that a lot of people had been injured and that it had been done on the orders of the government. He wanted to "put the saddle on the right horse." He may have suspected that the government gave specific instructions for the police to be violent. There is no evidence to show that the members of the Royal Commission, or even the plaintiffs' counsel, Mitchell, were privy to the warning from Paris. The questions and answers during the hearings give no such hint either.[56]

When the Home Office transmitted the Royal Commission's report to Mayne, it included a list of recommendations and comments. The remarks show that the Home Office was concerned mainly with the violence by individual policemen, and with Superintendent Hughes's leadership. Mayne was not directly criticized by the Home Office, nor were the basic police arrangements (aside from numbers) considered inadequate. Harrison wrote that the Chartist threat prompted Mayne to deploy unusually large numbers of police. In fact both the Royal Commission and the Home Office stated that the police numbers were inadequate, which would have been an unlikely occurrence if the authorities had had reason to fear unusual events beforehand.

Criticism of Mayne for the events of 1 July 1855 was muted. The Home Office was no doubt reluctant to bear down heavily on a generally very competent Commissioner, especially one who had directed the police since their founding and who had been knighted for his services during the Great Exhibition. Mayne was respected by the upper and middle classes, and his police were felt to be as good as could reasonably be expected. Even though the Royal Commission was convened to consider only the events of 1 July 1855, it seems unlikely that they ignored the police forbearance in subsequent weeks. The holding of the Commission and the airing of police deficiencies were prudent steps for the government in assuaging the anger of the articulate members of the public. The disturbances, however, were not over for the summer. Continued high grain prices prompted a series of six demonstrations (accompanied by some hooliganism) that were loosely organized by the Workingmen's Provision League. The price of bread had been high all year, and this no doubt contributed to the discontent behind the summer disorders.[57]

HYDE PARK AS A PUBLIC FORUM

For the public, the disturbances of 1855 set something of a precedent for using Hyde Park as a public forum to express grievances. The demonstrations heralded the beginning of a series of battles in the 1860s over the legal question of the public's right to assemble in the royal parks. Although the Royal Commission upheld complaints about police excesses it did not recognize Hyde Park as a forum for the discussion of "popular and exciting topics." The park's proper purpose, they said, was recreation. In 1856, because of "blasphemous" religious speeches, the First Commissioner of Works, Sir Benjamin Hall, forbade all meetings in Hyde Park, thus refusing to recognize any public right to assemble in the park.

With the rapid growth of London, the traditional venues of demonstrations, Coldbath Fields, St. George's Fields, and Spa Fields, had been covered with bricks and mortar, leaving Trafalgar Square and the royal parks as the only adequate central grounds. Kensington Gardens, Hyde Park, Green Park, St. James's, and Regent's Park were popular and convenient for the West End, and people in other parts of London were willing to travel considerable distances to use them. There was a lack of public open spaces in many parts of mid-Victorian London. This helps account for the continuing popularity of the privately owned pleasure gardens that were located in some of the suburbs. Although fashionable in the eighteenth century, they had lost some of their social glitter by the nineteenth and catered largely to a middle-class clientele. But even those closed in time; of the best known Vauxhall survived until 1859, and Cremorne Gardens shut its gates in 1877, much of its site having been covered with houses.[58]

A Londoner, especially one of the working classes whose recreational opportunities were limited, was likely to feel that his "birthright" was being violated by high-handed police proclamations that limited his freedom to use the park. It was clear that Mayne's park notices against people gathering "in large numbers" on 1 July were taken as a serious provocation on the part of the police, which probably made the disorders worse.

The riots also channeled public anger away from sabbatarianism and made the police the issue, tarnishing their image—exactly what Mayne feared. There had never been any doubt in his mind that the passage of the Wilson-Patten Act limiting Sunday pub hours was at the root of the trouble. Mayne was not alone in this feeling, and Parliament not only threw out Grosvenor's Sunday trading bill immediately, but repealed the Wilson-Patten Act. Pubs were allowed to stay open eight hours on Sunday instead of five and a half, being forced to close only from 3:00 P.M. to 5:00 P.M. The 10:00 P.M. final closing hour was moved up to 11:00 P.M., allowing thirsty travelers to get their refreshment. These limitations were enough to appease both sides of the argument, and more immediately, to quell popular indignation. For the police the cause of public order could be served without undue hardship.

While the riot was becoming less and less the tool to express popular demands, the events of 1855 showed that "outdoor" working-class pressure was nonetheless effective, even without more sophisticated institutionalized procedures. The public meeting, the independent newspaper, the petition, the reforming campaign, the steady democratization of Victorian life, all represented at least a change in the way in which working-class pressures were applied, if not an absolute gain in the political power of the masses in mid-nineteenth century Britain.[59]

Sabbatarians never gave up hope of purifying England, but memories of 1855 made Parliament steer clear of imposing further limitations on the less godly majority of the population. Englishmen of a religious bent could at least take grim satisfaction in knowing that the *dimanche anglais* was by now a famous institution that never failed to evoke amazement or a shudder from foreign visitors like Hippolyte Taine from France, or the Russian Alexander Herzen. A Frenchman, said Herzen—and no doubt himself—could "never resign himself to the 'slavery' of restaurants being closed on Sundays, and the people being bored to the glory of God."[60]

NOTES

1. Karl Marx and Frederick Engels, *Marx and Engels on Britain* (Moscow: Foreign Languages Publishing House, 1953), p. 415. *The People's Paper*, 7 July 1855. *The Times* (London), 3 July 1855. For my analysis of the sabbatarian background to the Hyde

Park disturbances I have drawn from Wilbur Miller's *Cops and Bobbies*, pp. 129-38, and from his article "Never on Sunday: Moralistic Reformers and the Police in London and New York City, 1830-1870," in *Police and Society*, ed. by David Bayley (Beverly Hills, Calif.: Sage, 1977), pp. 127-48. Most useful of the secondary sources has been Brian Harrison, "The Sunday Trading Riots of 1855," *Historical Journal*, VIII, No. 2 (1965), 219-45. Whereas my focus is understandably on the police Dr. Harrison puts the events in a broader framework. His article is essential reading for a more complete understanding of the event.

2. Harrison, "Sunday Trading Riots," pp. 220-21, 228-30. *The Times* (London), 14, 21, 28 Oct.; 4, 11, 18 Nov. 1855.

3. Royal Commission, 1855, q. 6164.

4. Hypatia Bradlaugh Bonner, *Charles Bradlaugh* (London: T. Fisher Unwin, 1894), I, 54.

5. Royal Commission, 1855, *Report*, p. vi. *Minutes*, q. 6165. *Marx and Engels on Britain*, p. 419.

6. Royal Commission, *Report*, p. xxvii. Minutes, qs. 6216, 6196.

7. *Minutes*, q. 6229.

8. *Minutes*, qs. 6229-31, q. 12,522. *Report*, p. vi. *The Times* (London), 1 Aug. 1855.

9. *The Times* (London), 2 July 1855. *Marx and Engels on Britain*, pp. 417, 421-22. *The People's Paper*, 7 July 1855, p. 6, estimated a crowd of 150,000.

10. *Spectator*, 7 July 1855, p. 697.

11. H.O. 45/6092 (7 July 1855,) Hughes's rpt. Royal Commission, 1855, q. 12,564.

12. Royal Commission, 1855, *Report*, pp. vi-vii. H.O. 45/6092 (2 July 1855), Hughes's rpt.

13. Royal Commission, 1855, qs. 6259, 6249.

14. Ibid., q. 12,57. *Report*, p. vii.

15. Royal Commission, 1855 q. 6259. *Report*, p. vii. H.O. 45/6092 (2 July 1855), A Div. rpt. and Sgt. Thurger's rpt. *Marx and Engels on Britain*, p. 423.

16. *Marx and Engels on Britain*, p. 423. Harrison, "Sunday Trading Riots," p. 232.

17. Royal Commission, 1855, qs. 6259-61.

18. Ibid., *Report*, p. viii.

19. Ibid., *Report*, p. viii. *Minutes*, qs. 2,359-12,400. H.O. 45/6092, C Div. rpt.

20. Royal Commission, 1855, q. 12,571. *Report*, p. viii.

21. H.O. 45/6092/25 (8 July 1855), reports. Royal Commission, 1855, q. 7160.

22. Bonner, *Charles Bradlaugh*, p. 55. Harrison, "Sunday Trading Riots," p. 233.

23. Royal Commission, 1855, *Report*, p. ix.

24. *Lloyd's Weekly London Newspaper*, 8 July 1855, p. 6. *The Times* (London), 2, 3 July 1855, editorials. *Reynolds' Newspaper*, 8 July 1855, pp. 1, 2.

25. Harrison, "Sunday Trading Riots," p. 231.

26. *Hansard*, Vol. 139 (2 July 1855), cols. 368-71.

27. Ibid., col. 530. *The Times* (London), 7, 9 July 1855.

28. *Hansard*, Vol. 139 (6 July 1855), cols. 525, 528-29.

29. H.O. 45/6092/25 (8 July 1855), orders.

30. Ibid. 6092/11 (6 July 1855), Gregory to Grey. Professor Carl Woodring of Columbia University has reminded me that Browning's popular poem, "The Pied Piper of Hamelin," which appeared in 1842, was reprinted in 1849. It could have been an inspiration for Gregory's idea.

31. H.O. 45/6092/25 (9 July 1855), A Div. rpts.

32. Ibid., 6092 (9 July 1855), F.O. to H.O.

33. Ibid. B Div. rpt.

34. Ibid. (8 July 1855), rpt. from Seymour.

35. Ibid. (9 July 1855), Webb's rpt.

36. Ibid., S Div. rpt.

37. Ibid. (8 Jul. 1855), C Div. rpt.

38. *Spectator*, 21 July 1855, p. 747.

39. *The Times* (London), 16 Oct. 1855.

40. *The Times* (London), 10 July 1855 and after.

41. Royal Commission, 1855, *Report*, p. v.

42. Ibid., qs. 13,820-836; q. 12,271.

43. Ibid., q. 6165.

44. Ibid., q. 6393. The phrase was first used in *Reynolds' Newspaper*, 8 July 1855, p. 1. Mayne always paid attention to what all the London newspapers had to say about the police.

45. Ibid., *Report*, pp. x-xi; *Minutes*, q. 513.

46. *The Times* (London), 25 July 1855.

47. Royal Commission, 1855, *Report*, pp. xi-xii. See also H.O. 65/20 (18 Nov. 1855), H.O. to Mayne. *The Times* (London), 23 Nov. 1855.

48. Thomas Frost, *Forty Years' Recollections* (London: Sampson Low, Marston, Searle, and Rivington, 1880), pp. 260-61.

49. Royal Commission, 1855, *Report*, pp. ix, xxxii. Keller, "Public Order in Victorian London," p. 180.

50. Royal Commission, 1855, *Report*, p. xii.

51. H.O. 65/20 (18 Nov. 1855), H.O. to Mayne.

52. MEPOL 2/5814 (4 May 1848), memo from Mayne.

53. H.O. 65/20 (3 March 1856). MEPOL 1/47 (30 Dec. 1867), Mayne to Lindsay.

54. H.O. 45/6092/1.

55. Harrison, "Sunday Trading Riots," p. 226.

56. Ibid., pp. 234-35. Royal Commission, 1855, qs. 6332-6409. Harrison's interpretations have been accepted by John Stevenson, "Civil Disorder," in *Crime and Law in Nineteenth-Century Britain*, ed. by W.R. Cornish, et al. (Dublin: Irish University Press, 1978), pp. 163-64.

57. *The Times* (London), 14, 21, 28 Oct.; 4, 11, 18 Nov. 1855.

58. Keller, "Public Order in Victorian London," pp. 155-62. Sheppard, *London 1808-1870*, pp. 356-58.

59. Harrison, "Sunday Trading Riots," p. 219.

60. Alexander Herzen, *My Past and Thoughts* (New York: Alfred A. Knopf, Inc., 1968), III, p. 1025.

7 The Garibaldi Riots

If the events of 1855 saw the beginning of a tradition of using Hyde Park and other parks for public meetings, they also brought out for the police and the government the ambiguities in the laws on the right of assembly and freedom of speech in parks ordinarily open to the public. It was an ambiguity that haunted the authorities in the Garibaldi Riots, and in the Reform Bill demonstrations in 1866-1867, treated in Chapter Nine. The police were again caught in the middle of a political process over which they had little control, as happened in 1855 and would happen again.

The Garibaldi Riots concerned international, religious, and ethnic issues distasteful, or at least obscure, to most respectable Londoners. The fact that many foreigners were involved in the weekly skirmishes in the park reminds us that the "alien question" was not completely dead. The problem for the police lay not in crowd control tactics, but in the legal confusion about park use and the right of the police to prohibit meetings, a problem that would not be fully resolved, although the Garibaldi Riots did result in a Sunday ban on demonstrations in the royal parks.

RULINGS ON PARK MEETINGS

It was in the nineteenth century that Hyde Park and Trafalgar Square came to be associated with free speech and public meetings—a reluctant tolerance by the various governments for the use of the parks for rallies. It was the Office of Works and Public Buildings that had jurisdiction over royal parks and Trafalgar Square. The major parks of London (Hyde Park, Regent's Park, etc.) were Crown property, and the Office of Works laid down the conditions under which the public would be admitted. These conditions were enforced by the park keepers, gate keepers, and the Metropolitan Police. The regulations defining park use had never been specific; therefore, the Office of Works was in the position of creating its own rules for its trusteeship of the Crown lands since the Crown had laid down no conditions when the parks were opened to the public.

The government assumed the policy that "public" use meant conditional use, and that the parks were primarily for recreation, not for speeches.

The Office of Works' most drastic ruling on park use came in 1855 in the aftermath of the 1855 disorders, when the First Commissioner of Works forbade all meetings in the parks under its jurisdiction. In light of this Mayne was able to draft a memo in 1859 prohibiting a demonstration by master builders in Hyde Park during the building trades strikes. In 1860, however, the Office of Works, now under W.F. Cowper, had a change of heart and decided not to interfere with social and religious discussions in the parks, unless the language was shocking or blasphemous. Cowper reversed himself after the Garibaldi Riots and "other inconveniences" in 1862, and banned all Sunday meetings.[1]

There was no unrestricted right of assembly in any part of London, and the police, in addition to helping keep order in the parks, had to enforce laws that prevented obstruction of the roads. A demonstration in, say, Trafalgar Square could be dispersed for that reason alone—an issue very much in question in the 1880s when Trafalgar Square became the scene of demonstrations sponsored mainly by Socialists.

Public meetings anywhere in London that were likely to be violent could be prevented by the authorities, but attempts to do so sparked some of the violence in 1855, in 1866 during the Reform Bill Riots, and in 1887 in Trafalgar Square. In 1833 the Whig government of Lord Grey declared a meeting about to be held in Coldbath Fields was "dangerous to the public peace and illegal." It was the first serious riot the police faced. In 1842 Peel's government banned a meeting on Clerkenwell Green. In 1848 the Chartists were stopped on the passage to Westminster, and in 1855 the police forcibly interfered with the crowds protesting Lord Robert Grosvenor's bill.

Uncertain of the law on park demonstrations after 1855, the government called upon the Law Officers of the Crown for their views on meetings. Their opinion, rendered in 1856, said that the public had no prescriptive right to the parks. If the parks were otherwise open individuals could be excluded, but only for previous misconduct. The lawyers recommended that this action, while legal, was not practicable. Individuals who began to preach, orate, or play instruments could be turned out, but they must have been notified beforehand, preferably by notices on the park gates, that their actions were illegal.[2]

The policy of blocking a park meeting hinged on the expectation that a breach of the peace would occur that might interfere with the "recreation and quiet of orderly people." If such was anticipated, the Commissioner of police, on the orders of the Secretary of State, could ban the meeting, by placing posters to that effect on the park gates and in other prominent places. Since there was no statute that guaranteed the abstract right of public meetings, the laws were conceived to consider individuals and not groups, and to grant individuals the right to do things not specifically banned. The right to assemble in the parks was the right (privilege, in fact, on Crown lands) of an individual to be in the park. It followed that interference with a meeting was an attack not on public right but on an individual.[3]

The issue was little more clarified in 1868 when the Law Officers of the Crown again delivered an opinion, saying that an assembly could not be banned simply because it "might tend to a breach of the peace." This could only be done if the object of a meeting or the conduct of the participants was such as to "inspire terror in Her Majesty's subjects and to tend to the disturbance of the peace." This reduced the government's discretion somewhat. The opinion was vague but sufficed until at least 1886.[4]

The fact that the Commissioner of police could issue a proclamation banning a meeting, as in 1855, had galled many who believed that Mayne was acting under his own authority as a "minister of police." In the House of Commons Sir John Shelley was particularly concerned with the proclamation issued in Mayne's name in 1855, and suggested that the posters should bear the words "By order of the Secretary of State for the Home Department." Home Secretary Grey said that this was inconvenient, and unnecessary, since the Commissioner signed proclamations by virtue of his status as a justice of peace. Furthermore all important proclamations were approved by the Home Office anyway, as had happened in 1855.[5]

Circumstances did force the government to prevent Sunday park meetings, and this was the direct result of the series of "Garibaldi" riots in 1862. Unlike 1855 or the Reform demonstrations in 1866-1867, the issues here were obscure to most Englishmen, and because of this the resulting disturbances did not evoke much sympathy from the propertied classes. In this light the government could more easily disallow park meetings without facing a barrage of criticism that rights were being usurped—the public order question appearing paramount here.

THE GARIBALDIANS VERSUS THE IRISH

The riots concerned Italian politics and pitted secularists and pro-republican English workingmen against Irish papal sympathizers over the question of Garibaldi's activities in Italy. The issue clearly brought out the different Irish and English working-class loyalties, with the Irish being papist and monarchist where the pope was concerned, and the English tending toward secularism and republicanism, and even anti-Catholicism.

George Holyoake and the secularists had championed European nationalities struggling against Austrian and Russian rule, and were especially sympathetic to Garibaldi and his nationalistic struggle against French and papal control in Italy. Together with the Workingmen's Garibaldian Committee they solicited funds for Garibaldi and the English legion which had joined him in Italy. When the groups announced a demonstration in Hyde Park for 28 September 1862 no one anticipated the angry response of the pro-papal Irish workingmen of London who also turned out in force.[6]

At 3:00 P.M. there were about 10,000-20,000 people in the park. Some 50 of the crowd of Garibaldians, including Charles Bradlaugh, climbed atop a mound of earth near the Grosvenor Gate between the Serpentine and Bayswater Road. Bradlaugh tried to speak, when a mob of Irish, some of them women, and some armed with sticks and rocks, attacked the Garibaldians and drove them off their mound. On two nearby mounds the Irish also started singing "God and Rome." The battle was on. The Garibaldians were aided by a group of Grenadier Guards wielding walking sticks, who were soon joined by yet more Guardsmen. The Guardsmen led some 200 or so Garibaldians and rushed into the mass of yelling Irishmen. Ten minutes of fighting sent the Irish fleeing off their mounds, with the troops in pursuit. Resuming the meeting, Bradlaugh and associates passed a resolution condemning French troops in Rome. Other speeches were made, but were interrupted by a large group of Irish who rushed into the crowds in greater force than before, swinging clubs and fists, and regaining the Garibaldian mound at about 3:30 P.M. There they stayed for an hour until torrential rains drove everybody out of the park, providentially putting an end to the day's excitement.[7]

The police had had no previous suspicion of trouble and were unable to do much. The constables and the park keepers could do little but make sudden sallies into the boiling crowds and try to arrest the most violent men they could get their hands on. By the end of the day these numbered only five Irish Londoners, but no Garibaldians. The Irishmen were tried the next day at the Marlborough Street Court, where the magistrate imposed relatively light fines, but recommended that no further park meetings of that nature be allowed—a point Mayne was all too happy to take up.[8] The numerous newspaper accounts are often contradictory, confusing, and generally anti-Irish. In spite of comments that the Irish were free with their use of clubs and knives, few sticks were evident, and no knives.[9]

September 28 proved to be only the first installment in a series of disturbances on successive Sundays. There was the expectation that 5 October would see another skirmish, and Mayne instructed his superintendents to find out what they could about the possibility. Most of the reports that came in from the divisions said that nothing could be learned of any meeting; and only several divisions, particularly A and C, thought there might be some trouble. Judging from the talk around Grey's Inn Road among the "low Irish" no one was absolutely sure.[10] Mayne could have deduced as much from reading the newspapers. He had seen a leaflet that said: "Working men of London! Let us crowd in thousands in Hyde Park next Sunday," but was not aware that the Workingmen's Garibaldi Committee had canceled that meeting. The Metropolitan Police, as we have seen, were often weakest in intelligence matters, and frequently depended on perfunctory and crude sources of information. Nevertheless, preparations were made—prudently, it turned out—to deal with a repeat of the previous Sunday's fracas.[11]

Waddington at the Home Office wrote: "There will be some disturbance, I daresay, tomorrow—but Mayne will have a good strong force in the neighbourhood to prevent the combatants from coming to extremities." Like Mayne he favored not prohibiting the meeting, hoping that crowd "extremities" would force the government into banning all park meetings in the future. They both felt that too many meetings had been held since 1860 to ban them now without an obvious reason. In the short run he and Mayne were only too happy to give the demonstrators enough rope to hang themselves with.[12]

MORE DISTURBANCES

Four hundred and ten men under Assistant Commissioner (Captain) Harris were assigned to a dozen locations in and around the park. Six plainclothesmen were to mingle with the crowds to relay messages to the various commanders and to Mayne, who remained at his home in Chester Square in Belgravia, receiving periodic reports. The police were told not to provoke the speakers or to interfere, except in case of a breach of the peace, and only if the police had sufficient force to do so. Mayne wrote to Alfred Austin, the Permanent Secretary at the Office of Works, assuring him that the police would make arrangements to "apprehend the rioters and suppress the disturbances of the public peace should there be an actual breach of the peace."[13]

By 2:30 P.M. on 5 October some 200 Irish were on the mound (nicknamed the "redan") awaiting the Garibaldi Committee which never came. Soon a large number of Guardsmen and Garibaldi sympathizers carrying sticks forced them off the mound, only to be replaced shortly after by the bludgeon-wielding Irishmen. The off-duty soldiers were out in force, with their numbers increasing all the time. Soon a mixed party of them, including Coldstreams, Grenadiers, Life

Guards, and Buffs, plus a scattering of Garibaldians, charged back up the mound striking with their heavy belts, sticks, and umbrellas. The Irish again retreated showering them with stones and abuse. And so it went. The troops made forays into the crowds of Irish, stampeding people across the park. Eventually the Irish regained the mound. Other bands, numbering 200 Irish in all, moved across the park striking indiscriminately about them in affrays involving about 2,000 people on all sides. Mayne later reported to Waddington that there were about 15,000 people by 3:20 P.M., and that there were "various acts of violence" but not enough to call out the reserves. He thought the police patrols were sufficient. The 500 soldiers were trying to subdue the bands of Irishmen and hand them over to the police. The police, as on the previous Sunday, limited themselves to making sorties of four or five into the crowds to seize outstandingly violent contestants. Many foreigners were also present in the park, mostly Italians, "and made free use of the knife," according to the Commissioner of Hyde Park. This was considered characteristic of Italians. One Italian was later imprisoned for stabbing a man.

Late in the afternoon Mayne asked the commander of the Wellington Barracks to get the soldiers out of the park. Military guards arrived and ordered them out. By this time the crowds had been thinned out by a timely shower and were milling around. There were some individual scuffles. Finally Mayne gave the word for the police reserves to move in, and by 7:00 P.M. the park was cleared. Mayne himself was vague as to when the police actually dispersed the crowds. Park Commissioner Mann said 7:00 P.M.; *The Times* said 6:00 P.M.[14] Several arrests were made, and Mayne afterwards called the riots a "great scandal," at which "seditious and blasphemous language" was constantly used. The secularists blamed the Garibaldi Committee's poor organization; the Committee blamed the press for not announcing the cancellation of the formal meeting; the press blamed Mayne, and Mayne blamed the Guardsmen for provoking trouble. He denounced in particular the policy of allowing meetings at which such evils as "Chartism, Socialism, and Infidelity" were preached. The fact that the *mêlée* had lasted as long as it did seemed an outrage to many who would naturally blame the police for not being willing or able to stop it.[15]

BANNING SUNDAY MEETINGS

Mayne's point about park rallies had been got across, and on 9 October, with the permission of the Office of Works and the Home Office, future Sunday meetings in the parks were prohibited, including the expected gathering on 12 October. The public notice to this effect was a masterpiece of studied ambiguity.

Whereas numbers of persons have been in the habit of assembling and holding meetings on Sundays in Hyde Park and other parks in the metropolis, for the purpose of delivering or hearing speeches, and for the public discussion of popular and exciting topics; and whereas such meetings are inconsistent with the purposes for which the parks are thrown open to and used by the public.... Notice is hereby given, that no such meeting or assemblage of persons for any of the purposes aforesaid will be allowed hereafter to take place in any of the parks in the metropolis; and all well-disposed persons are hereby cautioned and requested to abstain from joining or attending any such meeting or assemblage.[16]

It is not absolutely clear whether all meetings were banned, or merely those for the discussion of ''popular and exciting topics.'' No specific reference was made to preaching; but it was preaching in Hyde Park that had forced the Office of Works to ban all meetings from 1856 to 1860. The printed notice appears to block meetings any day of the week, though this was not the case. The police order that was issued two days later on 11 October 1862 specified that the ban was for Sundays only. Even in preventing all Sunday meetings, rather than specifying individual gatherings as they came up, the government appeared to be stretching the law. Still, the general impression in the mind of the public was that all meetings were banned, and the police and Home Office did not mind a little confusion on that point.[17]

While there was scant sympathy for these particular riots, the press had been skeptical of Mayne's discretion in prohibiting meetings (since in their eyes he had bungled), and deciding which ''popular and exciting topics'' were likely to cause disturbances. The *Saturday Review* wrote that Mayne should have no such power and that it was preferable to ban all meetings, or ban none at all, rather than allow such discretion to the police. Mayne wrote to *The Times* justifying the policy of banning meetings, and reminding his critics that with Home Office approval he was empowered to issue prohibition notices in his own name.[18]

Unlike the Sunday Trading Riots or the Reform demonstrations in 1866-1867, the Garibaldi Riots attracted little interest or sympathy—especially where Irish Catholic laborers were involved—from the more respectable classes of London, as expressed in articles and letters to *The Times* and other newspapers. The subject of the brawls was of peripheral concern for most Londoners, and one that invoked more disdain than alarm. References in the *Spectator* and the *Saturday Review* show that part of their indignation was vented because the disorders were not confined to working-class areas. As in 1855, the traditional Sunday retreat of the respectable Londoners was being turned into a Sunday battlefield. The *Saturday Review* recommended that ''Mr. Weston's Music Hall and the Crown and Anchor are the proper places for this sort of thing.'' In 1866 the same magazine wondered why the Hyde Park Reform meetings could not be held in Victoria Park, close to the homes of most of the reformers.[19] Had the police been conspicuously brutal in 1862 instead of in 1855 few would have cared, and there would have been no Royal Commission to investigate their behavior.

Notices prohibiting the 12 October meeting were posted at all the London park entrances and on leading thoroughfares. The police orders of 11 October also said that communication with leaders in the Italian community should be made, to discourage Italians from coming to the park on 12 October, and to warn that any who came with knives or other offensive weapons would be arrested.[20] The "redan" in Hyde Park was also leveled by Office of Works laborers.

The police were determined now to stop any meeting. One thousand one hundred and sixty-five men, a few in plain clothes, were deployed in Hyde Park, Regent's Park, Victoria Park, and Battersea Park. They were to block anyone from speaking or preaching. Police orders included the usual warning that constables were to ignore any offensive language used against them and to avoid making arrests if possible.[21]

As expected, crowds assembled in Hyde Park, but they were quickly broken up by police patrols. Speakers were also silenced and military pickets stood at the park gates to turn away any uniformed soldiers. At 2:30 P.M. groups of Irish laborers came up from Westminster along Birdcage Walk, up Constitution Hill and into the park. There were wild chases across the grass and sporadic fighting between Irish and Garibaldians; but a convenient rain dispersed most of the participants by three o'clock. As on the previous Sunday all but a few of those arrested were Irish, giving substance to the charge that the police had allied themselves with the Garibaldians by showing a marked prejudice against the Irish.

There were repeat performances in various parks in the several weeks following, but with diminishing numbers of participants and violence. There were still occasional brawls around London, usually in pubs. Most of the outbreaks occurred in the West End slums, in the area to the north of Hyde Park, and in Irish areas of west central and northwest London from St. Giles to Holborn and St. Pancras to Clerkenwell. These were districts that had borne the brunt of recent Irish immigration. There was little fighting in other parts of the West End or south of the river. London was not the only place where such fighting took place: other towns, notably Birkenhead, had disturbances.[22]

The Garibaldi events were not quite at an end. In 1864 Garibaldi himself received a triumphant reception in London in early April and was scheduled to speak in numerous towns all over England. After his well-fêted visit to London, ill health compelled him to leave England. His sudden departure was, however, widely assumed to be the result of government intrigue.[23]

On Saturday 23 April, a group of working men turned a tree-planting ceremony on Primrose Hill in honor of the 300th anniversary of Shakespeare's birth into a protest meeting against Garibaldi's alleged expulsion. The meeting was peaceful but a nervous Superintendent Loxton became alarmed that it might turn violent and ordered the meeting broken up. The crowd of about 50,000 left peacefully but with loud grumbling about high-handed police behavior.[24]

The whole episode proved to be an embarrassment for the police since Loxton had no authority to break up a peaceful Saturday assembly. The police orders only banned outright, park meetings on Sunday. Loxton claimed that he was acting in the spirit of the public notice of 1862, preventing all meetings of a "popular and exciting" kind. Sir George Grey had to admit in the Commons that the police had been wrong, and Mayne was forced to reprimand Loxton for his action and for not having on hand a sufficient body of police had the meeting turned violent; that it dispersed peacefully was beside the point.[25]

THE POLICE, THE PUBLIC, AND HYDE PARK

Mayne was still hoping that all park meetings, not just on Sundays, would be banned. He wrote to Waddington at the Home Office suggesting as much, and quoting the Royal Commission of 1855 in saying that the parks were not appropriate forums for public speeches. This would certainly have been "preventive policing" in another sense. Waddington, as before, agreed wholeheartedly; Grey disapproved, so Mayne had to satisfy himself with posting notices on the park gates merely reminding people of the standing orders forbidding Sunday meetings.[26]

For the law and order public the issue in 1862 was seen primarily as one of disorder which had to be stopped. In this light the ban on Sunday meetings could be imposed without provoking criticism that Englishmen's rights were being abridged.

Police popularity with the working classes was scarcely enhanced by the Garibaldi disorders of 1862 and 1864. Mayne's widely known distaste for park meetings and his attempts to suppress the Reform Bill demonstrations in Hyde Park two years later won him the undying hatred of radicals as well. On another level the events of 1862 created even more of an estrangement between the police and the London Irish, a shortcoming that put the police at a disadvantage for information, especially during the Fenian alarms five years later.[27]

The Garibaldi Riots had done little to define the question of the public's right to assemble for speeches in the parks. There was no unrestricted right of assembly in any part of London and the law allowed the expulsion from Crown lands of individuals who misbehaved. Demonstrations could be banned in parks or elsewhere if they were likely to create an obstruction (say, in Trafalgar Square), or if violence was likely. After 1868 legal opinion held that a meeting could not be banned just because it might become unruly, but only if its purpose was to create disturbances. This made it slightly more difficult for the government to ban demonstrations, whether in the parks or in the streets.

By 1862 Hyde Park was firmly established as a forum for political meetings of one sort or another, just as was Trafalgar Square. Hyde Park had become a symbol of free speech. As Mayne learned in 1866, and a later Commissioner learned in the late 1880s, restrictions on mass gatherings created the very issue that could lead to violent confrontations. From the standpoint of the police the problem was, as in 1855, one of law not of enforcement, and police procedures for mob control remained unchanged.

On the political level the dispersal of the Primrose Hill assembly in 1864 led directly to the formation of the Reform League. The League was successful in blending the Garibaldi and nationalist movements with radical and working-class elements, and so creating a mass movement for parliamentary reform that was largely successful because it straddled class lines.[28] Hyde Park would become the scene of mass demonstrations for reform and once again a challenge to the government over park use.

NOTES

1. H.O. 45/6794 (2, 3 May; July 1860). MEPOL 2/69 (Aug. 1859). *Hansard*, Vol. 184 (24 July 1866), col. 1409.

2. Williams, *Keeping the Peace*, p. 70. Walpole, *History*, II, pp. 171-72. *Hansard*, Vol. 184 (19, 24 July 1866), cols. 1074-75 (Walpole), 1393. P.R.O., Office of Works 16/790, Law Officers' Opinion (L.O.O.), 18, 21 Nov. 1856.

3. A.V. Dicey, "On the Right of Public Meeting," *Contemporary Review*, LV (April 1889), 508-9.

4. H.O. 48/53 (1 June 1868), Law Officers' Opinion, 179.

5. *Hansard*, Vol. 140 (8 Feb. 1856), col. 473.

6. Sheridan Gilley, "The Garibaldi Riots of 1862," *The Historical Journal*, XVI, No. 4 (1973), 699-700. Dr. Gilley's is the first scholarly study of the hitherto neglected riots.

7. Bonner, *Bradlaugh*, pp. 215-16. Gilley, "Garibaldi Riots," pp. 704-5.

8. H.O. 45/6794/6 (1 Oct. 1862), Mann to Office of Works.

9. Gilley, "Garibaldi Riots," pp. 705-06. Broadlands MSS, WFC/LL/1 (1 Oct. 1862), Mann to Waddington.

10. H.O. 45/6794/7, police rpts.

11. Gilley, "Garibaldi Riots," p. 709.

12. H.O. 45/6794/5a (Oct. 1862), Waddington (note).

13. Ibid., 6794/7. MEPOL 7/23 (4 Oct. 1862). Broadlands MSS, WFC/LL/1 (4 Oct. 1862), Mayne to Austin.

14. H.O. 45/6794/7 (6 Oct. 1862), Mayne to Waddington. Ibid., 6794/6 (6 Oct. 1862), Mann to G. Russell. Gilley, "Garibaldi Riots," pp. 709-10. *The Times* (London), 6 Oct. 1862.

15. H.O. 45/6794/7 (6 Oct. 1862), Mayne to Waddington. Gilley, "Garibaldi Riots," p. 715.

16. *The Times* (London), 11 Oct. 1862.

17. H.O. 65/24 (9 Oct. 1862), H.O. to Office of Works. Ibid. (10 Oct. 1862), Waddington to Mayne. MEPOL 7/23 (11 Oct. 1862), order. *P.P.* 1864 (252), XLVIII, p. 787. Keller, "Public Order in Victorian London," p. 344.

18. MEPOL 1/47 (13 Oct. 1862), Mayne to Delane.

19. *Saturday Review*, 11 Oct. 1862, p. 432; 28 July 1866, p. 96.

20. MEPOL 7/23 (10, 11 Oct. 1862).

21. Ibid. (11 Oct. 1862).

22. Gilley, "Garibaldi Riots," pp. 711-12, 717, 722, 726. MEPOL 7/23 (18, 25 Oct.; 1, 22 Nov. 1862). *Spectator*, 11 Oct. 1862, p. 1122.

23. Frances E. Gillespie, *Labor and Politics in England* (Durham, N.C.: Duke University Press, 1927), pp. 217-19.

24. *P.P.* 1864 (272), XLVIII (22 April 1864), Police Orders, pp. 784, 788. *Hansard*, Vol. 175 (27 May 1864), cols. 775-76. F.M. Leventhal, *Respectable Radical: George Howell and Victorian Working Class Politics* (London: Weidenfeld and Nicolson, 1971), pp. 48-49.

25. *P.P.* 1864 (272), XLVIII, pp. 783-84, Loxton's and Stokes's rpts. *Hansard*, Vol. 175 (27 May 1864), pp. 775-76. MEPOL 7/25 (7 May 1864).

26. H.O. 45/6794/11 (4 May 1864). MEPOL 7/25 (5 May 1864).

27. Gilley, "Garibaldi Riots," pp. 730-31.

28. Leventhal, *Respectable Radical*, p. 50.

8 Hyde Park and Reform Bill Agitation, 1866-1867

It would be natural for an Englishman to assume that free speech and the right of assembly were threads woven into the Constitution centuries ago, as venerable as (and as old as) the Magna Carta and the Bill of Rights, a birthright always there but in a sense "rediscovered" in the nineteenth century and exercised in a manner consonant with the political fashion of the age. To assume that open-air speaking on political matters was a hallowed institution is to compress a process that was largely defined in the Victorian age. In fact, the assertion of freedom of speech and assembly is the foremost theme in the study of public order in the nineteenth century.

Public meetings in London were significant not merely for the issues at hand, whether sabbatarianism, Italian politics, or political reform, but for the very fact of meeting in the first place. For the Reform League and its supporters the park demonstrations were nominally about the extension of the franchise, but were really about the question of the right of assembly. The police and the Home Office, backed by ambiguous laws, had the uneasy task of trying to preserve order without provoking disorder and without making themselves the issue, as happened in 1855 and to a lesser extent in 1862. The events of 1866-1867 did not resolve the park issues: that would be done with further legislation and after other challenges. But the Reform League did in a real sense "win" the battle for Hyde Park, making that park in particular the main public forum in London. Trafalgar Square would also be a popular meeting ground later.

As we shall see the government's decision in 1866 to close Hyde Park to the Reform League's meeting only led to violent confrontations between the police and reformers, in which the police were aided directly by the military for the first time. In 1867, the government's decision, made privately, that it would not keep reformers out of the park marked not a capitulation to mob rule, as alarmed conservatives complained, but a necessary accommodation which aided the process of public order in the long run. The use of Hyde Park, and later Trafalgar Square, for political gatherings symbolized the right of assembly and of free speech. Police attempts to block meetings seemed to be a rejection of those freedoms which were now becoming institutionalized in the form of peaceful and organized political rallies.

THE REFORM LEAGUE

With the advent of the Reform League the cause of parliamentary reform and manhood suffrage found a strong voice. It was primarily a working-class body, though conceived as a result of negotiations between a group of labor leaders and a number of advanced liberals who contributed money for "earnest agitation." Self-help was part of the guiding spirit of the League, a narrower conception of social change than that of the Chartists. While talk of revolution was occasionally heard in the 1860s, this usually meant the social reconstruction that would result from extended manhood suffrage and the secret ballot.[1]

The year 1866 was a year of economic depression, especially in London. In May the banking house of Overend and Gurney collapsed sending severe tremors throughout the entire British financial establishment. In late spring and summer the country saw food prices and unemployment mounting. The exceptionally harsh winter of 1866-1867 brought more hardship, a cholera epidemic, bad harvests, and a series of bread riots in various parts of the East End, together with the virtual breakdown of the machinery of poor relief there. The period also heralded the collapse of the Thames shipbuilding industry which further impoverished the East End, an area already taking on a separate identity as "outcast London," the abode of the shiftless, the chronically poor, the criminal.[2]

Of all the agitation in the 1860s, none was so threatening as that over the question of extending the franchise. Parliament had already rejected reform bills in 1852, 1854, 1859, and 1860, but with the death of Palmerston and the reshuffling of the parties, reform was taken up again with determination. Yet another reform bill of Lord John Russell was rejected in May 1866 bringing down his government.

The Reform League's first show of strength came when they scheduled a giant protest rally aimed at the new Tory administration under Lord Derby. A meeting was planned for Trafalgar Square on 2 July, which Mayne had intended to ban, on the grounds that it would block traffic. He had a change of heart and reluctantly permitted the meeting, but wrote to Edmund Beales, the Reform League president, warning him that the police would not tolerate any window-smashing rampages in the West End. Just to make sure, Mayne ordered constables to patrol in front of houses of prominent people where disorderly crowds might assemble to "excite terror or alarm in the minds of Her Majesty's Subjects." Mayne also dispatched a group of plain-clothes officers to obtain whatever information they could about the upcoming meeting. In spite of official anxieties, the meeting was peaceful, with an attendance of about 80,000.[3]

The success and the enthusiasm of the demonstration, when viewed against government instability, encouraged the League to try for bigger events, by planning a monster rally in Hyde Park with bands and banners, to impress the new Derby government with the need for reform.

CLOSING HYDE PARK

The government was sufficiently alarmed by the prospect of more Hyde Park meetings that it decided to get a legal sounding. Sir Henry Thring prepared a memorandum embodying the 1856 decision of the Law Officers of the Crown and sent it to the new Home Secretary, Spencer Walpole. It said: "The Government do not think they are justified in suppressing the meeting with force. The meeting will be permitted to assemble; but in the event of its becoming disorderly, a stop will be immediately put to it." Basically the government had no right to disperse a peaceful meeting—only one that became disorderly. People could not be excluded from the park except individually as trespassers, and then for previous misconduct, or for attempting to make speeches. Any prohibition on speaking would have to be posted beforehand, however. The government did have another option: in its capacity as landlord (acting for the Crown) it could simply close the park altogether.[4]

Walpole doubted that the police could evict "trespassers" from Hyde Park without causing a riot. He preferred to let the assembly take place and to break it up if it became disorderly. Derby was certain that any meeting was bound to become violent and rather than risk another Peterloo massacre, overruled Walpole and ordered the gates of Hyde Park closed. He assumed that the League would back down.

The order closing Hyde Park on Monday, 23 July was duly signed by Lord John Manners, the First Commissioner of Works, and transmitted to the Reform League. Edmund Beales was angry at this and wrote Mayne, demanding to know how the government could ascertain in advance whether or not a meeting would be violent. He thought it an unwarranted interference with the right of the people to use their own public property.[5]

The government's action forced the League into a tactical dilemma since the authorities showed no inclination to rescind the ban. Should they defy it and force their way into the park, or should they simply back down and call off the meeting? Beales and his associates decided to leave the meeting as announced, to try to enter the park, but if refused, to proceed to Trafalgar Square and meet there, having made their point.

The police meanwhile had the notices banning the gathering printed and distributed on 18 July all over London, especially in pubs and shops, and on park railings—excellent advertising that no doubt increased park attendance. The posters declared the meeting to be illegal as it was "calculated to lead to riotous and disorderly conduct, and to endanger the public peace." The park gates were to be closed at 5:00 P.M. and anyone attempting to speak would be told not to, and arrested if he persisted. People already in the park were to be allowed to remain. The police assigned a total of 1,613 men, including 105 in plain clothes and 60 on horseback, in locations around the park, with double patrols in the park itself. Since the processions were to form at a dozen locations all over London and would march toward Hyde Park, the police assigned extra reserves at the police stations nearest the assembly points. They were instructed not to interfere with the various processions moving toward Hyde Park, but were simply to make sure the roads were not obstructed. As usual the police orders also said that arrests should be avoided if possible, and that the crowds should only be dispersed if sufficient police were on hand. Mayne himself planned to be in the park—a break with his usual practice—though the tactical control of the police was to be with the two Assistant Commissioners, Harris at Marble Arch and Labalmondiere at Hyde Park Corner.[6]

JULY 23, 1866: THE RAILINGS COME DOWN

Finally the day arrived. There were essentially three processions, composed of smaller contingents joining all along the way, that would approach the park gates. Edmund Beales and the first group left from the Reform League offices in Adelphi Terrace and proceeded by way of Regent Street to Marble Arch. At Oxford Circus their numbers were swelled by a large second contingent from the Holborn branch, who were preceded by a brass band and a large tricolor of red, green, and blue. After that the Clerkenwell branch of the League joined the others at Marble Arch before entering the park. By then the numbers, according to Henry Broadhurst, were about 15,000, marching to bands. "The whole scene, except for the absence of glittering arms and uniforms, resembled the orderly progress of a disciplined army rather than a hastily arranged procession of civilians."[7] One man who observed Marble Arch gate from a nearby rooftop described the scene in a letter to *The Times*. He saw some young boys in the dense crowds throw dirt in the eyes of the police inside the park, while some older youths were successful in prying open one of the gates with a lamppost they had torn down. A column of police immediately marched between them and the gate and drove them away.[8] As the marchers approached Marble Arch the rumors began to fly that the park gates were open, or alternatively, that they were closed. The answer was soon clear when the marchers saw a line of constables blocking the locked gates. Part of the procession went straight along Bayswater Road, but the larger part turned south down Park Lane to test the other gates. At Marble Arch when the carriages bearing the leaders of the Reform League arrived, barricades of omnibuses blocked the entrances and there was a double line of mounted constables drawn up before the entrance; inside stood a line of foot police. Beales, Applegarth, Howell, and Major Dixon were in a carriage that was drawn as near the gates as possible and surrounded by a crowd so thick that the men had trouble dismounting. They were told that they could not enter the park. At that point the crowds rushed around Beales, and the police started beating them back with their truncheons. Having made their symbolic protest in front of the closed gates, Beales and some of the other leaders set off for Trafalgar Square as planned and addressed a large rally. The South London contingent also turned off to go there when they saw that the park gates were closed. Charles Bradlaugh and other lieutenants stayed by Hyde Park to divert the arriving processions and handed out leaflets that urged departure for Trafalgar Square. Many of the leaflets were thrown on the ground unread.[9]

Henry Broadhurst, then a stonemason, gave a full account of the 23 July scene. At about 7:00 P.M. he and his colleagues reached Hyde Park corner where the crowds were already thick. They tried to make their way north along Park Lane but were stopped by the dense mobs moving south, shouting and swaying. Crowd pressure forced people against the park railings and the police attempted to drive the masses back by pounding on the railings with their truncheons. Suddenly the railings gave way, first on Bayswater Road, then discontinuously down Park Lane, helped along by the crowds who swung on the fences and forced them down for some 1400 yards. Many sections still remained standing. The police used their truncheons to keep the crowds back, but to little avail, since breaches allowed easy access. There were numerous scuffles.[10]

The masses fell or jumped into the park while the police swung their truncheons at the first ranks, but were themselves easily brushed aside by the sheer numbers of people. Broadhurst saw little personal violence after that, although he did hear a great deal of shouting. He also observed one laborer being carried out on a stretcher with his head bloody. Stones were thrown at the police, and a mounted officer was knocked off his horse by missiles. Forty or fifty arrests were made near Marble Arch. Mayne, now in the park and on horseback, was struck several times; one stone hit him in the side of the head causing blood to stream down his face. Before that the seventy-year-old Commissioner had taken the time to remonstrate with a startled woman for bringing her baby into the park. Soon the mobs had spread over the park while speakers like Baxter Langley started haranguing various noisy rallies, which the police made no attempt to stop.[11]

Troops had been held in readiness should they be needed. The Foot Guards had been confined in the Chelsea barracks in readiness, and some Coldstream Guards were also available to Mayne if he needed them. By 7:30 P.M. Mayne called up the 50 soldiers in the Magazine barracks in Hyde Park to try to bridge the gap in the railing on both sides of Marble Arch gate, but the force was too small to do this. Five companies of reinforcements from local barracks were also brought over to try to bridge the fence gaps. The police and the military units were simply not adequate to do this and to drive the enormous crowds out of the park. Altogether Mayne and General Paulet had mobilized the first and second battalions of Life Guards, a battalion each of Grenadier, Coldstream, and Scots Fusilier Guards. Life Guards also protected the new carriage road being constructed from Marble Arch to Victoria Gate, which had piles of stones that the demonstrators were grabbing to throw at the police.[12]

The arrival of the military seems to have caused more curiosity than alarm, even when fixed bayonets were used to push back the crowds. As in 1855 the soldiers were popular with the masses and were roundly cheered. Broadhurst and others were fascinated by the colorful troops. Many people simply stood and cheered, never really fearing that the soldiers would open fire, as the troops marched and countermarched. At one point someone yelled, "Three cheers for the Guards—the people's Guards!" "The commanding officer possessed more discretion than the Home Secretary, otherwise Peterloo might have been re-enacted on a hundredfold larger scale."[13]

A correspondent to *The Times*, who signed himself "C," asked one laborer why the police were booed and hissed while the soldiers were cheered. The answer was: "The soldiers are men and the others ain't. . . . The police have no feeling for the working man; they sell themselves for 2s a day." But not the soldiers?, he was asked. "They are poor devils, hard up; they haven't a shilling to bless themselves with." "C" took his leave, little enlightened by the explanation.[14] As in 1855 and to a great extent in 1862 the soldiers were popular with many of the working classes and were looked upon almost as protectors of the public against the police. This feeling arose only because of the existence of a professional police force and the removal of troops as the first line of defense against public disorder. A further irony is that the London police, for the first time since 1829, required the direct assistance of the military in battling disorderly crowds.

After watching the soldiers a while the crowd gradually dispersed, and Lord Paulet ordered the troops back to the barracks. There had been no real army casualties, "though some of the men were hit by stones intended for the police." The darkness soon put an end to the day's excitement. In spite of some of the violence the mood of the crowds was generally cheerful, "a disorderly though good-humoured mob," as the Home Secretary's son later described it.[15] Thomas Frost claimed that the crowds of reformers who marched with banners did not push down the railings. Rather, it was the sympathizers, aided by "roughs" and "idlers" who did the damage and who skirmished with the police, hurling rocks and half-bricks at them. *The Times* also noted that many of the people appeared to be "quiet and respectably dressed," and seemed to be motivated by curiosity. In contrast there were a few "roughs" who tangled with the police.[16]

The excitement was not limited to Monday. At about 1:00 A.M. the next day, 24 July, isolated bands of youths smashed windows in the Lord Chancellor's house and other buildings in Great Cumberland Street. At one o'clock in the afternoon a number of people were tearing up plants near Marble Arch, when a group of 50 A Division police reserves marched into the park. The reserves were not numerous enough to disperse what *The Times* called "knots of the lowest and most disorderly 'roughs'—the yiesty [*sic*] scum of the previous day's turmoil." Reinforcements from D, S, Y, and X Divisions soon arrived and skirmished with the mobs, which resisted efforts to disperse them. The police were assailed with stones, bricks, parts of the fallen fences and even branches that had been torn off the trees. The skirmishes with what were for the most part youths went on all afternoon, the police using their truncheons freely. Mayne finally decided that the police numbers were still inadequate and that the crowds were becoming "very turbulent," and so called in the Second Regiment of the Life Guards and two companies of Coldstream Guards. General Paulet came into the park at about 5:00 P.M. and was surprised to find that Mayne had already summoned the troops who were assembled by the Serpentine. He and Mayne waited near Marble Arch after assigning a squadron to the Bayswater Road. As the working day ended the crowd numbers grew, and there was a noticeable increase in the proportion of young hooligans. Paulet ordered up yet more troops including cavalry.

In the evening some of the Reform League officers tried to persuade the people to leave the park, but without much success. The police and troops could do little but try to keep the paths and roads in the park clear. There were no major confrontations and by 8:30 P.M. the police and military advanced in a line across the park, clearing it easily in about half an hour. The troops remained until ten o'clock.

As on the previous night bands of people went on window-smashing rampages, this time attacking the Athenaeum and United Services Clubs. The next day saw more turbulence, consisting mostly of youthful vandalism and some assaults on well-dressed park visitors.[17]

WALPOLE UNDER ATTACK

While this was going on Spencer Walpole had the unenviable task of trying to convince his fellow parliamentarians that the government's policy had been the right one. He said he agreed with Derby (a change of heart) and that closing the gates had been the best course after all and that the damage to the railings could not have been prevented, short of opening the park. Whether or not the government's critics concurred that the gates should have been closed, it was widely thought to have been foolish and provocative to keep the police in the park skirmishing with the demonstrators. Once the crowds were inside there was little point in marching the police and the troops around.[18] Walpole had two alternatives, said the *Spectator:* either withdraw the police and allow the speeches, or read the Riot Act and call in the cavalry. Walpole did neither, but allowed Mayne to let the police "turn rioters too, and make little dashes into the crowds, who at worst were only trespassers, which of course ended in savage fighting." The more conservative *Saturday Review* also took the view that Walpole was within his rights to close the park, but since rioting broke out anyway, the soldiers and the police should have been withdrawn. The legal responsibility for the violence should then have rested solely on the heads of the Reform League leaders.[19]

After the first two days of disturbances Beales and Holyoake headed a deputation of Reform League leaders to meet with Walpole at the Home Office in an effort to stop the disruptions in Hyde Park. The League had prided itself on its self-discipline and ability to maintain order, but it was clear that the growing numbers of ruffians and idlers in the crowds threatened to discredit the reform movement. Beales offered to try to restore order in Hyde Park if the police and soldiers were withdrawn. Walpole accepted this and was reportedly so relieved that he wept. Beales also wanted permission for another park meeting the following Monday. Walpole told him that he would have to consult the cabinet and seek legal advice on the matter. Meanwhile, the League should put that request in writing and await the government's decision on a further meeting.[20]

The League's written request reached the Home Office at about six o'clock on 25 July; but before any answer could be given, Beales issued a placard that appeared to announce a park meeting on Monday, 30 July. Beales had apparently assumed after the interview that the government was ready to allow a meeting rather than risk another bout of violence. The posters that were put up by the League were ambiguous in their layout, and if not read in full appeared to condone the meeting, which was no doubt what the framers had in mind to pressure the government to grant permission. The poster read as follows (preserving the format as reproduced in Sir Spencer Walpole's account):

The Government, by the Right Honourable Spencer Walpole, the Home Secretary had this day agreed with the Council of the Reform League to facilitate, in every way, their obtaining a speedy decision, either in Parliament or in a court of law, as to the right of the people to hold public meetings in the parks, and it is earnestly requested that, in the meantime, and until a question is decided, no further attempt be made to hold a

> MEETING IN HYDE PARK
> Except by arrangement with the Government
> ON MONDAY AFTERNOON
> July 30th, AT 6 O'CLOCK[21]

Walpole was immediately heaped with abuse for appearing to capitulate to the League in allowing a park meeting. It was widely assumed that he had made a deal to withdraw the police from Hyde Park and allow another demonstration in return for the League's help in quelling the disturbances. A confused Walpole immediately denied that any such deal had been made and said that he had not authorized another demonstration. Holyoake upheld Walpole's claim. With the cabinet's backing Walpole proceeded to ban any attempt to assemble in Hyde Park on Monday. The League also withdrew the misleading poster and admitted that there had been some misunderstanding.

Nevertheless, the whole episode put Walpole and the cabinet in a worse light than the Reform League leaders. "If this be strong government, we should like to be told where anarchy begins," wrote the *Spectator*. And so the matter rested, "leaving in impartial minds the conclusion that Mr. Walpole is weak, Sir Richard Mayne an old soldier, the British 'rough' no politician, and Mr. Beales a goose."[22]

Walpole could at least derive some consolation from the compliments bestowed on him from the other side of the political fence. The Reform League officials, not expecting much from a Tory Home Secretary anyway, found Walpole an agreeable and reasonable man with whom to deal. Cremer described him as "a really amiable Conservative" whose actions kept the reformers from being revolutionaries. Holyoake admired Walpole's moderation and said that as far as he knew he was the first Home Secretary who ever "showed consideration for the people at his own peril."[23]

On Saturday 28 July the Law Officers of the Crown gave the opinion that the government had no right to disperse a peaceful meeting whether or not announcements had been put up beforehand banning the assembly. Furthermore, unless there was a riot, the people could only be removed as trespassers one at a time, and with "just so much force (and no more) as is necessary for that purpose." The only real options were as before: close the gates and block a meeting, or simply allow a meeting to take place and do nothing unless it turned riotous. This was little comfort for the government; they could only hope that the League would not mount a challenge. Outside of official circles the government's weakness on the legal issue was not generally known. It would be almost a year before the Reform League would try to force the matter once again.[24]

In the meantime moderate radicals such as John Stuart Mill did not want the League to antagonize the public and cause a reaction, if a park meeting were held on 30 July. Much to Walpole's and Mayne's relief the place was then switched to the large Agricultural Hall in Islington where about 25,000 cheered to speeches by Mill, P.A. Taylor, Beales and Bradlaugh, and appropriate quotations from Shelley's "Masque of Anarchy." In case of trouble Mayne had ordered 3,680 policemen to be at various points around London, including Hyde Park and the Agricultural Hall. In addition Horse Guards and Hussars were moved into London from Aldershot and from Hounslow respectively. The meeting was peaceful.

Large crowds attended reform meetings in other parts of Britain too. In Birmingham John Bright attracted 100,000 in August and filled Manchester's Free Trade Hall in September. In Leeds a procession of workmen stretched for four miles. There were also fall meetings in Glasgow and Edinburgh. The League's marshals were successful in maintaining order at all of these assemblies.[25]

THE EVENTS OF 1866 IN THE PUBLIC MIND

Many sensitive observers saw far more in the events of July 1866 than questions of the public use of the parks or Reform League tactics. Karl Marx, ever eager to look for revolutionary potential in any public gathering, felt that a bloody encounter with the "ruling powers" would be necessary for any working-class progress. If more police had been knocked about, the military would have been forced to intervene decisively, and "then there would have been some fun." It had been a close run on 23 July. "Here the government has nearly produced a revolt. The Englishman first needs a revolutionary education, of course, and two weeks would be enough for that if Sir Richard Mayne had absolute control."

Thomas Frost likewise saw a revolution narrowly averted. "We were not far from it on the evening when the Hyde Park railings were demolished. The sterling common sense of Englishmen availed, however, to avert a collision and a crash that in France would have been inevitable."[26]

In the pessimistic though perceptive essay quoted before, Frederic Harrison saw the fall of the railings as accidental and exonerated the Leaguers from having intended violence; but more ominous were the dangerous "political" elements who came after the riot. "I know of men of good position who travelled up to London from the North to fight, and that clerks in business houses had their rifles beside their desks." He felt that the masses had been worked up and that real violence might be coming. In the face of that it was not worth risking "blood and fire" for a "petty change in the electoral system."[27] The *Saturday Review* saw international repercussions: British authority itself had been weakened.

For the past week London has virtually been in the hands of the dregs of its population. . . . The fact will remain, and will be regarded as proving that boasting, wealthy, powerful England is smitten with paralysis at the heart. A country which cannot control the fermenting scum of its city Arabs, what power can it have in the councils of Europe, or the politics of the world?[28]

As for the demonstrations themselves, even some of the most conservative critics were willing to concede that the roughs in the crowds and not the reformers caused most of the mischief. Both Derby and Walpole played down the violence as having been largely unintended. Derby said that a great portion of the crowds were "boys and young men, who had no serious views with regard to the demonstration, but joined in it merely for the purpose of assisting in any row or disturbance that might take place."[29] The *Spectator* was even clearer on the distinction, both about the police as well as the demonstrators. "The mob was composed of reformers and roughs, of whom one set protected flowers and another bonneted everybody within reach; and that the police displayed two characters, one section of them being utter ruffians, who hit hardest when least opposed, and the other disciplined men, who took stones, and rubble, and wounds as part of the day's work."[30]

Police behavior had come under criticism from several sides, as in 1855. The working-class newspaper, the *Morning Star*, called the police savages who hit people indiscriminately. The report of the Sub-Committee of the Reform League also mentioned specific cases where the police had even assaulted people outside the park who were not apparently involved with the demonstration. Other observers thought that the police, on numerous occasions during the three days, had set upon people unnecessarily and without sufficient provocation.[31]

The police still had been vastly outnumbered and took the brunt of the personal injuries. Some 265 were suffering from injuries, out of whom 1 superintendent, 2 inspectors, 9 sergeants, and 33 constables had permanent wounds; a few of the men had to be removed from active service. Sympathetic citizens, however, sent in contributions to the police, totaling some £800, distributed as gratuities.[32]

By winter the reformers began to speak of more vigorous action. In December Lord Ranelagh allowed the use of the grounds of Beaufort House in Kensington for a peaceful reform meeting at which some 25,000 men attended. They had originally planned to meet in Hyde Park but accepted the government's decision to prohibit it there. In February, after the reassembly of Parliament, the League held a large demonstration that marched from Trafalgar Square to Islington.[33] It was also in these early months of 1867 that there were more bread riots in East London and unemployment that reached unprecedented proportions.

CONFRONTATION, HYDE PARK, 1867

The left wing within the Reform League wanted to press on with agitation and pressured Beales to try once again the right to hold public meetings in Hyde Park. Another big demonstration was planned for Hyde Park on Good Friday during the Easter recess of Parliament, but the indignation of the more religious League members caused it to be put off until 6 May. The League decided to press on regardless of government opposition, knowing full well at this point that a reform bill was not a question of ''whether,'' but rather of ''how much.'' With the date set, 40 billboard men, hundreds of posters and 35,000 handbills made sure that the public received the news.[34]

The cabinet mooted the question of what to do if the League held its meeting in the park as they planned. Would a few police approach the speakers and remove them, and thus invite resistance from the crowd, which would in turn mean calling up more police and even troops? Derby said that it would not have been prudent to try to force Crown rights on the park meeting issue. A ''temporary violation'' of the law was nothing compared to what could happen if an angry mob engaged the police a second time. Derby realized that a serious clash with the crowds might well drive the Conservatives from office for a long time to come, aside from any other repercussions. Furthermore, there was the lingering fear of a possible coalition between the Reformers, the Irish, and the trade unions, an unholy alliance, in the minds of the propertied classes, that would only be facilitated by more violent confrontations.[35]

The cabinet soon decided what was to be done: nothing, provided the meeting was peaceful. The government planned to bluff, to mount a giant show of strength, and to hope that the Reform League would change its mind about 6 May.[36]

The government circulated notices warning against the meeting. The authorities had originally considered issuing a royal proclamation to this effect, but finally decided to have Sir Henry Thring draw up a notice. The word "illegal" was not used to describe the demonstration. Three policemen carried the notice to a Reform League delegate meeting on 1 May, and also informed the Leaguers that they would make themselves liable to prosecution for trespass if they persisted and held the demonstration.[37] The notice read:

Whereas it has been publicly announced that a meeting will be held in Hyde Park on Monday the 6th of May, for the purpose of political discussion; and whereas the use of the Park for the purpose of holding such meeting is not permitted, and interferes with the object for which Her Majesty had been pleased to open the Park for the general enjoyment of her people; now all persons are hereby warned and admonished to abstain from attending, aiding, or taking part in any such meeting, or from entering the Park with a view to attend, and, or take part in such a meeting.
S.H. Walpole. Home Office, Whitehall, May 1st 1867.[38]

The notice indicated that such meetings were not permitted and warned people from taking part, but made no mention that the gates would be closed. The implication was that even a peaceful meeting would be stopped. Walpole later claimed that while the meeting was not banned (though this was scarcely obvious from the wording), he hoped that the notice could serve to warn the leaders that they would be subject to legal proceedings if violence ensued. Presumably this might also scare away some of their followers. The lingering impression, which the government did nothing to dispel, was that any meeting would be broken up.[39]

The York Branch of the Reform League wrote to Walpole to request that the ban be lifted and warned the government that "ill judged repressive measures," might provoke a collision with the "People." The petition also went on to remind Walpole of the "serious results" that followed the "government interference" with the previous meeting in July 1866. The League had no intention of backing down at that stage and hoped to force the whole question into the courts. The League chose ten leaders upon whom summonses would probably be served by the police after the speeches began in the park. The men were instructed to leave the park without resistance in the company of the police and register their names and addresses. The meeting would then disperse without further ado, allowing the legal machinery to begin. The League did not want violence on its hands.[40]

The cabinet realized that it would be impossible to prevent the demonstration and immediately sought to strengthen its legal hand in relation to park assemblies by introducing a Royal Parks Bill that would require Crown permission to hold a public meeting in a royal park. Violations would result in a fine or jail term. The timing could not have been worse. Bright and Beales immediately and correctly took this as a sign that the government's position was weak and that it could not handle the situation with the existing law. The government had waited in introducing the bill, assuming that the League planned to bring the issue to court after the 1866 riots. Also with the end of a parliamentary session coming up and with no further challenges then foreseen on park use, the cabinet dragged its feet in introducing a bill until the League forced it to act.[41]

Walpole tried to explain his position in Parliament, stating that the gates would be left open; but he would not say what he planned to do if the meeting were held, except to give assurance that a large police force aided by special constables would be standing by to preserve the peace. Some of the cabinet ministers were using tough language, implying that demonstrators would be thrown out of the park. The government's exact plans were not mentioned until days later. Bright argued that the alarm was "preposterous and absurd." He assailed in particular the use of special constables, who could only exacerbate class tensions. Furthermore, mass meetings were held all over England, he said; why not in London? Walpole claimed that the government had no wish to interfere with public meetings for political purposes, and that the charge would be trespass, not a criminal offense. He added that the League would be solely responsible for any breach of the peace.[42]

The government's policy was made to look panicky by their hasty attempt to call up special constables to patrol in the police divisions left undermanned by the massing of policemen near Hyde Park. If Walpole had hoped to whip up the spirit of 1848, he was to be disappointed by the lethargic and irritated responses from many of the parish vestries (the governing bodies of the parishes) who were called upon by the Home Office to handle arrangements for swearing in the specials. A few parishes flatly refused to do anything, claiming that the government was manufacturing a crisis.

In spite of this the government managed to bring in some 12,000 to 15,000 special constables. Workers at the Woolwich Arsenal worked Sunday producing staves for them. Even troops from Aldershot were called in to stand by, and rumors spread that Armstrong guns were being brought into the Metropolis.

Mayne assigned 4,398 police to duty in the Hyde Park vicinity, with about 1,000 actually in the park, though instructed not to interfere with the meeting.[43]

As late as five o'clock on 6 May Beales reported that the government had given the League leaders further warning of arrests. His derisive comments about this were uttered at the 8 May meeting of the League's General Council. "The Government gave them all to understand that they had an enormous array of military force—infantry, cavalry, and artillery—(laughter)—yes, artillery at the railway stations—cutlasses without end at Scotland-yard, [*sic*], batons fabricated at Woolwich, and special constables—(great laughter)—ridiculous and absurd as they were, sworn in in all directions."[44]

Finally the hour arrived. At six o'clock on 6 May the League officers appeared at Marble Arch and entered without resistance. They were followed by a band playing the "Marseillaise" (which raised a cheer from the spectators) and then the Clerkenwell and Holborn branches of the Reform League, carrying a red flag topped by a cap of liberty. The demonstrators immediately spread out over the park, their numbers reaching 100,000 to 150,000 within half an hour, though figures reported in the newspapers varied greatly. The leaders entered and started speaking from at least ten platforms, evoking cheers for Beales and the League and boos and hisses for Walpole and the police. A few stones were thrown at the police, who stayed in the background, watching impassively. Nothing else happened. The crowds probably reached a peak of about 200,000, including many well-dressed people in carriages.

After the meetings, as it began to get dark and the people drifted away, the police moved in to prevent any hooliganism. The day's events were probably best summed up in John Bright's sardonic entry in his diary: "Great meeting in Hyde Park perfectly peaceful; Government in discredit and humiliated by their foolish conduct on this question."[45]

This was mild compared to some of the abuse hurled at Walpole. The *Saturday Review* outdid itself in assailing the government's capitulation to the "dangerous classes."

Perhaps no more disgraceful day has ever marked the political character of this country. The dangerous classes, in their most dangerous aspect, have been formally assured by authority that authority is impotent to preserve the peace and order of society whenever it suits illegal violence openly to defy and challenge the law.... This is the result of last Monday on the British Empire and the British Constitution. It is, as they say, an era, and may as well be marked with the blackest charcoal. We now date constitutional history from the Walpole period.

The article did, however, concede that having based his actions on the advice of the Law Officers of the Crown in 1866, Walpole could only invoke the cumbersome law on trespass. Instead of doing that he tried to scare away the Reform League and failed.[46]

THE REFORM LEAGUE CLAIMS A VICTORY

On 9 May Lord Derby admitted in the House of Lords that the government had tried to bluff, hoping that the Reform League would be deterred from meeting. He did not want a repeat of July 1866, nor did he have any intention of having individual "trespassers" evicted. The government chose to do nothing when the meeting was held even though it caused "some slight humiliation in the public mind, as having sanctioned or allowed a violation of the law." Lord Russell, the opposition leader, attacked the government's policy of making weak threats they were not prepared to follow up. Russell believed that future meetings should be allowed, and that the people would become bored with them and not bother to attend.[47]

The Reform League claimed that it had won an even greater victory than in the previous July. It had shown at other meetings in other places that it was capable of maintaining order; now it seemed to be able to impose its will on the government, having forced a capitulation over the use of Hyde Park for its gatherings. The League's prestige increased greatly.

Though the government's stand was taken collectively, in the public eye Walpole bore much of the blame for allowing Hyde Park to be used as a radical forum. Many thought he was too weak to face down the Reform League. The events of 6 May 1867 only seemed to prove the point that he was simply not up to the job; consequently, he resigned as Home Secretary, though retaining a cabinet seat without portfolio—itself an embarrassment. Derby praised him in the Lords and Disraeli did likewise in the Commons. Walpole was convinced that Disraeli was responsible behind the scenes for trying to discredit him, and for authoring (he suspected) an attack on him in a journal article. When Disraeli became Prime Minister, Walpole refused to serve under him and resigned his cabinet seat.[48]

Walpole's historian son, Sir Spencer Walpole, wrote the entry on his father in the *Dictionary of National Biography* and devoted the bulk of space to the two episodes in Hyde Park. The events of 1866-1867 also loom large in the son's *History* as an attempt to clear away some of the criticism that hung over his father by those who believed that Walpole alone had failed.

What Mayne felt about it all can only be guessed from his previous sentiments on park meetings. Like a good civil servant he could hardly attack his superiors publicly. One correspondent of Beales's, who signed himself "A Policeman," said that Mayne was furious at Walpole and the government for not meeting the demonstration with force. Mayne supposedly had little regard for Walpole anyway since the latter's meeting with Beales at the Home Office in 1866.[49]

The stormy events preceding the passage of the Reform Bill made a deep impression on many in London's middle and upper classes. The Reverend Henry Solly addressed a packed meeting of the Society of Arts in 1868. "What could a force of 8,000 or 9,000 police be against the 150,000 roughs and ruffians, whom, on some sufficiently exciting occasion, the Metropolis might see arrayed against law and order?... How different a London mob is from a docile agricultural peasantry or orderly Lancashire operatives...." His speech revealed the attitude that after about 1850 London had replaced the industrial North as the problem focus of industrial age anxiety.[50]

Other observers such as Matthew Arnold and Frederic Harrison saw in the success of the Reform agitation and the seeming governmental weakness a portent of popular unrest that threatened the whole basis of government as they had known it, and narrowed the line between government and anarchy.

A separate incident reported with alarm by Matthew Arnold seemed to confirm the views of contemporaries that the lower orders were becoming lawless. The colonel of the City of London Militia led his men to Hyde Park, and as they approached, a number of bystanders were openly set upon and robbed. The colonel did not interfere because he was afraid that his men would be overpowered and their rifles taken from them.[51]

Such things made the fissures and stresses of civilized society appear more alarming as the prospects of a mass electorate drew nearer. Though exaggerated in retrospect, the pessimistic views were shared by many, particularly in London, although the unease began to wane quickly. As Harrison put it:

It was very easy to abuse an unlucky set of ministers about Hyde Park. But what were they to do? To have used the army would have been the end of the British constitution. There were seven thousand policemen, but what were they among so many? The Executive in this country has absolutely nothing to fall back upon but the special constable, the moral support of the cheesemonger and the pork-butcher.[52]

Ultimately, of course, Harrison was correct: the government had little to fall back on, unless the extremes were considered. But few were prepared to act out the extremes in 1867, least of all the Reform League or Derby and his cabinet, at that time minus the "strong men" such as Carnarvon, General Peel, and Cranborne.

Harrison underestimated the power of a disciplined body of police acting in concert by plan. Such police, though relatively small in numbers, would usually have an advantage over larger mobs. It was likely that if Mayne and his police had had orders to disperse the crowds of 6 May, this could have been done at the outset without great resistance. The League would thus have suffered a rout, despite its slight attempts at organizing its own constabulary. Furthermore, Beales and associates had no desire to provoke a riot with the authorities. Reform, not revolution, was their aim.

A NEW PARKS BILL

Another parks bill was proposed in July by the new Home Secretary, Gathorne Hardy, that was tougher than the previous proposal. This one would also require Crown permission for park assemblies, and it would empower the police not merely to evict people from a park, but also to take them before a magistrate for unauthorized speaking. The Reform League was set on fighting it directly and would not be deterred from entering parks, which they considered public property. The bill was by no means a popular one in Parliament and was delayed, debated, put off, amended and debated again. A later amendment dropped the provision that would allow the Crown to approve meetings, and banned all political and religious demonstrations.

The problem boiled down to one of maintaining the historic right of assembly and guaranteeing that there was some place to carry it out, reasonably close to the center of London. Finally the bill was simply dropped, ironically on the same day that the second Reform Bill passed through Parliament, the second great measure of electoral reform in the nineteenth century.[53]

Eventually a Parks Regulation Act was enacted in 1872 that put park use on a statutory basis, and laid down uniform guidelines for all royal parks and gardens in Britain. Outdoor assemblies were now guaranteed under statute law for the first time. There were general regulations that spelled out basic policy for all the parks, plus rules that could be applied to specific parks.

The statute enabled the Office of Works to regulate the use of parks, and empowered the police and the park keepers to enforce the rules. In fact the Ranger of Hyde Park issued rules that September that only allowed speeches to be delivered within forty yards of the notice board. In 1896 public addresses were permitted in other parts of Hyde Park. For other parks open-air gatherings were allowed, but permission had to be obtained beforehand. Nevertheless, Hyde Park had clearly become the main public forum. From the 1870s it saw numerous demonstrations on such subjects as the Eastern Question, the Russo-Turkish War, the arrest of Land Leaguers, the Irish Coercion Bill, and unemployment.[54]

In any democratic society legal questions about freedom of speech and the right of assembly are unlikely to be "resolved" once and for all, especially where the issues at hand are tied closely to the question of public order. The events of 1866-1867 did at least bring an end to the series of "battles" for the right of assembly in Hyde Park. The Reform League had clearly won, but this is not to say that the government lost, if the long-term maintenance of public order was better served by allowing peaceful meetings to be held in the park. It may have been a League victory, but it was not the whole war, for the question of the right of assembly would be raised again in 1887 in Trafalgar Square, against the backdrop of more serious crowd violence. Within several years of that, demonstrations would be permitted at certain times in Trafalgar Square.

As an exercise in the maintenance of order, we cannot say that the events of 1866-1867 changed police tactics. What was obvious—if it had not been before— was that the police were only as effective as the laws and the government let them be. The disarray in decision making by the government only put the police in a position where hostility, if not violence, would be likely, thus compromising the non-partisan, non-political role the police tried to maintain.

It was clear that the government's attempt to ban the reform meetings in London, sponsored by an organization that in the past had shown itself capable of keeping its own order, was unwise. This action seemed to reject what many Englishmen felt was their right to hold organized political rallies.

The activity of the Reform League and the London Workingmen's Association represents only one part of the impetus that finally brought about the extension of the franchise. The weight of current scholarship would lean toward parliamentary maneuvering as the main force for reform. But no little credit must go to the League for acting as a voice for organized labor and for keeping the issue in the public eye through public meetings. Certainly many contemporaries thought that League pressure had been influential, and that if reform had been denied, the government would eventually have been confronted in the streets with a far more implacable movement than Mr. Beales and his League.

To forestall this and to prevent a possible alliance between the respectable working classes and the casual "residuum" Parliament passed a sweeping reform bill.[55] In this light 6 May 1867 could be seen less as a defeat for the government than a recognition of the inevitability of political change. Perhaps it is some measure of the political accommodation that had taken place already to compare the government's resolve in facing down the Chartists at Kennington Common in 1848 with the vacillating policies of 1866-1867.

For the Metropolitan Police there would be a lapse of almost twenty years before they were again confronted with large-scale crowd disorder. The police, meanwhile, were becoming more and more involved with a threat of a different nature, that of Fenian unrest, which would reach a peak in England in the fall and winter of 1867. The Fenians would subject the police organization and practices to more strain and public criticism than the park disturbances.

NOTES

1. Royden Harrison, *Before the Socialists: Studies in Labour and Politics* (London: Routledge & Kegan Paul, 1965), p. 80. Bishopsgate Institute (London), Howell Collection, Reform League Council Minutes, manifesto leaflet.

2. Jones, *Outcast London*, pp. 15-16, 241-42. Harrison, *Before the Socialists*, p. 85. Leventhal, *Respectable Radical*, p. 72.

3. Walpole, *History*, II, 170. The author was the son of the Home Secretary. Bonner, *Bradlaugh*, p. 222. MEPOL 7/27 (2 July 1866), Mayne to Beales and police orders.

4. *The Times* (London), 25 July 1866. Walpole, *History*, II, 173-74, 174 n. 2.

5. Leventhal, *Respectable Radical*, p. 74. *The Times* (London), 20 July 1866.

6. MEPOL 7/27 (18, 21 July 1866).

7. Henry Broadhurst, *The Story of His Life from a Stonemason's Bench to the Treasury Bench, Told by Himself* (London: Hutchinson & Co., 1901), pp. 35, 37.

8. *The Times* (London), 26 July 1866, letter by "A Vagrant."

9. A.W. Humphrey, *Robert Applegarth: Trade Unionist, Educationist, Reformer* (London: National Labour Press, Ltd., n.d.), pp. 60-61. Howard Evans, *Sir Randal Cremer: His Life and Work* (London: T. Fisher Unwin, 1909), pp. 44-45. Donald Richter, *Riotous Victorians* (Athens, Ohio: Ohio University Press, 1981), p. 53.

10. Humphrey, *Robert Applegarth*, pp. 44-45. Broadhurst, *Life*, pp. 38-39.

11. Broadhurst, *Life*, p. 39. Walpole, *History*, II, 173-74. *The Times* (London), 24 July 1866.

12. H.O. 45/7854 (24 July 1866), Paulet to H.O.; Mayne to Paulet.

13. Broadhurst, *Life*, p. 40.

14. *The Times* (London), 25 July 1866, letter from "C."

15. H.O. 45/7854 (23 July 1866), Paulet to H.O. Walpole, *History*, II, 174.

16. Frost, *Recollections*, p. 309. *The Times* (London), 24 July 1866.

17. *The Times* (London), 25, 26, 28 July 1866. H.O. 45/7854 (24 July 1866), Mayne to Paulet; Paulet to H.O.

18. *Hansard*, Vol. 184 (24 July 1866), cols. 1373-99.

19. *Spectator*, 28 July 1866, p. 821. *Saturday Review*, 28 July 1866, p. 108.

20. Leventhal, *Respectable Radical*, p. 75. Harrison, *Before the Socialists*, pp. 82 ff. Richter, *Riotous Victorians*, p. 55.

21. Walpole, *History*, II, 175-76.

22. *Spectator*, 28 July 1866, pp. 817, 821. *Hansard*, Vol. 184 (26 July 1866), col. 15. Holyoake, *Sixty Years*, pp. 186-90.

23. Evans, *Randal Cremer*, p. 45. Holyoake, *Sixty Years*, p. 190.

24. Walpole, *History*, II, 172. *Hansard*, Vol. 187 (9 May 1867), col. 220. Office of Works 16/793, Law Officers' Opinion (L.O.O.) (28 July 1866).

25. Leventhal, *Respectable Radical*, p. 76. Bonner, *Bradlaugh*, p. 226. MEPOL 7/ 27 (30 July 1866). H.O. 45/7854 (30 July 1866), Quartermaster Gen., Horse Guards, to Waddington. Richter, *Riotous Victorians*, p. 56.

26. *Marx and Engels on Britain*, Marx to Engels (27 July 1866), p. 495. Frost, *Recollections*, p. 308.

27. F. Harrison, *Order and Progress*, pp. 183, 184 n. 2.

28. *Saturday Review*, 28 July 1866, p. 109.

29. *Hansard*, Vol. 184 (24 July 1866), col. 1371.

30. *Spectator*, 4 Aug. 1866, p. 847.

31. *Morning Star*, quoted in Bonner, *Bradlaugh*, p. 225. Howell Collection, Reform League Papers, No. 45, Hyde Park Cases, *Report of the Subcommittee*, 1866. *Spectator*, 28 July 1866, pp. 817-18.

32. *Hansard*, Vol. 184 (3 Aug. 1866), col. 1986. "Police of London," *Quarterly Review*, CXXIX, 124-25. MEPOL 1/47 (11 Aug. 1866), Mayne to *The Times*. MEPOL 7/27 (8, 17 Aug., 12 Dec. 1866).

33. Harrison, *Before the Socialists*, pp. 86-87. Sheppard, *London 1808-1870*, p. 342. *Annual Register*, Chronicle (11 Feb. 1867), pp. 121-22. MEPOL 7/29 (9 Feb. 1867).

34. Walpole, *History*, II, 196. Harrison, *Before the Socialists*, p. 90.

35. Jones, *Outcast London*, p. 242.

36. *Hansard*, Vol. 187 (9 May 1867), col. 226.

37. Ibid., cols. 225-26. Walpole, *History*, II, 197.

38. *The Times* (London), 2 May 1867.

39. Evans, *Randal Cremer*, pp. 47-48. *Hansard*, Vol. 187 (9 May 1867), col. 225. Walpole, *History*, II, 196-97.

40. H.O. 45/7854 (2 May 1867). Howell Collection, Reform League Papers, Misc. MSS No. 20 (5 May 1867).

41. *Hansard*, Vol. 187 (9 May 1867), col. 223. Ibid., Vol. 196 (3 May 1867), cols. 1955-56, 2025.

42. Ibid., Vol. 187 (9 May 1867), cols. 216-17. Ibid., Vol. 196 (3 May 1867), cols. 1937, 2026. *Annual Register* (6 May 1867), pp. 169-70.

43. H.O. 45/7854. Harrison, *Before the Socialists*, p. 92. Leventhal, *Respectable Radical*, p. 90. MEPOL 7/29 (6 May 1867).

44. Howell Collection, *Minutes of the General Council of the Reform League* (8 May 1867).

45. *Annual Register*, Chronicle (6 May 1867), pp. 54-55. Harrison, *Before the Socialists*, p. 94. *The Diaries of John Bright* (London: Cassell & Co., Ltd., 1930), p. 304.

46. *Saturday Review*, 11 May 1867, pp. 583-85.

47. *Hansard*, Vol. 187 (9 May 1867), cols. 220, 227, 230.

48. Walpole, *History*, II, 198-99.

49. Howell Collection, "A Policeman" to Beales (25 May 1867).

50. Quoted in Jones, *Outcast London*, p. 243; see also pp. 11-12.

51. Matthew Arnold, *Culture and Anarchy*, ed. by R.H. Super (Ann Arbor: University of Michigan Press, 1965), pp. 131-32.

52. F. Harrison, *Order and Progress*, p. 183.

53. *Hansard*, Vol. 188 (22 July 1867). Ibid., Vol. 189 (29 July, 13, 15 Aug. 1867). Howell Collection, Reform League Papers No. 54 (25 July 1867). Ibid., Special meeting, Council of Reform League (n.d.).

54. *Public General Statutes*. Williams, *Keeping the Peace*, pp. 72-73. Keller, "Public Order in Victorian London," 252, 355. Richter, *Riotous Victorians*, p. 90.

55. Jones, *Outcast London*, p. 57.

9   The Police and the Fenians

"It is disgusting that such things can take place in a well governed country.... Strong measures will soon be called for," wrote an indignant Gathorne Hardy in his diary in 1867. The "well governed country" to which he referred was Ireland, and the events that aroused his displeasure were the activities of the Fenians. Two years before, Lord Wodehouse, the Lord Lieutenant of Ireland, had written to Sir George Grey, expressing somewhat the same sentiments. "It is difficult to bring oneself to believe people capable of such egregious folly, but the matter must be treated as serious."[1] If Hardy and Wodehouse were puzzled by the conduct of their ungrateful Irish subjects, they shared their confusion with most of their countrymen. Both men at least took the Fenians seriously.

The Metropolitan Police also learned to take the Fenians seriously, for the Fenians challenged the police in a variety of ways, brought out deficiencies in the force and its leadership, and revealed their inexperience and lack of knowledge in dealing with urban terrorism. It may be fitting that this final chapter combines elements of both sides of policing considered in this book: political policing, including detection, surveillance, and intelligence work; and considerations of public order, the banning of demonstrations, the calling up of special constables and military reserves, and the maintenance of security for people and property.

We shall see that the greatest difficulty the police had was in the area of detection, because the detectives were too few in number, and too inexperienced in the kind of intelligence work required to develop an adequate knowledge of Fenianism in England. This deficiency could also be charged against other English police forces. The police suffered in any case from fragmentary support from the working classes, and most critically, from inadequate ties with the London Irish community and their priests, who were generally unsympathetic to Fenian disorders.

The police were not without some highly capable and intelligent men, detective Williamson being an example. Unfortunately, Commissioner Mayne did not take advice readily, and thus did not draw enough on the expertise his men gained in the streets. Mayne's tight control over the police, understandable in view of his desire to insure accountability and lawful behavior from his men, had the unfortunate effect of stifling initiative from within police ranks. Criticism of the police properly fell on the head of the remote and aged Commissioner.

The old anxieties about a "spy" system were not heard so much in the late 1860s, and had Mayne requested somewhat greater police powers he might have gotten his way at this time, for the articulate public was willing to accept a more intrusive police presence, if only to weather the Fenian crisis. From the police, the public demanded greater protection and effectiveness than they got during the Fenian alarms.

THE BACKGROUND TO FENIANISM

Fenianism had been founded in the United States in 1856, under the name Fenian Brotherhood, by the Irishman John O'Mahony. The organization's purpose was to supply arms and officers for revolutionary efforts to sever Ireland from British rule and create a republic. In 1858 the Irish counterpart organization, the Irish Revolutionary Brotherhood (later the Irish Republican Brotherhood), was established on the same principles by James Stephens. Both organizations were heavily supported by Irish-Americans, many of whom, after 1865, were able also to contribute combat experience gained in the American Civil War. O'Mahony and Stephens and others, who had taken part in the Young Ireland Insurrection of 1848 and afterwards fled to Europe, imbibed the ideas of the Continental revolutionaries. And in New York in 1866 Stephens apparently met with a group of European soldiers of fortune, including Gustave Cluseret, who was later involved in the Paris Commune in 1871.[2]

By the mid-1860s small uprisings were taking place in southern Ireland, which alarmed the authorities and led to numerous arrests. The Fenians, as they were commonly called, were by then organized into "circles" numbering between 800 and 2,000 men each. The circle was divided and sub-divided twice again in groups of nine, so that at the lowest level of organization, a group of nine men formed a section. The idea was that secrecy would be preserved by allowing the men to know only those in their section.[3]

Most Fenian activity was confined to Ireland (or North America) until 1867, when several events in England gave rise to fears that England itself was threatened with violence on a widespread scale. London was less the scene of Fenian organizing than Liverpool, Birmingham, and Manchester, until the Clerkenwell jail explosion in December 1867 focused attention on the capital. Then the London Metropolitan Police got the first of many lessons in urban terrorism.

FENIANS IN ENGLAND

Early police involvement in England was relatively slight, compared to the constant vigilance of the Irish authorities that was directed from Dublin Castle, the seat of the Lord Lieutenant. London detectives, however, had kept their eyes on the movements of suspected Fenians, and in April 1866 Home Secretary Grey dispatched a London and a Dublin policeman to Paris to identify James Stephens and his associates. Apparently the plan was for more London detectives to show up abroad "at intervals," as "one cannot do much good."[4] Mayne and the Home Office began to doubt the prudence of this, fearing that the conspicuousness of the detectives might cause embarrassment. In writing to the British Consul at Le Havre, Mayne said that this would establish a precedent: the French would have agents watching French political suspects in London. "This practice altho' I know it is followed yet [sic] it is without the knowledge of our authorities, and would I am sure cause excitement here and condemnation." Also he believed that this would be of little benefit to the Fenian trials in Ireland.[5]

In spite of Mayne's reservations other evidence makes it likely that he had a change of heart about this. In July 1867 he wrote to Lord Naas (later Lord Mayo), the Irish Chief Secretary in Derby's government, saying that he would send a police observer to a Dublin trial but asked that the officer not be made a witness unless necessary, "as of course it would become public that police are employed in Paris for observation of political offenders." Other references in the private out-letters of the Police Commissioner refer to reports from Paris, particularly about the surveillance of the American Fenian, Roberts, and other suspected Fenians there.

There had been no real question of sending detectives to the United States, since the Foreign Office, through its officials there, provided information that was "very full." Also the American Fenians were anything but discreet in their plans.[6]

It is clear that by 1866 the Metropolitan Police were being looked to as the center of intelligence on Fenian matters in England; their detectives were being used regularly in other parts of the country for investigations. In February 1866 the Jersey authorities requested a couple of detectives from London to watch for possible disaffection of troops quartered on the island. In fact, practically the whole detective force, as well as uniformed constables, was used at one time or another for investigations in England, Ireland, and on the Continent, following suspects and watching ports. Sergeants Mulvaney and Druscovitch spent £400.19 in keeping an intermittent watch on Stephens in Paris from August 1867 to January 1868. Inspector Williamson also spent some time in Paris. Other London policemen appeared in Antwerp and Dieppe, as well as in Ireland. All of the policemen later received gratuities for their efforts.[7]

In 1866 and early 1867 Liverpool seemed to be the center of the Fenian conspiracy. In August 1866 a tip-off from an informer led to the recovery in Liverpool of a number of swords and rifles, which had earlier been stolen from the headquarters of the London Irish volunteer companies, and even from the Tower of London. Mayne dispatched detectives Williamson and Mulvaney to Liverpool to work with the Liverpool and Irish police, in an attempt to contain and crush Fenianism there. The Home Office had also instructed Major Greig, the Head Constable in Liverpool, to cooperate with the London police and take whatever advice Mayne might send on how to deal with the Fenians. Soon the detectives were sending back regular reports of their investigations, which tended to deflate the seriousness of the Fenian activity there.[8]

On 24 September Mayne sent £10 to Liverpool to pay the informer whose information had led to the recovery of the weapons and the arrests of four men. At the same time the Commissioner wrote that "it is of great importance that information be now obtained on which the conspiracy should be defeated in Liverpool, where it seems to be so widely spread."[9] The center of Fenian fund raising and planning, however, seemed to be moving to London. Inspector Thompson of the Metropolitan Police had arrested Richard O'Sullivan Burke and John Casey there for Fenian activities; and the Dublin police were convinced that James Stephens and Colonel Kelly, the man who replaced Stephens as the head of the I.R.B., stayed in London frequently, and that their strategic planning was done there. Indeed, it was in London that Kelly and the important Irish leaders met to form a Provisional Government to direct the civil affairs of the Fenian organization in Ireland and to plan an uprising in Ireland for March 1867. Sprawling London, with its Irish areas, no doubt seemed a safer refuge than informer-riddled Dublin, or even Birmingham, Manchester, or Liverpool.[10]

The Reform Bill demonstrations also raised the inevitable speculation that Fenian activity might benefit by these disturbances. The Tory journal, *Blackwoods Edinburgh Magazine*, indicated a connection between the two, but drew back from charging the Reform League leaders with knowingly aiding the Fenians. Nevertheless, the specter of violence was invoked.

Who can doubt, had the attack on Chester Castle [an abortive attempt in February 1867 to steal 10,000 government weapons] succeeded, but that in St. Giles's, perhaps at Islington, not less than in Kerry, disturbances would have broken out? And, blood once drawn, especially in the metropolis, it would be hard to say what consequences might not follow.[11]

There had been a meeting between Fenian leaders and Reform League officials, and of the latter, Bradlaugh, Cremer, and Odger were prepared to offer their support only if Fenian principles were merely democratic and not anti-English. They said they would have to confer with Edmund Beales, the head of the Reform League. Nothing further came of this, but Kelly was not surprised: he did not really expect to elicit English support. Always sensitive to public charges of disloyalty, the Reform League went out of its way to disavow any connection with secret organizations that advocated violence and assassination. This was later confirmed in December 1867 when the explosion at the Clerkenwell House of Detention in London was roundly condemned by the League.

While it is true that there was some lukewarm enthusiasm from Reform leaders like Odger, it is also true that Fenianism attracted very little support from among the British working classes, or indeed from any social level in Britain. On the contrary there is ample evidence of widespread anti-Irish feeling. Irish immigration had produced difficulties in social and economic integration which were still acute in some parts of England in the 1860s.[12]

THE MANCHESTER RESCUE

In September 1867 in Manchester, the Fenian leaders Kelly and Deasy, who had finally been captured several days before, were being conveyed in a police van from the Court House to the county jail, guarded by 12 unarmed policemen. The van was assaulted by a band of 30 armed men, who, in trying to shoot the lock off the door to release the prisoners, killed Manchester Police Sergeant Brett inside. Kelly and Deasy were released and spirited away, prompting a vigorous search for them. They eventually made their way out of the country. Twenty-nine men were quickly rounded up, and three of them were eventually convicted and executed for the murder.[13]

The Home Secretary, Gathorne Hardy, was angry that the police of the cities, including Manchester and London, did not take Fenianism seriously, as evidenced by the inadequate protection of the prisoners in Manchester. From Dublin Lord Mayo, the Irish Chief Secretary, had frequently criticized the English police for their incompetence in dealing with the Fenian situation in their own country. In a note to Disraeli, Mayo said that the affair showed what he had always said, that there was no such thing as police in England. "The English Police always ridicule everything we tell them. So I have lately left them alone." Mayo also wrote to Gathorne Hardy:

The whole time I have been in office all the warnings the Irish Government have given to the English Police have been disregarded. For a long time we have been almost certain that if any Fenianism existed in the United Kingdom it had its centre at Liverpool and Manchester.... There is much more Fenian activity on your side of the Channel than here.

He also suggested that Detective Adolphus Williamson should be placed at the head of a "Fenian Police Department." Lord Malmesbury even proposed to Sir James Ferguson of the Home Office that Hardy should visit the prefect of the Paris police while in France "and learn how they catch conspirators! I believe our police have much to learn!"[14]

Hardy wrote back to Mayo on 21 September, "I agree with you that the Police have been supine and if the information which has reached me tonight that Deasy has got to France be correct negligence as well as apathy must be imputed to them."[15] The Dublin police and the Royal Irish Constabulary were also beginning to resent the arrogance of the English police, having themselves been more zealous and efficient in sniffing out Fenians than their confreres across the Irish Sea. The Dublin police chief forwarded to Lord Mayo a report by one of his own "G-men" (Dublin G Division), Edward Entwissell, who had been sent to Manchester to help search for the escaped prisoners. Mayo made sure the report got to Gathorne Hardy. Entwissell and a companion claimed that they worked hard day and night searching houses, "almost as if the Fenian business were at its glory in Dublin.... And as you know, Sir, our companions, English policemen, are not cheap at any price. I never met such thirsty fellows in my life.... They know as little how to discharge duty in connection with Fenianism as I do about translating Hebrew or marshalling troops to fight a battle, but of course a Dublin officer is only an officer from Dublin, and London leads the day—of that more anon." When Hardy read the report he commented to Mayo that "your Royal Irish clearly did not think much of the London and Manchester police, or of their knowledge of how to handle the Fenian problem."[16] Unfortunately, Hardy had little idea of how to handle the problem either.

In Manchester the search for the escaped men was still going on. Inspector Williamson and his three associates there had little luck in learning the whereabouts of Kelly and Deasy. Rewards were offered, and ports and railways were observed. Train stations in London were watched as well, and by two Manchester policemen, whose presence was known to Mayne.[17]

The police and the Home Office were becoming alarmed that Fenianism was showing signs of taking permanent root in England. Already the attempt on Chester Castle, the theft of weapons from volunteer companies, and the Fenian recruitment going on in British military units were cause enough for alarm. It was feared that widespread violence, sabotage, and assassination in England would be a prelude to a concerted armed uprising in Ireland which the English (thus preoccupied) would be incapable of suppressing. More intelligence was needed and the Home Office issued a circular in September to all the chief constables and mayors in Britain instructing them on how to obtain "correct information" on the Fenians. "It is desirable that a system should be established by which a constant watch should be kept on persons believed to belong to such organization, and regular information be transmitted to this office." The head constables were to appoint a number of "discreet," trusty, and intelligent policemen to do nothing but watch Irish quarters and report all suspicious activity. The information obtained was to be kept strictly secret. With that done Hardy wrote in his diary: "These Fenians are troublesome but I can do nothing personally but hope that a circular I sent will help arrangements."[18] Soon word came that a group of 30 to 40 armed Fenians was on its way to Scotland to seize the Queen on one of her excursions to Balmoral. Immediately a party of 12 plain-clothes policemen from London was sent North to guard the train stops along the way and to keep an eye on all suspicious parties, particularly near Balmoral. Troops were likewise sent to Ballater a few miles to the east. Hardy wrote to Derby that the "Horrible Fenians" had kept him busy at the Home Office. He hoped to persuade the Queen to travel only by day. "There is great uneasiness in all parts of England where Irish are, and, though exaggerated, it is not without foundation." Nothing came of that particular scare.[19]

Outside of official circles there did not appear to be any extreme concern for the Fenians in England. Newspapers and journals seemed relatively muted in their coverage of Fenianism, usually discussing Irish affairs more broadly. What "scare" there was in London took place immediately after the Clerkenwell explosion in December 1867 and was short-lived. Nevertheless, there was uneasiness, and the Home Office reluctantly issued pistols and swords to various provincial towns who were requesting them for their police, in case of emergencies. Extra police were detailed to the Royal Gunpowder Factory at Waltham Abbey, to the small arms factory at Enfield, and to other potentially sensitive places.[20]

On 18 November Hardy refused to see a deputation of 60 to 80 men, led by an Irishman named James P. Finlan, who were hoping to get a reprieve for the three condemned men who had been convicted of the murder of Police Sergeant Brett in Manchester. Finlan and his followers stormed into the Home Office and held an "indignation meeting" which included several short speeches and a denunciation of Hardy. They soon left voluntarily and *The Times* wrote: "We have never reported a more disgraceful outrage."[21] There was little sympathy for the condemned men from that quarter, or indeed, from any, outside of the resident Irish in England.

Finlan and other London Irish held a meeting on Clerkenwell Green on 21 November, in a desperate attempt to win a last minute reprieve for the condemned men. They also sent a deputation to Windsor in a futile attempt to present a petition to the Queen. Nevertheless, the executions took place as planned on 23 November, thus creating the "Manchester Martyrs." Memorial "funeral" processions which wound their way through London to Hyde Park were organized the next day. There were many women among the 2,000 present, listening to speeches and prayers for the hanged men. The police made no attempt to interfere with the peaceful gathering.

The Irish sympathizers attempted to hold a commemoration meeting the next month on Clerkenwell Green. Mayne decided that such things had gone far enough, declared the meeting illegal, and ordered Finlan arrested if he tried to speak, either in Clerkenwell or in Hyde Park. The next year Finlan and his associates planned other memorial meetings in London for 22 and 29 November 1868, but both were banned by Mayne, who ordered the police to break up any assemblies immediately.[22]

CLERKENWELL

"Desperate men are abroad & desperate means may be tried," wrote Gathorne Hardy in his diary. His worst fears were to be confirmed less than a month later when a barrel of gunpowder blew down some 60 yards of the wall of the Clerkenwell House of Detention, demolished houses on the street opposite, killed 12 people and maimed 120. It was a thwarted attempt to free Richard O'Sullivan Burke, the man who had planned the escape of Kelly and Deasy in Manchester, and who was himself detained on a charge of being a Fenian arms agent.[23]

Burke had arranged his own rescue through friends outside. According to John Devoy's account, a priest supplied the powder—but far too much of it was used for the job to be done.[24] As was routine, warning of the escape attempt got to Dublin through an informer. Superintendent Ryan of the Dublin police sent the report on to Dublin Castle on 11 December 1867. The message was passed on to London, where it arrived at the Home Office at noon the next day. The note said: "The rescue of Richard Burke from prison in London is contemplated. The plan is to blow up the exercise walls by means of gun powder; the hour between 3 and 4 P.M.; and the signal for all right, a white ball thrown up outside when he is at exercise."[25] A copy of the message was sent to Mayne and to

Mr. Pownall, the Chairman of the Middlesex Sessions. By 12:45 P.M. Mayne had sent out orders to the police to inform the Governor of Clerkenwell, and to check the prison walls to see if they were mined. At least 5 uniformed constables, plus 3 in plain clothes, were assigned to the immediate vicinity of the House of Detention to check the walls and to watch any people loitering nearby. The police inspector at the King's Cross Police Station was also to take note of unusual activity. For 13 December Mayne ordered a double patrol (of 2 constables) to be posted, with an extra 5 uniformed and 3 plain-clothes policemen to watch the area around the walls as had been done the day before.[26]

On 12 December a woman in a neighboring house saw a man wheel a cask up to the prison wall and light it. A white rubber ball was thrown over the wall and was picked up by a curious warder who pocketed it. Seeing the ball, Burke retreated to a corner of the exercise yard, to await the blast that was to blow a hole in the wall; the blast did not occur. When the powder failed to ignite the man returned and quickly took it away from the wall.

The next afternoon another ball came flying over the wall. Burke, meanwhile, was being guarded closely by extra warders and was held in the female section of the prison, his cell being changed frequently, by orders of Pownall of the Middlesex Sessions. Another cask of powder was trundled up to the wall, covered with a piece of tarpaulin, and ignited by a second party, who quickly retreated. This one worked: a deafening explosion took place that killed 12, injured 100, and blew nearly all the clothes off Constable Moriarty, who was walking near the cask.[27] A policeman near the prison ran after the man who had allegedly lit the fuse, but was unable to catch him. Two other men and one woman were arrested on the spot. Altogether the police rounded up several conspirators involved, four of whom confessed and volunteered to become witnesses. Two of them were refused because their evidence would incriminate a useful Fenian informer in Dublin. The prime planner had been a Captain Murphy, who escaped.[28]

The destruction and loss of life caused by the Clerkenwell blast not only shocked the public, but also caused a split in the Fenian ranks. There was criticism from the more moderate Roberts American wing which assumed (wrongly) that Kelly was behind it. They felt that the Manchester and Clerkenwell affairs had only weakened the movement in the United Kingdom. Frederick Engels wrote to Marx: "The stupid affair in Clerkenwell was obviously the work of a few specialized fanatics; it is the misfortune of all conspiracies that they lead to such stupidities."[29]

The condemnation of Mayne and the police for their lack of vigilance came in from all sides, and Gathorne Hardy was indignant and embarrassed that the warning had come "from *Ireland*!" no less, even specifying the exact time and place of the blast. He wrote in his diary, "Strict enquiry is needed," and "more detection force & skill needed. . . . I must decide whether to ask for more powers." Some of the criticism that hung over the police was based on the false assumption that no precautions had been taken to guard the outside of Clerkenwell immediately after the warning from Ireland had been received. The fault lay in the failure of the police on the spot to catch the conspirators before they could do any damage.[30]

Shortly after the Clerkenwell explosion Disraeli wrote to Derby:

It is my opinion that nothing effective can be done in any way in these dangers, if we don't get rid of Mayne. I have spoken to Hardy [Home Secretary] who says he "wishes to God he would resign," but, surely, when even the safety of the State is at stake, there ought to be no false delicacy in such matters . . . I think you ought to interfere.[31]

The Under-Secretary of State Liddell supposedly said: "We told Mayne that he had made a damned fool of himself, but we weren't going to throw him over after his long public service." Mayne admitted that he had been at fault for the lax security. By that time he was seventy-one and six years beyond the mandatory retirement age for civil service.[32]

Several months later Hardy was still trying to explain in Parliament what went wrong. It came out that Mayne had interpreted the warning as meaning that the walls were to be blown "up" (from beneath) and not blown "down." Mayne accordingly instructed Inspector Gernon to watch the walls for "mining." The passing policeman thus paid little attention to the cask that was placed by the wall. This only convinced people that Mayne and his police were incompetent buffoons.[33] Lord Mayo was quick to remind Hardy that they had been well warned. He told Derby: "You will see that we gave ample notice of the Clerkenwell outrage and that it occurred exactly at the hour indicated. . . . Truly the ways of the English Police are wonderful."[34] Derby agreed and told Disraeli, the Chancellor of the Exchequer: "It is really lamentable that the peace of the metropolis, and its immunity from wilful devastation, should depend on a body of Police, who, as Detectives, are manifestly incompetent; and under a chief who, whatever may be his other merits, has not the energy, nor, apparently, the skill to find out and employ men fitted for peculiar duties." Derby even toyed briefly with the idea of asking that Habeas Corpus be suspended in England, as it was in Ireland periodically. He wanted a select committee to see if more extraordinary measures were needed.[35]

LIEUTENANT COLONEL FEILDING

The government in any case was beginning to wonder whether the London Metropolitan Police were adequate for dealing with such secret conspiracies. Derby and Disraeli were convinced that a new investigation organization had to be formed. On the day of the Clerkenwell blast, Disraeli wrote to Hardy saying that Derby had received information "which determined him to take immediate steps for establishing some organization for looking after English and especially London Fenianism." After Derby conferred with Mayo, it was agreed that "a certain person from Ireland would probably undertake the chief management of the enterprise."[36] The person in mind was Lt. Col. W.H.A. Feilding, the Senior Army Intelligence Officer in Ireland, who had been efficient in hunting down Fenians among his own troops. Feilding was to marshal a temporary secret service organization in London, assisted by Captain Whelan of the 8th Regiment, and by a barrister, Robert Anderson. Their expenses would be met from Secret Service funds. Feilding was reluctant to take a secret post, which meant that he was essentially a spy. This was not consistent with his being an officer and a gentleman, so he was "seconded" to the Home Office for "special services," an official position that would also make his duties more acceptable to Mayne who would have objected to any other arrangement—not that Mayne's opinion was sought. Feilding's reports would go to Liddell at the Home Office, not to Mayne. Disraeli was impressed with Feilding at their first meeting and felt that he was the right man to strengthen the intelligence arm of the government (where the police were weak) and to protect the public better, against the "system of organized incendiarism afloat." And how would Mayne react when he realized the scope of Feilding's duties? *"Let him resign,"* if he does not like it, said Disraeli, emphasizing the words. Hardy approved Feilding's request to have three detectives assigned to him, accountable to Feilding and not Mayne; Feilding would have nothing to do with Mayne, who he thought "would thwart everything." Hardy, however, was skeptical of finding trustworthy detectives for the job and said: "There are really no men in the force who, either from lack of honesty or intelligence, can be trusted."[37]

Feilding was to follow his own intuition in his duties to attempt to discover what, if any, links existed between the Fenians in England and the Continental revolutionaries, or with other incendiary groups in England. Derby was doubtful that such a connection existed, but was prepared to exert efforts to find out, including having an agent in Italy try to determine if the Fenians were successful in enlisting the support of Garibaldi and Mazzini. In fact, Mazzini had been approached in late 1866 or early 1867 and scarcely gave the Fenians the time of day. He felt that England was the most constitutional government in Europe and the only asylum for political refugees, and did not want to see England bothered. Derby wrote to the Queen, mentioning the new group.

Though for the most part [the police] perform their ordinary duties efficiently, they are not equal to the present extraordinary demand. They are especially deficient, however, as a detective force, which is at this time urgently required; and steps have already been taken to supply this deficiency by a separate and secret organization; and at the same time to diminish the pressure upon the regular force by an increase of their numbers.[38]

It is clear from the foregoing that the Metropolitan Police were being virtually superseded in this area by the special agents of the government. Mayne no doubt was soon aware of Feilding's duties, but was kept in the dark on many details. On 23 December Mayo wrote to Hardy saying that before three weeks were over his agents would be into the most secret Fenian councils. He told Hardy to make sure that the Metropolitan Police made no preventive arrests, and not to let the police know anything of the matter until the time for action came. Hardy also had agents in Paris making investigations, of which Mayo heartily approved. Mayo said that Hardy was "quite right not to do anything on the Continent through London Police."[39]

In one instance early in January Mayne, without Hardy's knowledge, had a young woman released who was suspected of being a Fenian messenger, and who was potentially a good source of information. Mayo was furious at letting go such a person, who might have been able to break the Clerkenwell conspiracy. On another occasion Feilding complained to Hardy that Mayne's police had arrested one of Feilding's men who was on the trail of Kelly, the leading Fenian rescued in Manchester, and who was suspected of being about to sail from Liverpool. Mayne was ordered to release the man immediately.[40]

The needs of the Metropolitan Police were not ignored, in spite of all of this. Hardy and Mayne were determined to increase police numbers including "a considerable addition" of detectives. The Home Office told Mayne to look for skilled persons for the detection of crime and also for "special and delicate services, which may be entrusted to them in other places." These men could be temporarily employed as Mayne saw fit. Hardy wanted a report of how his recruiting fared. At the same time Hardy called for a confidential report on the management of the police, which was not to be made public. He even refused Harvey Lewis' request in Parliament to see the report.[41]

It was becoming evident to Feilding and his employers that the Clerkenwell explosion was not part of a major conspiracy, but had been planned by Burke himself and several London associates, whose ill-conceived attempt and the resulting bloodshed only split the Fenian ranks further. Feilding's group was disbanded in April 1868 in the light of this knowledge.

LONDON, 1867: PREPARATIONS FOR DISORDER

Meanwhile, the alarm of December and January had caused a great deal of official anxiety, enhanced by the usual flood of warnings, crank letters, and practical jokes with firecrackers. The Home Office warned the railroads that there might be attempts to cut the telegraph wires and destroy the rails, and so isolate London. Mayne was also apprehensive that a major attack would occur in the country and warned the Chief Constable of Kent, and probably others, to watch pubs and lodging houses and the railroads for "suspicious persons arriving."[42]

The City of London Police were eager to be connected by telegraph to Scotland Yard so that a civil or military force could be hastily summoned into the City in case of disturbance. The City Commissioner also wanted Hardy's permission to issue forty-two revolvers, similar to the ones he heard had been issued to the Metropolitan Police. Truncheons, he said, were simply not adequate for a real threat. Hardy reluctantly agreed to the issuance of pistols to be kept in certain City police stations for emergencies only.

The police orders of 28 January 1868 described various types of explosives and how to extinguish "Greek fire." Suspicious packages thought to contain explosives were to be taken to a police station "as quietly as possible." Derby believed that "incendiary fires" appeared to be "the form of outbreak most to be apprehended." The Home Office allocated £70 to be spent to make the ground floor windows and doors of Scotland Yard bulletproof.[43] In case of an outbreak Mayne or either of the two Assistant Commissioners could requisition troops if needed. In such case Mayne would stay in Scotland Yard, Harris at the King's Cross police station, and Labalmondiere at either the Vine Street police station or Southwark, "if the disturbance be in that quarter." Mayne had a telegraph to each police station by this time.[44]

Security for Queen Victoria at Osborne, on the Isle of Wight, was improved by the presence of troops and 18 London policemen. "The Queen," she wrote, "does *not* consider Windsor *at all safe*. And to London *nothing* will make her go, *till* the present state of affairs is *altered*. Such precautions are taken here that the Queen will be little better than a *State* prisoner." By 11 January she was confident enough of her own protection at Osborne to have the numbers of

Scots Fusilier Guards reduced to 100. As the weeks passed she also began to chafe at the extra protection and ridiculed Derby for it.[45]

In London special constables were also enlisted as an emergency force if needed, and were organized by Lt. Col. R.E. Ewart of the Royal Engineers. The Home Office issued a circular to the London parishes calling on "well-disposed persons." "As it is possible that owing to the designs of wicked and evil-disposed persons the ordinary police force of the Metropolis may, at the present time, be found insufficient in numbers to perform the duties required of them; therefore [special constables must be sworn in] . . . for the preservation of the peace and in affording protection to life and property."[46] Magistrates were to swear in the special constables who would then elect officers from their numbers to receive specific orders and directions from the police superintendents. The men were organized in the police divisions with a particular police station as their assembly point, in case an alarm should be raised. As in 1848, no uniforms were to be worn except for arm bands or patches; the men would carry staffs or truncheons when on duty, and if possible a police lantern on their belts. They were supposed to learn rudimentary military drill, and when patrolling, to walk in pairs, preferably near other patrols. They had the authority to interfere immediately in apprehending the instigators of riots or breaches of the peace, and could make arrests. By law, special constables were commissioned to act in the metropolis for two months, or in the counties for three. Their expenses could be reimbursed by magistrates.

The responses from the volunteers were certainly more enthusiastic than the preceding summer, and the numbers of special constables in London alone grew from 46,201 on 14 January 1868 to 53,113 on 7 February. For all of Britain, including London, the total number of special constables was 113,674 on 7 February. At Woolwich Arsenal alone, 5,000 were sworn in, 3,000 of them being available for protection of private property in adjacent parishes.[47]

In preparing for the worst (which did not come) the authorities ordered that devices for firing chemical lights be installed by the Engineers on public buildings, and other structures in central London, such as the Duke of York Column, the Nelson Monument, the Big Ben Tower, and Buckingham Palace. The devices would provide emergency lighting in case the gas supplies were cut off. Later it was decided to use Ladd's portable (battery-powered) electric lights. Police and army sappers inspected the sewers regularly and fastened the covers securely.[48]

Gathorne Hardy was being urged by the Queen to step up anti-Fenian activity. She suggested that Parliament should be called to pass new laws and to suspend Habeas Corpus for three months. "What is the use of trying to stop these outrages without strong measures to enable us to punish these horrible people? And is it right to wait till *fresh* outrages take place & more innocent lives are sacrificed *before* we resort to such measures.'' Her fury reached a peak in May when she heard that there was only enough evidence to condemn one Clerkenwell ''criminal,'' Michael Barrett, who had the dubious honor of being the last man publicly executed in England. She said the Fenians should be ''lynch-lawed'' on the spot ''as that would deter them far more than trials which continually break down.''[49] The Queen was not alone in thinking that if the conviction of one man was the best the police could bring about, they were woefully lacking. Derby himself was not sure that he could hold out against repression. Since public confidence was down he feared a new burst of anti-Catholicism against the Irish in England.[50]

THE FEARS SUBSIDE

In spite of official preparations for disorder, few believed that a concerted uprising would occur in England. The *Saturday Review* played down the threat and said that special constables could best be used to guard prisoners during trials. The magazine also wrote that few of the Fenian schemes and threats were to be taken seriously. Two weeks after the Clerkenwell explosion, Disraeli, after reading a report on the Fenians, commented to Hardy that they did not appear especially formidable, ''tho' they could do a lot of mischief.''[51]

The London explosion caused far more indignation than terror, but for a brief time, recalled Sir Robert Anderson, the Metropolis was ''thrown into a state of panic.'' Anderson noted that some private secretaries at Whitehall carried pistols. Of other actual Fenian mischief in England, there was almost nothing. In Newcastle, on 17 December, three men were killed by an explosion of nitroglycerin, which was at first suspected as an Irish deed; however, an enquiry determined that the blast was an accident. Certainly, within a short time fears had subsided, though in March 1868, there was an attempt on the life of the Duke of Edinburgh in Australia by an avowed Fenian. In April two Fenians were arrested near Buckingham Palace with combustible materials on them. These incidents served to remind Englishmen that there were Fenians and that they could be dangerous.[52]

While preparations against disorder were being made, Fenianism as a serious threat had slipped away almost unnoticed, if indeed it had ever been a serious threat in the 1860s. Hopelessly riddled with dissension and sapped by penury and ill-spent funds, the Fenians could do little to further the avowed aim of creating an uprising to free Ireland, especially in the face of a hostile British public. The publicity generated was not without effect, for it quickened the determination of Butt and Gladstone to do something to pacify Ireland. To the extremists, disestablishment of the Irish (Protestant) Church and land reforms were simply temporary palliatives that would only delay the establishment of an Irish-run Ireland. It would not be long before British politicians would reluctantly be forced to conclude the same. For a time the dust of Clerkenwell would be allowed to settle, and men were beginning to agree with Mr. Ayrton who spoke in Parliament in June 1868 about "a dozen drunken tailors" trying to liberate Ireland. "All London was alarmed at the doings of these drunken tailors, and the Home Secretary swore in 25,000 [53,000 in reality] special constables to protect the metropolis against them."[53]

JUDGING THE POLICE

For the police the Fenian scares made it obvious that the detective force of 15 men was inadequate to cope with the widespread investigative work called for in dealing with secret plots. The lack of adequate liaison with European police departments—admittedly a political matter, and not exclusively a police failing—hampered the international investigations that were necessary.

There was a lack of communication with and sympathy for the London Irish community by the Metropolitan Police, which put the police at a disadvantage for information. The police had been embarrassed in 1865 when officers from Dublin and Liverpool seized a leading Fenian in Islington and got his stock of *Irish People*. Irish informers were plentiful and could have been more assiduously cultivated, as could the Irish priests, who were the natural community leaders and usually took the side of law and order, especially after the vehement denunciations of Fenian violence by the Catholic Church leaders. Assigning Irish policemen to Irish areas, a reversal of Mayne's usual policy, might have helped the Metropolitan Police build stronger ties with these areas of London.

Whatever failings the Fenians revealed, we cannot ignore the fact of simple human error on the part of the police in such things as the release of suspects or the misinterpretation of warnings. There were mistakes made in many of the episodes described in this book, but no alteration in police organization or personnel could insure against them. Changing the Commissioner was no guarantee either.

Although respected, the remote and somewhat austere Richard Mayne was never really popular with the public. The Clerkenwell blast, especially, brought criticism and questions about his competence to serve. It was widely expected that the seventy-one-year-old Commissioner would either resign or be fired, but Mayne obliged his critics by dying in December 1868. His successor, Edmund Henderson, increased the detectives to 33 and established the divisional detectives. He also altered police organization somewhat to allow for greater decentralization of power.

Mayne's unquestioned integrity and rigid control of the police may have served the police well in gaining public confidence that the institution was truly accountable, but his qualities had the drawback of inhibiting fresh perspectives. In a sense Mayne's own conservatism in wanting to preserve much of the preventive side of policing was due to the struggles he and Rowan had to have the police accepted in the early days. Even though the struggles had been largely won, Mayne's attitude did not change much.

The shortcomings that the police had under Rowan and Mayne were overshadowed by the enlightened vision of the two Commissioners, implanted in the public mind, that it was possible to maintain order by use of an essentially unarmed police, acting without the authoritarian demeanor or paramilitary trappings of police forces in other countries. Most Victorians, if given a choice, would still have regarded inefficiency as a small price to pay to maintain what they saw as their liberties.

NOTES

1. Great Britain. Suffolk Record Office, Ipswich. Cranbrook (Gathorne Hardy) MSS, T501/260 (17 Feb. 1867), *Diary*. Broadlands MSS, GC/GR 2578/3 (12 Sept. 1865), Wodehouse to Grey.

2. Ó Broin, *Fenian Fever*, p. 1. Lawrence J. McCaffrey, *The Irish Question: 1800-1922* (Lexington: University of Kentucky Press, 1968), pp. 82-83. Sir Robert Anderson, *Sidelights on the Home Rule Movement* (London: John Murray, 1906), p. 63.

3. Ó Broin, *Fenian Fever*, p. 2.

4. Oxford University, Bodleian Library, Clarendon Deposit C99/88 (8 April 1866), Wodehouse to Clarendon.

5. MEPOL 1/47 (6 Dec. 1866), Mayne to British Consul, Le Havre.

6. Ibid. (19 July 1867), Mayne to Naas. Broadlands MSS, GC/GR/2579.

7. H.O. 45/7799/93 (28 Feb. 1866), Lt. Gov. of Jersey to Waddington. Ibid., 65/8 (2 April 1868). MEPOL 7/30 (7 Nov. 1868).

8. H.O. 45/7799/120 (15 Sept. 1866), Williamson's rpt.

9. MEPOL 1/47 (Aug. & 24 Sept. 1866), Mayne to Greig. H.O. 45/7799/118 (12 Sept. 1866). Desmond Ryan, *The Phoenix Flame* (London: Arthur Barker, Ltd., 1937), p. 144.

10. Browne, *Rise of Scotland Yard*, p. 141. H.O. 45/7799/935-36, 938 (8 April 1867), Ryan to Naas. Ó Broin, *Fenian Fever*, p. 124. Anderson, *Sidelights*, p. 64.

11. *Blackwoods Edinburgh Magazine* (March 1867), p. 381.

12. Howell Collection, Reform League Papers, Nos. 66, 68, 70; speech by Odger (n.d., 1867); General Council statement (18 Nov., 19 Dec. 1867). Ó Broin, *Fenian*

Fever, p. 125. Norman McCord, "The Fenians and Public Opinion in Great Britain," in *Fenians and Fenianism*, ed. by Maurice Harmon (Seattle: University of Washington Press, 1970), p. 52.

13. Ó Broin, *Fenian Fever,* pp. 195-97.

14. Dublin. National Library of Ireland. Mayo MSS 11189 (11), Mayo to Hardy, 19 Sept. 1867. H.O. 45/7799/221 (19 Sept. 1867), Mayo to Hardy. Cranbrook MSS, T501/270 (7 Oct. 1867), Ferguson to Hardy.

15. Quoted in Ó Broin, *Fenian Fever,* p. 196.

16. Mayo MSS 11189 (11), Entwissell's Rpt., 25 Sept. 1867. Ibid., Hardy to Mayo, 30 Sept. 1867.

17. H.O. 45/7799/221 (19 Sept. 1867), Ferguson to Hardy. MEPOL 1/47 (11 Oct. 1867), Mayne to Capt. Palin.

18. H.O. 45/7799/226 (28 Sept. 1867). Cranbrook MSS, T501/260 (1 Oct. 1867), *Diary*.

19. Queen's College, Oxford (Lord Blake), Derby MSS 164/6 (14 Oct. 1867), Hardy to Derby. H.O. 45/7799/225 (14 Oct. 1867). MEPOL 1/47 (14 Oct. 1867), Mayne to Chief Constable, Aberdeenshire.

20. H.O. 65/8 (2, 7 Nov. 1867).

21. *The Times* (London), 20 Nov. 1867. Cranbrook MSS, T501/260 (18 Nov. 1867), *Diary*. Malmesbury, *Memoirs*, II, 374-75.

22. Cranbrook MSS, T501/265 (23 Nov. 1867). *The Times* (London), 22, 25 Nov. 1867. MEPOL 7/29 (21, 23, 24 Nov. 1867). MEPOL 7/30 (21, 29 Nov. 1868).

23. Cranbrook MSS, T501/260 (29 Nov. 1867), *Diary*.

24. John Devoy, *Recollections of an Irish Rebel* (London: Irish University Press, reprint, 1969), p. 248.

25. Ireland. Dublin Castle. Irish State Paper Office. Chief Secretary's Office, Registered Papers, 21787, Ryan's rpt. (11 Dec. 1867). According to Anderson, *Sidelights*, p. 78, even non-Fenians had foreknowledge of the Clerkenwell plot.

26. *Hansard*, Vol. 190 (9 March 1868), cols. 1215-17. H.O. 65/8 (11 March 1868), Ferguson to Mayne. Browne, *Rise of Scotland Yard*, p. 141. Browne is incorrect in saying that no extra precautions were taken on 12 December, the day the blast was first expected.

27. *Hansard*, Vol. 190 (9 March 1868), cols. 1215-16. Dublin Castle, Chief Secretary's Office, Registered Papers, 1867/21787 (13 Dec. 1867).

28. Ó Broin, *Fenian Fever*, p. 211. *Annual Register*, Chronicle (December 1867), p. 174.

29. Ó Broin, *Fenian Fever*, p. 211. *Karl Marx and Frederick Engels on Ireland* (London: Lawrence & Wishart, 1971), p. 141.

30. Cranbrook MSS, T501/260 (15 Dec. 1867).

31. Queen's College, Oxford (Lord Blake), Derby MSS 146/3, Disraeli to Derby (16 Dec. 1867).

32. Margaret W. Prothero, *History of the Criminal Investigation Department at Scotland Yard from Earliest Times Until To-Day* (London: Herbert Jenkins, 1931), p. 72. Browne, *Rise of Scotland Yard*, p. 143.

33. *Hansard*, Vol. 190 (9 March 1868), col. 1216.

34. Quoted in Ó Broin, *Fenian Fever*, pp. 211-12. Cranbrook MSS, T501/270 (19 Dec. 1867), Mayo to Hardy.

35. Ó Broin, *Fenian Fever*, p. 216.

36. Cranbrook MSS, T501/266 (13 Dec. 1867), Disraeli to Hardy.

37. Derby MSS 164/6 (n.d.), Hardy to Derby. Ó Broin, *Fenian Fever*, pp. 79, 213-15. Derby MSS 146/3 (16 Dec. 1867), Disraeli to Derby.

38. Cranbrook MSS, T501/270 (n.d.), letter to Feilding. *Letters of Queen Victoria*, 2d ser., I, 479, Derby to Queen (19 Dec. 1867).

39. Cranbrook MSS, T501/270 (23 Dec. 1867), Mayo to Hardy. Ibid. (25 Dec. 1867).

40. Ibid. (5 Jan. 1868). Ibid., T501/260 (18 Jan. 1868), Feilding to Hardy.

41. H.O. 65/8 (26 Dec. 1867), Ferguson to Mayne. *Hansard*, Vol. 192 (8 June 1868), col. 1222.

42. H.O. 45/7799/307 (23 Dec. 1867), H.O. to railway companies. MEPOL 1/47 (14 Dec. 1867), Mayne to Buxton.

43. H.O. 45/7799 (n.d.), City Commissioner to Hardy. MEPOL 8/3 (28 Jan. 1868). *Letters of Queen Victoria*, 2d ser., I, 479, Derby to Queen (19 Dec. 1867).

44. MEPOL 1/47 (30 Dec. 1867), Mayne to Lindsay. H.O. 65/8 (22 Jan. 1868), H.O. to Police Receiver.

45. *Letters of Queen Victoria*, 2d ser., I, 484, Queen to Derby (20 Dec. 1867). Cranbrook MSS, T501/211 (11 Jan. 1868), Ponsonby to Hardy.

46. H.O. 45/7799/299 (16 Dec. 1867), Circular.

47. Ibid., 7799/349 & 359.

48. Ibid., 7799/320, 321, 328 (Dec. 1867).

49. Cranbrook MSS, T501/265 (19 Dec. 1867, 1 May 1868).

50. Ó Broin, *Fenian Fever*, p. 216.

51. *Saturday Review*, 11 Jan. 1868, pp. 45, 38. Cranbrook MSS, T501/226 (26, 27 Dec. 1867), Disraeli to Hardy.

52. Joseph Irving, *Annals of Our Time, 1837-1871*, pp. 800, 820. Anderson, *Sidelights*, pp. 277-78.

53. *Hansard*, Vol. 193 (29 June 1868), col. 346.

10 Conclusion: The Police and Society

With the temporary cessation of the Fenian threat and the death of Sir Richard Mayne in 1868 the mid-Victorian period symbolically came to an end for the police. London was to have a respite from large-scale crowd disorder until 1886, though the intervening years were to see numerous small park meetings. As we have seen, the police organization in the 1850s and 1860s underwent no drastic changes, but, rather, evolved steadily along the lines set in the earliest days of the force. The constable of the 1830s could easily fill the role of the constable of the 1880s.

THE POLICE RECONSIDERED

Perhaps it was to their credit that the British subordinated police efficiency to constitutional and political considerations. The Victorian bobby may have been portrayed frequently as a figure for ridicule but almost never as a figure of terror. One might even be tempted to hazard the perverse observation that the police enjoyed an extra measure of support because they were not always very good at what they did. A certain inefficiency could be reassuring that the police were not a threat to liberty.

The non-military, watchman role of the Metropolitan Police was stamped on the force by Rowan and Mayne, who guided the organization in its first forty years. Presiding over an agency composed mainly of young men from rural areas, the Commissioners maintained a tight discipline. Training of the constables was brief, but was generally sufficient for the duties of the constables, which more often required a strong arm, courage, and common sense.

Much of the police effectiveness lay in the growing confidence the public had in them. The police structure and prevailing philosophy was that it was an organization wielding impersonal authority, and free from the trammels of partisan politics and local control. Police discretionary powers were carefully circumscribed by regulations as well.

The confidence in the police held by the propertied public was enhanced by the obvious usefulness of the constables in heading off mob disorders, as was apparent in the 1830s and 1840s, and again in the successful crowd control at the Great Exhibition in 1851. Nevertheless, by mid-century, if the police were perceived by many Londoners as successful, such a judgment was more likely based on police effectiveness in dealing with day to day crime, keeping the streets orderly, and exercising a variety of service functions, rather than on dramatic confrontations with crowds.

The crowd control ability of the police was developed by trial and error. The unarmed police quickly learned the necessity of exercising restraint and avoiding provocation of crowds, and they also learned the importance of coordination and timing in dispersing a crowd at the optimum moment before violence got out of hand.

As we have seen, specific incidents such as the riots in Hyde Park in 1855 brought some discredit upon police behavior and police leadership. The Garibaldi Riots and the Reform Bill demonstrations were frustrating and difficult for the police because of the legal ambiguity over park use. The constables were thrust into a situation over which they had limited control. The difficulties were created by inadequate laws and by the vacillation and confusion of the government over its policies. The problem was one of law, not of enforcement. The police were simply as effective as the laws allowed them to be.

Since the Metropolitan Police was conceived as a preventive "high profile" organization, the Detective Department was created with some reluctance by the Commissioners, who were aware of the traditional English aversion to spying or other "Continental" police practices. As we have seen, the small group of detectives proved to be inefficient in rooting out Irish Fenians, although we would have to see their surveillance and evaluation of aliens in the 1850s as reasonably effective, thanks especially to Sgt. John Sanders whose perceptive reports contributed to a more level-headed response to the aliens by the police and the government. Intelligence gathering was, nonetheless, a weak aspect of the police, but this is understandable when we recall that detection in the nineteenth century was rudimentary at best and depended heavily on the personal qualities of the men assigned to such duties. An increase in the number of detectives would not necessarily have guaranteed quality. Calling for specialized skills and getting them are often two different things.

We have looked in detail at the police and have been able to examine both their successes and failures, and it now remains to try to put the police in a larger framework. We could ask the question of just how effective police deterrence was, but more important, whether one could separate the police from the myriad of urban improvements that made the metropolis more livable.

If indeed we accept the view that London became a more orderly and less crime-ridden place, as did other cities, why was this so? Why was there a kind of "equipoise" in the mid-Victorian years with which this book is most concerned? To attempt some explanation, we shall cast a net over a wider society, under the assumption that the processes affecting London were evident to a greater or lesser degree in other parts of England. We must consider a number of factors that have contributed, but none of which can be said to be singularly decisive.

First, one could identify the mid-Victorian "equipoise" as characterizing a society that has "matured," in which the social classes put aside their conflict and accepted institutionalized roles. The progress from conflict to consensus was a kind of natural development that brought with it a drop in crime.

The problem with the consensus idea is simply that the absence of overt conflict does not necessarily signify a real consensus. It may reflect some kind of operational consensus—that is, a stand-off—not a harmony of interests that would denote a true consensus. Brute repression alone in a society can mask conflicts, and it would be a mistake to see an authoritarian government as having effected some true accommodation among the competing social and economic groups within it. A close look at any society would reveal conflicts. "Even liberal society may, if we shift our perspectives a little, be regarded as normally disintegrative in its tendencies, riddled with conflict and tension as its unavoidable condition."[1] Victorian society, as this book has shown, was laced with tensions.

SOCIAL CONTROL

Another explanation to account for mid-Victorian stability and for the taming of Victorian cities over a longer spell is the approach that sees social control as the key. The term has been used with varying degrees of clarity by a number of social historians in the past few years, and is generally employed to denote the imposition of behavior and beliefs by one class upon another. This implies a belief that an orderly society is the result of many social processes and institutions that regulate work and leisure habits, religion, and education in an effort to infuse the mores of a higher class—mainly the middle class—into the working classes. Agencies of overt coercion such as the law, the police, and prisons would be excluded as forms of social control unless it is argued that all attempts to maintain law and order are a form of social control, in which case the concept becomes so diffused as to be of little use to historians.[2]

In interpreting social control, if a crude reductionism is applied, all things like public health, leisure, social work, schools, etc., are seen as if the social control element were their central aim; that the humanitarian, the clergyman, the social worker, and the educator are but policemen "without boots" to use A.P. Donajgrodzki's phrase. Such an approach would assume an acceptance by both the governors and the governed of their respective roles. This puts the working classes on the receiving end of dictates from a remote state and from bourgeois schemers who wish to define law and order to their own self-interest, and to make their world safe for capitalism.

As F.M.L. Thompson points out, it is unwarrantably condescending to the humble masses of the nineteenth century to assume that they were not capable of any self-improvement or cultural development unless the impetus came from outside. The working classes often had minds of their own. There is plenty of evidence that they generated their own values and attitudes, and were able to shape to their own liking much of their schooling, their leisure activities, and their public and private behavior, as a way of coping with life in an industrial society. The working classes may well have wished to be respectable because it suited them, not because some middle-class reformers told them to.

Much of what is seen as social control is control imposed from within a class, not from outside, and might more properly be referred to as socialization, wherein people learn to adapt to a group of which they become a part, by behaving in acceptable ways and by assuming the attitudes of that larger group. Emulation, that is to say, keeping up with the Joneses, also plays an important part in this process. Viewing social control through teleological lenses clouds our understanding of the subtleties of the real social processes at work, which more often than not operate independently of some conscious control process. Social controls did play some role, but they were not necessarily overt or even intentional.[3]

Even if one chooses to see the police as part of social control, it is difficult to portray their function as an interfering one that automatically served bourgeois interests, if this meant forcing unwelcome restrictions on working-class life or intervening in leisure activities, just because some slight disorder might occur. As we have seen, the police interest in keeping order often meant avoiding provocation. This does not mean, of course, that the police did not bring great pressure to bear on popular amusements like prizefighting, footracing in the streets, or even kite flying, things that were not in themselves illegal. Vague statutes often gave the police considerable latitude in deciding what was a public nuisance or a disorder.

In general their attitude was to enforce statutes, but not to become professional busybodies. The police were in the business of keeping order: they had no wish to erode support for themselves by antagonizing any section of the public unless absolutely necessary. Richard Mayne's opposition to sabbatarian legislation in 1855 was well founded, in light of what happened in Hyde Park in that year.

The police confidence that public gatherings could be kept orderly (even fairs, the bane of hardcore moralists) was shared to a great extent by the propertied public, and this posture worked against moves to suppress such gatherings after the 1840s. Here we can see the police fostering a relaxation and liberalization of attitudes.

In looking for explanations for mid-Victorian stability, some labor historians have pointed to the embourgeoisement of the working classes and especially to the alleged absorption by the skilled workers—the "labor aristocrats"—of middle-class values. By embracing the tenets of self-help and individualism, and by gaining some degree of prosperity, these men came to identify themselves more with the rulers than with the working classes of which they were a part. This allegedly broke the collectivity of the working classes which in the two decades before 1850 had put the Victorian rulers on the defensive.

ACCEPTING THE RULE OF LAW

While there is undoubtedly merit in the ideas of consensus, social control, and the fragmentation of the working classes in the mid-Victorian period, we must find other explanations for the relative stability of Victorian England, and for the diminution of violence. The reasons probably lie in the growing acceptance of the rule of law and in material improvements. To an extraordinary degree even the working classes by the middle of the century accepted the legitimacy of the legal system and were willing participants in it in defense of their own property.

This, of course, was not carved in stone: it depended on forbearance and flexibility on both sides. Since the government drew its mandate from a broader public in the mid-Victorian years, it was less willing to risk naked confrontations with the people and was more apt to be accommodating to competing interests. There was a delicate balance, but the rulers and the ruled realized that their interests were better served if they sought justice in the law rather than in provoking political turmoil. Even foreign observers frequently commented on the orderly constitutional nature of English political activity, and the English habit of litigiousness.[4]

One must be careful not to exaggerate the orderliness of English society, since many working communities had been deeply alienated from the police and law. In London, just as the middle and upper classes were won over to acceptance of the London police, so too did the working classes show some grudging support for the police by the early 1870s.[5] The public had been educated in this attitude by the fact that with the cheapening of the costs of litigation, the procedures of law and order were available to the poor who were now more ready to bring charges. At the same time the police and the courts were becoming more efficient and were making inroads into the world of crime. People were more inclined to see the justice system in a friendlier light and were more willing to report crimes, to prosecute, and to give evidence.

This increasing cooperation with the law also meant that recorded crime mounted steadily until about 1840, giving some alarmed contemporaries the anxiety that crime itself was climbing, when in fact it was not. The increase in reporting of crimes meant that the figures of known crimes climbed closer to the number of crimes actually committed—the "dark figure." With the diminution in recorded serious crime after 1840, one could surmise that the police were either not catching criminals or that people were not reporting crime, but the indications, as we have seen in the introduction, point to the opposite, a real drop in serious crimes. The police were beginning to pay off.[6]

The criminal world itself was peculiarly vulnerable to the actions of the police in a way that it had not been before and perhaps never will be again. The Victorian criminal was rarely very sophisticated, and when a crime was committed it was not too hard to find the offender. This was due not so much to the effectiveness of the police—indeed, parts of this book belabor police inadequacies—but to the relative defenselessness and weakness of the criminal world. Much of criminality simply had not changed for centuries, and even in London the underworld elements who could be thought of as professional were not particularly sophisticated. The criminal rookeries of London, each with its specialties, its hierarchies, its territories, had developed since the Middle Ages without being bothered by the state or by the dominant values of the propertied classes. They were very much part of popular culture, but still a world apart from the rulers of society. Just as the poor were segregated in certain areas, crime was largely hidden from the eyes of the respectable and was not considered a serious threat to the social order until the 1820s and 1830s. Before that it was felt that the forces of order were sufficient to meet a threat.

In the early Victorian period the camouflage began to disappear as the policeman, the reformer, the railroad, and city renewal, began to pierce and destroy the criminal rookeries and opened them to the assaults of outside control. The rookeries became obsolete and nothing took their place.

Since the mid-Victorian police had almost no scientific aids, the policeman was expected to match his native intelligence against the evasion of the criminal, and this was often sufficient. In Gatrell's words, those who "broke the law were not well defended against those who sought to bring them to justice." This of course would shift in our century. Even when the available technology improved, the criminals simply did not adapt until after World War I when mass education and much greater mobility made them potent adversaries for the police.[7]

Even with all the police deficiencies noted, the police and the law were indeed effective, when we consider the relative vulnerability of the lawbreakers, and also when we appreciate the growing acceptance of the rule of law throughout English society. The mid-Victorians were also favored by an improving economic climate, relatively free from the unfortunate combination of economic depression, high food prices, and unemployment that had created tensions in the 1830s and 1840s, and which would appear again in the twentieth century, along with an increase in crime.

Stepped-up police vigilance can reduce criminal behavior when there exists an improving socioeconomic system, but policing alone cannot counter the destructive effects of social fragmentation or serious economic dislocations. We must see the success of the mid-Victorian London police as partly due to some organizational skill, resourcefulness, and restraint, but also to improving living conditions in London and to the availability of more consumer goods and services; to the absorption of potentially riotous and criminal elements into the full-time labor market; to education for children; to the movements towards universal suffrage; to temperance and to the moralizing messages of reformers. Also we must consider other factors such as civic improvements and public health measures. The poor law procedures had a profound effect on working-class attitudes and were a powerful incentive to maintain respectability and avoid the stigma of the workhouse.

If the poor behaved better at the end of the nineteenth century than at the beginning, as contemporaries believed, we must be reminded again that the urban industrial age brought with it a battery of disciplines. Factory work, or at least work in large organizations like the railroads, put a premium on discipline, punctuality, sobriety, and regularity. Also many employers were able to influence their workers through the services they provided outside the workplace, such as factory villages, workers' outings, chapels, schools, clubs, and organized sports.[8]

Englishmen, then, were accommodating themselves to the prevailing social order, to the rule of law, and to the necessary restraints an industrial world thrust upon them. The police did help reduce disorder, but their actions were only part of the demand—created by a new economic order—for a more disciplined and orderly society.

If the nineteenth century saw changes in the quality of urban life, so much has been altered since then that the London of Queen Victoria seems very remote to us today. It can only be recaptured in photographs and in the recollections of those whose memories stretch back before the turn of the century. The writer Leonard Woolf was impressed by the improvements he observed. Writing in 1960 he gave the following description, which might well serve as a fitting conclusion to this work:

I am struck by the immense change from social barbarism to social civilization which has taken place in London (indeed in Great Britain) during my lifetime. . . . The slums and their unfortunate and terrifying products no longer exist. No one but an old Londoner who has been born and bred and has lived for fifty or sixty years in London can have any idea of the extent of the change. It is amazing to walk down Drury Lane or the small streets about Seven Dials today and recall their condition only fifty years ago. Even as late as 1900 it would not have been safe to walk in any of those streets after dark. The whole locality was an appalling slum, and its inhabitants, like those of the innumerable slums scattered over London, were the *animaux farouches.*[9]

NOTES

1. Gatrell, "The Decline of Theft and Violence," p. 254.
2. F.M.L. Thompson, "Social Control in Victorian Britain," *The Economic History Review*, XXXIV, No. 2 (May 1981), 197.
3. In the introduction to his book, Donajgrodzki elaborates on these and other misconceptions of social control. Donajgrodzki, *Social Control*, pp. 9, 11, 15. Some of the same points are made by Gatrell, "The Decline of Theft and Violence," p. 256. See also Thompson's highly perceptive analysis in "Social Control," pp. 189-90; 195-96.
4. Philips, *Crime and Authority*, pp. 285-86.
5. Miller, *Cops and Bobbies*, pp. 138-39.
6. J.M. Hart, "Reform of the Borough Police, 1835-1856," *English Historical Review*, LXX (July 1955), 414. Gatrell, "Decline of Theft and Violence," pp. 244, 249-54.
7. Gatrell, "Decline of Theft and Violence," p. 258.
8. Thompson, "Social Control," pp. 195-96.
9. Leonard Woolf, *Sowing: An Autobiography of the Years 1880 to 1904* (New York: Harcourt, Brace & Co., 1960), pp. 63-64.

Bibliography

MANUSCRIPT SOURCES AND LIBRARIES USED

Great Britain and Ireland

British Library (British Museum) and British Library Newspaper Collection, Colindale, London.
Borough of Camden Libraries, London.
Cambridge University Library.
Chadwick MSS, University College, University of London.
Clarendon Collection and other sources, Bodleian Libraries, Oxford University.
Cranbrook (Gathorne Hardy) MSS. Suffolk Record Office, Ipswich.
Derby MSS, in the keeping of Lord Blake, Queens College, Oxford.
Disraeli Papers, London School of Economics and Political Science.
Guildhall Record Office, London: Minutes of the Proceedings of the Court of Common Council and Police Committee Minutes.
Howell Collection, Reform League Papers. Bishopsgate Institute, London.
Irish State Paper Office, Dublin Castle: Chief Secretary's Office, Registered Papers.
Mayo MSS. National Library of Ireland, Dublin.
Metropolitan Police Records (MEPOL), Home Office (H.O.), Foreign Office (F.O.), and other MSS. Public Record Office, Kew, Surrey.
Police Staff College (Police College), Bramshill House, Hampshire.
Palmerston and Spencer Walpole MSS. British Museum, London.
Palmerston, Broadlands MSS. Royal Commission of Historical Manuscripts and National Register of Archives, London.
Sessional Papers, House of Lords. Department of Trade and Industry Library, London.
University of London Libraries.

The United States

Boston Public Library.
Bryn Mawr College Library.

Columbia University Libraries.
Harvard University Libraries.
Haverford College Library.
John Jay College of Criminal Justice Library.
New York Public Library.
Pennsylvania State University Library.
Saint Joseph's University Library.
University of Pennsylvania Library.
University of Texas (Austin) Library.

SELECT COMMITTEES AND ROYAL COMMISSIONS CITED

Great Britain. Parliament. Parliamentary Papers.

1816 (510), V, *Report on the State of the Police of the Metropolis.*
1817 (233), VII, Reports on police and licensing.
1817 (484), VII, Reports on rewards, convictions and prisons.
1818 (423), VIII, *Police of the Metropolis.*
1822 (440), IV, *Police of the Metropolis.*
1828 (533), VI, *Police of the Metropolis.*
1833 (627), XIII, *Report From the Select Committee on the Petition of Frederick Young and Others* (Popay incident).
1833 (675), XIII, *Select Committee on the Metropolitan Police.*
1833 (718), XIII, *Select Committee on Cold Bath Fields Meeting.*
1834 (600), XVI, *Select Committee on the Police of the Metropolis.*
1837 (451), XII, *Select Committee on the Metropolis Police Offices.*
1837-1838 (578), XV, *Select Committee on the Metropolis Police Offices.*
1839 (169), XIX, *First Report of the Commissioners Appointed to Inquire as to the Best Means of Establishing an Efficient Constabulary Force in the Counties of England and Wales.*
1852-1853 (71), XXXVI, *Select Committee on Police.*
1856 (2016), XXIII, Royal Commission of 1855. *Report on the Alleged Disturbances of the Public Peace in Hyde Park on Sunday, 1 July 1855.*

BOOKS AND ARTICLES

Anderson, Sir Robert. *Sidelights on the Home Rule Movement.* London: John Murray, 1906.
Annual Register: A Review of Public Events at Home and Abroad, 1867, New Series. London: Longmans, Green, 1867.

Arnold, Matthew. *Culture and Anarchy*. Edited by R.H. Super. Ann Arbor: University of Michigan Press, 1965.

Ascoli, David. *The Queen's Peace*. North Pomfret, Vt.: David & Charles, 1980.

Bailey, Victor. "The Metropolitan Police, the Home Office and the Threat of Outcast London." *Policing and Punishment in Nineteenth Century Britain*. Edited by Victor Bailey. New Brunswick, N.J.: Rutgers University Press, 1981.

Ballantine, William. *Some Experiences of a Barrister's Life*. Vol. II. London: Richard Bentley & Son, 1882.

Beales, Derek. *England and Italy, 1859-1860*. London: Thomas Nelson & Sons, Ltd., 1961.

Best, Geoffrey. *Mid-Victorian Britain, 1851-1875*. St. Albans, Herts, U.K.: Panther Books, Ltd., 1973.

Bonner, Hypatia Bradlaugh. *Charles Bradlaugh*. Vol. I. London: T. Fisher Unwin, 1894.

Brewer, John. "An Ungovernable People? Law and Disorder in Stuart and Hanoverian England." *History Today*, XXX (Jan. 1980), 18-27.

Bright. *The Diaries of John Bright*. London: Cassell & Co., Ltd., 1930.

Broadhurst, Henry. *The Story of His Life from a Stonemason's Bench to the Treasury Bench Told by Himself*. London: Hutchinson & Co., 1901.

Brock, Peter. "Polish Democrats and English Radicals, 1832-1862: A Chapter in the History of Anglo-Polish Relations." *Journal Of Modern History*, XXV (June 1953), 139-56.

Browne, Douglas G. *The Rise of Scotland Yard: History of the Metropolitan Police*. London: Harrap & Co., 1956.

Buckle, G.E., ed. *The Letters of Queen Victoria*. 2d ser., 1862-1878. Vol. I. London: John Murray, 1926.

Burtchaell, George D., and Sadleir, Thomas Ulick, eds. *Alumni Dublinenses*. New edn. Dublin: Alexander Thom & Co., Ltd., 1935.

Calman, Alvin R. *Ledru-Rollin après 1848 et les proscrits français en Angleterre*. Paris: F. Reider & Cie., Éditeurs, 1921.

Carr, E.H. *The Romantic Exiles*. London: Penguin Books, 1968.

Cavanagh, Timothy. *Scotland Yard Past and Present*. London: Chatto & Windus, 1893.

Chadwick, Edwin. "Preventive Police." *London Review*, I, No. 1 (Feb. 1829).

Clarkson, C.T., and Richardson, J.H. *Police! History of the Metropolitan Police*. London: Field and Tuer, Leadenhall Press, 1889.

Collins, Philip. *Dickens and Crime*. 2d ed. London: Macmillan and Co., Ltd., 1965.

Critchley, Thomas Alan. *A History of Police in England and Wales, 1900-1966*. London: Constable, 1967.

"Custos." *The Police Force of the Metropolis in 1868*. London: William Ridgway, 1868.

Devoy, John. *Recollections of an Irish Rebel*. Reprint. London: Irish University Press, 1969.

Dicey, A.V. "On the Right of Public Meeting." *Contemporary Review*, LV (April 1889), 508-27.

Dickens, Charles. "The Detective Police." *The Uncommercial Traveller and Reprinted Pieces*. London: Oxford University Press, 1968.

Dilnot, George. *The Story of Scotland Yard*. Boston: Houghton Mifflin Co., 1927.

Donajgrodzki, A.P., ed. *Social Control in Nineteenth Century Britain*. London and Totowa, N.J.: Croom Helm and Rowman and Littlefield, 1977.

Duncombe, Thomas H. *The Life and Correspondence of Thomas Slingsby Duncombe*. Vol. II. London: Hurst and Blackett, Publishers, 1868.

Emsley, Clive. *Policing and Its Context, 1750-1870*. New York: Schocken Books, 1984.

Evans, Howard. *Sir Randal Cremer: His Life and Work*. London: T. Fisher Unwin, 1909.

Fay, C.R. *Palace of Industry, 1851: A Study of the Great Exhibition and its Future*. Cambridge: Cambridge University Press 1951.

Fosdick, Raymond B. *European Police Systems*. Patterson Smith Reprint Series. Montclair, N. J.: Patterson Smith [1915], 1969.

Frost, Thomas. *Forty Years' Recollections*. London: Sampson Low, Marston, Searle, and Rivington, 1880.

Fuller, Robert A. *Recollections of a Detective*. London: John Long, Ltd., 1912.

Gatrell, V.A.C. "The Decline of Theft and Violence in Victorian and Edwardian England." *Crime and Law: The Social History of Crime in Western Europe Since 1500*. Edited by V.A.C. Gatrell, B. Lenman, G. Parker. London: Europa Publications, Ltd., 1980.

Gatrell, V.A.C., and Hadden, T.B. "Criminal Statistics and their Interpretation." *Nineteenth-Century Society. Essays in the Use of Quantitative Methods for the Study of Social Data*. Edited by E.A. Wrigley. Cambridge: Cambridge University Press, 1972.

Gillespie, Frances Elma. *Labor and Politics in England*. Durham, N.C.: Duke University Press, 1927.

Gilley, Sheridan. "The Garibaldi Riots of 1862." *The Historical Journal*, XVI, No. 4 (1973), 697-732.

Goddard, Henry. *Memoirs of a Bow Street Runner*. London: Museum Press Ltd., 1956.

Gurr, T.R. "Historical Trends in Violent Crime: A Critical Review of the Evidence." *Crime and Justice, An Annual Review of Research*, Vol. III. Edited by Norval Morris and Michael Tonry. Chicago and London: University of Chicago Press, 1981.

Gurr, T.R., Grabosky, P.M., and Hula, R. *The Politics of Crime and Conflict: A Comparative Study of Four Cities*. Beverly Hills: Sage Publications, 1977.

Gurr, T.R., and Graham, Hugh D., eds. *Violence in America: Historical and Comparative Perspectives*, rev. ed. Beverly Hills: Sage Publications, 1979.

Harrison, Brian. "The Sunday Trading Riots of 1855." *The Historical Journal*, VIII, No. 2 (1965), 219-45.

Harrison, Frederic. *Order and Progress*. London: Longmans, Green, and Co., 1875.

Harrison, Royden. *Before the Socialists: Studies in Labour and Politics*. London: Routledge & Kegan Paul, 1965.

Hart, Jenifer M. *The British Police*. London: Allen & Unwin, 1951.

―――. "Reform of the Borough Police, 1835-1856." *English Historical Review*, LXX (July 1955), 411-27.

Hay, Douglas. "Crime and Justice in Eighteenth- and Nineteenth-Century England." *Crime and Justice, An Annual Review of Research*, Vol. II. Edited by Norval Morris and Michael Tonry. Chicago and London: University of Chicago Press, 1980, 45-84.

―――. "Property, Authority and the Criminal Law." *Albion's Fatal Tree: Crime and Society in Eighteenth-Century England*. Edited by Douglas Hay, Peter Linebaugh, John Rule, E.P. Thompson, and Cal Winslow. New York: Pantheon Books, 1975.

Hearder, H. "Napoleon's Threat to Break Off Diplomatic Relations with England During the Crisis Over the Orsini Attempt in 1858." *English Historical Review*, LXXI (1957), 479-81.

Hibbert, Christopher. *The Roots of Evil. A Social History of Crime and Punishment*. London: Penguin Books, Ltd., 1966.

Hobhouse, Christopher. *1851 and the Crystal Palace*. London: John Murray, 1950.

Hobsbawm, E.J. *Industry and Empire*. The Pelican Economic History of Britain. Baltimore, Md.: Penguin Books, 1969.

Holyoake, George Jacob. *Sixty Years of an Agitator's Life*. Vol. II. London: T. Fisher Unwin, 1892.

Hone, J. Ann. *For the Cause of Truth: Radicalism in London 1796-1821*. Oxford: Clarendon Press, 1982.

Howson, Gerald. *Thief-Taker General: The Rise and Fall of Jonathan Wild*. London: Hutchinson and Co., Ltd., 1970.

Humphrey, A.W. *Robert Applegarth: Trade Unionist, Educationist, Reformer*. London: National Labour Press, Ltd., n.d.

Ignatieff, Michael. *A Just Measure of Pain: The Penitentiary in the Industrial Revolution, 1750-1850*. New York: Morningside Books, Columbia University Press, 1980.

Irving, Joseph. *The Annals of Our Time, 1837-1871*. London: Macmillan and Co., 1880.

Jones, G. Stedman. *Outcast London: A Study in the Relationship Between Classes in Victorian Society*. Middlesex, U.K.: Penguin Books, Ltd., 1976.

Keller, Lisa. "Public Order in Victorian London: The Interaction Between the Metropolitan Police, the Government, the Urban Crowd, and the Law." Ph.D. diss., Cambridge University, 1976.

Lane, Roger. "Crime and the Industrial Revolution: British and American Views." *Journal of Social History*, VII (Spring, 1974), 287-303.

―――. "Urban Police and Crime in Nineteenth-Century America." *Crime and Justice, An Annual Review of Research*, Vol. II. Edited by Norval Morris and Michael Tonry. Chicago and London: University of Chicago Press, 1980, 1-43.

Lee, W.L. Melville. *A History of Police in England*. London: Methuen & Co., 1901.

Leventhal, F.M. *Respectable Radical: George Howell and Victorian Working Class Politics*. London: Weidenfeld and Nicolson, 1971.

Linton, W.J. *Memories*. London: Lawrence & Bullen, 1895.

Literary Association of the Friends of Poland. *Report of the Twenty-First, Twenty-Second, Twenty-Third, Twenty-Fourth, Twenty-Sixth, and Twenty-Seventh Annual Meetings of the Literary Association of the Friends of Poland*. London: E. Detkins, 1853, 1854, 1855, 1856, 1858, 1859.

Lyman, J.L. "The Metropolitan Police Act of 1829: An Analysis of Certain Events Influencing the Passage and Character of the Metropolitan Police Act in England." *The Journal of Criminal Law, Criminology, and Police Science*, LV, No. 1 (1964), 141-54.

McCaffrey, Lawrence J. *The Irish Question, 1800-1922*. Lexington, Kentucky: The University of Kentucky Press, 1968.

McCord, Norman. "The Fenians and Public Opinion in Great Britain." *Fenians and Fenianism*. Edited by Maurice Harmon. Seattle: University of Washington Press, 1970, 40-55.

MacDonagh, Oliver. *Early Victorian Government, 1830-1870*. London: Weidenfeld and Nicolson, 1977.

McKichan, Finlay. "Constabulary Duties: The Lives of Police Constables a Century Ago." *History Today*, XXX (Sept. 1980), 38-43.

McLellan, David. *Karl Marx, His Life and Thought*. New York: Harper and Row, Publishers, 1973.

Malmesbury, The Earl of. *Memoirs of an Ex-Minister: An Autobiography*. 2 vols. London: Longmans, Green, and Co., 1884.

Maré Eric de. *London 1851. The Year of the Great Exhibition*. The Folio Press. London: J.M. Dent, Ltd., 1973.

Marin, J.P., and Wilson, Gail. *The Police: A Study in Manpower: The Evolution of the Service in England and Wales, 1829-1965*. London: Heinemann Educational Books, Ltd., 1969.

Marx, Karl, and Engels, Frederick. *Karl Marx and Frederick Engels on Ireland*. London: Lawrence & Wishart, 1971.

————. *Marx and Engels on Britain*. Moscow: Foreign Languages Publishing House, 1953.

Mather, F.C. *Public Order in the Age of the Chartists*. Manchester: Manchester University Press, 1959.

Mayhew, Henry. *London Labour and the London Poor*. 4 vols. London: Frank Cass and Co., Ltd., reprint 1967.

Midwinter, Eric C. *Social Administration in Lancashire 1830-1860: Poor Law, Public Health and Police*. Manchester: Manchester University Press, 1969.

Miller, Wilbur. *Cops and Bobbies. Police Authority in New York and London 1830-1870*. Chicago: University of Chicago Press, 1977.

————. "Never on Sunday: Moralistic Reformers and the Police in London and New York City, 1830-1870." *Police and Society*. Edited by David Bayley. Beverly Hills, Calif.: Sage Publications, 1977, 127-48.

Moylan, Sir John. *Scotland Yard and the Metropolitan Police*. London: Putnam & Co., 1934.

Munger, Frank. "Contentious Gatherings in Lancashire, England, 1750-1830." *Class Conflict and Collective Action*. Edited by Louise Tilly and Charles Tilly. Beverly Hills, Calif.: Sage Publications, 1981.

Ó Broin, Leon. *Fenian Fever: An Anglo-American Dilemma*. London: Chatto & Windus, 1971.

Payne, Howard C. *The Police State of Louis Napoleon Bonaparte, 1851-1860*. Seattle: University of Washington Press, 1966.

Payne, Howard C., and Grosshans, Henry. "The Exiled Revolutionaries and the French Political Police in the 1850s." *American Historical Review*, LXVIII, No. 4 (1963), 954-73.

Philips, David. *Crime and Authority in Victorian England*. London: Croom Helm and Rowman and Littlefield, 1977.

————. " 'A New Engine of Power and Authority': The Institutionalization of Law-Enforcement in England, 1780-1830." *Crime and Law: The Social History of Crime in Western Europe Since 1500*. Edited by V.A.C. Gatrell, B. Lenman, and G. Parker. London: Europa Publications, 1980, 155-89.

"The Police and the Thieves." *Quarterly Review*, XCIX (June 1856), 160-200.

"The Police of London." *Quarterly Review*, CXXIX (July-Oct. 1870), 87-129.

"The Police System of London." *Edinburgh Review*, XCVI (July 1852), 1-33.

Porter, Bernard. *The Refugee Question in Mid-Victorian Politics*. Cambridge: Cambridge University Press, 1979.

Post Office London Directory. London: W. Kelly & Co., 1850.

Prothero, Margaret W. *History of the Criminal Investigation Department at Scotland Yard from Earliest Times Until To-Day*. London: Herbert Jenkins, 1931.

Pulling, Christopher R.D. *Mr. Punch and the Police*. London: Butterworths, 1964.

Radzinowicz, Sir Leon. *A History of English Criminal Law and Its Administration From 1750*. Vol. II. London: Stevens, 1956.

Reith, Charles. *The Blind Eye of History*. London: Faber and Faber, Ltd., 1952.

————. *A New Study of Police History*. London: Oliver & Boyd, 1956.

Richardson, James F. *The New York Police: Colonial Times to 1901*. New York: Oxford University Press, 1970.

Richter, Donald. *Riotous Victorians*. Athens, Ohio: Ohio University Press, 1981.

————. "The Role of Mob Riot in Victorian Elections, 1865-1885." *Victorian Studies*, XV, No. 1 (1971).

Ridley, Jasper. *Lord Palmerston*. London: Granada Publishing, Ltd., 1972.

Robinson, Howard. *The British Post Office: A History*. Princeton, N.J.: Princeton University Press, 1948.

Rudé, George. *Hanoverian London: 1714-1808*. London: Secker & Warburg, 1971.

Rumbelow, Donald. *I Spy Blue: The Police and Crime in the City of London From Elizabeth I to Victoria*. London: Macmillan, St. Martin's Press, 1971.

Ryan, Desmond. *The Phoenix Flame. A Study of Fenianism and John Devoy*. London: Arthur Barker, Ltd., 1937.

Schoyen, A.R. *The Chartist Challenge: A Portrait of George Julian Harney*. London: William Heinemann, Ltd., 1958.

Sheppard, Francis. *London 1808-1870, The Infernal Wen*. London: Secker & Warburg, 1971.

Silver, Allan. "The Demand for Order in Civil Society." *The Police: Six Sociological Essays*. Edited by David J. Bordua. New York: John Wiley & Sons, Inc., 1967.

Smith, H. Llewellyn. "Influx of Population." *Life and Labour of the People in London*. 1st ser. Edited by Charles Booth. London: Macmillan and Co., Ltd., 1902.

Smith, Phillip Thurmond. "The London Metropolitan Police and Public Order and Security, 1850-1868." Ph.D. diss., Columbia University, 1976.

Stevenson, John. "Civil Disorder." *Crime and Law in Nineteenth Century Britain*. Edited by W. Cornish, J. Hart, A. Manchester, and J. Stevenson. Dublin: Irish University Press, 1978.

————. *Popular Disturbances in England, 1700-1870*. New York: Longman Group Ltd., 1979.

————. "Social Control and the Prevention of Riots in England, 1789-1829." *Social Control in Nineteenth Century Britain*. Edited by A.P. Donajgrodzki. Totowa, N.J.: Croom Helm and Rowman and Littlefield, 1977.

Storch, Robert. "Crime and Justice in Nineteenth-Century England." *History Today*, XXX (Sept. 1980), 32-37.

————. "The Plague of Blue Locusts: Police Reform and Popular Resistance in Northern England, 1840-1857." *International Review of Social History*, XX (1975), 61-90.

Thompson, F.M.L. "Social Control in Victorian Britain." *The Economic History Review*, 2d ser., XXXIV, No. 2 (May 1981), 189-208.

Tilly, Charles. "How Protest Modernized in France, 1845-1855." *The Dimensions of Quantitative Research in History*. Edited by W.O. Aydelotte, Allan Bogue, and Robert Fogel. London: Oxford University Press, 1972.

————. "The Web of Contention in Eighteenth-Century Cities." *Class Conflict and Collective Action*. Edited by Louise Tilly and Charles Tilly. Beverly Hills, Calif.: Sage Publications, 1981.

Tobias, J.J. *Crime and Industrial Society in the Nineteenth Century*. Middlesex, U.K.: Penguin Books, Ltd., 1967.

————. *Crime and Police in England 1700-1900*. New York: St. Martin's Press, 1979.

————. "Police and Public in the United Kingdom." *Police Forces in History*. Edited by G.L. Mosse. Beverly Hills, Calif.: Sage Publications, 1975.

Troup, Sir Edward. *The Home Office*. 2d ed. London: G.P. Putnam's Sons, Ltd., 1926.

Wallas, Graham. *The Life of Francis Place, 1771-1854*. London: George Allen & Unwin, Ltd., 1918.

Walpole, Sir Spencer. *The History of Twenty-Five Years*. Vol. II. London: Longmans, Green, and Co., 1904.

Williams, David. *Keeping the Peace: The Police and Public Order*. London: Hutchinson of London, 1967.

Wills, W.H. "The Metropolitan Protectives." *Old Leaves: Gathered From Household Words*. New York: Harper & Bros., 1860.

Woolf, Leonard. *Sowing: An Autobiography of the Years 1880 to 1904*. New York: Harcourt, Brace, Co., 1960.

Young, G.M. *Victorian England: Portait of An Age*. 2d ed. New York: Oxford University Press, 1969.

Index

About the Author

PHILLIP THURMOND SMITH is Assistant Professor of History at Saint Joseph's University in Philadelphia.

10696104